Press, Politics, and Power

Egypt's Heikal and *Al-Ahram*

(٭ ثمن الأهرام ٭)

في الاسكندرية عن سنة واحدة ثلاثة وعشرون فرنكا
وعن سنة اشهر خمسة عشر فرنكا واثمانها في الخارج خاصة

	فرنك	فرنك
في مصر وسائر الارياف الخديوية	٢٥	١٦
في الاستانة العلية	٢٥	١٦
في سورية وسائر الممالك المحروسة	٣٠	١٦
في اوروبا والجزائر وتونس	٤٠	١٧
في بلاد وكلكتة		١٧

لمن يكل ثمن الأهرام ذات اربع صفحات نصف فرنك

(٭ مكاتبات الأهرام ٭)

جميع المكاتبات التي ترسل الى الجريدة المتعلقة بالاهرام يرجى
ان تكون خالصة الاجرة باسم سليم افندي نقلا محرر الأهرام
ومحل ادارتها الى شارع البورس امام بنك العمومات

(٭ وكالة الأهرام في الخارج ٭)

اما وكلاء الأهرام فنذكر في احراء الجريدة عند وجودهم ويمكن
الحصول على الأهرام في الاماكن التي ليس بها وكلاء
بارسال حوالة الى مديرها على بارسال طوابع الوسطة من
اي نوع كان على قدر مدة الاشتراك

بالاسكندرية في يوم السبت ٥ اغسطس (اب) سنة ١٨٧٦

الاخبار البرقية الواردة الى الاسكندرية

باريز في ٣٠ تموز الساعة ١٢ ظلا لمرد الدول ان
قد دخل في عمل هدم والعساكر الشاهانية المهاجمة لجبل
الاسود رجعت في يوربنار

باريز في ٣١ تموز الساعة ١١ ان العساكر الشاهانية
انتصرت على الصرب في مدير الذي ورحفت ان بحافظ
ون مراكز الصرب غير مامونه

باريز في ٢ اب ان العساكر الشاهانية انتصرت على
العصاة الى لهرسك وقد ترك ترك بالديرالو

حوادث مختلفة

نخفل قريبا محاورة رضية في مجلس نواب امة
تكثر بخصوص الحوادث الحالية

نعد نشرف بالمثول لمام حضرة لمرشال مكمهون
رئيس الجمهورية الفرنساوية لمجرل شاكندي دوكده
جاعاولده ان حضرة كنا بمن جلالةملك بطانيا
يعلن نتيجة سير لمدير الحكومة الفرنسية نوبة نعيد تعديد
الكتاب قال اني باحزام اقدمة ان تعظكحوم حيث تلفي

هذا هو العدد الأول من السنة الأولى من جريدة الأهرام
المرتبة بعناية الحكمة السنية والمنعمة الاستعداد الحام
لان نجعل من يتصفح صفاتها وانها بان بطالعة لانها تلاقي
البحث لتقف على الفوائد الصحيحة في نفي مقدوق الجرائد
وتكب قبول الجمهور والاستقبال شاهد ...

...

كيف ما يجيء العاقل فكرة باحثا عن حركة العام
الانساني يرى في فروع الحوادث راجعة الى اصل واحد

Press, Politics, and Power

Egypt's Heikal and *Al-Ahram*

MUNIR K. NASSER

The Iowa State University Press / Ames

To

Iftikhar,

Nisreen,

and

Sarab

MUNIR KHALIL NASSER is Assistant Professor of Journalism at the Department of Communication Arts, University of the Pacific, Stockton, California. A native of Birzeit on the West Bank of Jordan, Professor Nasser worked as a journalist for Arabic newspapers and radio stations in Jerusalem, Amman, and Cairo. He earned the B.A. degree at the American University in Cairo, the M.A. degree at the University of South Carolina, and the Ph.D. degree at the University of Missouri—Columbia. Besides this book, he has written a number of articles and convention papers on the Middle East press.

Before joining the University of the Pacific, Professor Nasser taught journalism at the University of Iowa, Iowa City, and at Birzeit University on the West Bank of Jordan. He won the first-place award in the 1974 AEJ competition in international communication.

© 1979 The Iowa State University Press
United States and English language rights only

Composed and printed by The Iowa State University Press, Ames, Iowa 50010

First edition, 1979

Library of Congress Cataloging in Publication Data

Nasser, Munir K   1936–
  Press, politics, and power.

  Bibliography: p.
  Includes index.
    1. Haykal, Muhammad Hasanayn. 2. Al-Ahram, Cairo. 3. Egypt—Politics and government—1952–   4. Journalists—Egypt—Biography. 5. Statesmen—Egypt—Biography. I. Title.
PN5465.H3N3   070.4′092′4   [B]   79-11924
ISBN 0-8138-0955-X
ISBN: 0-8138-1290-9 (pbk)

C O N T E N T S

PREFACE

THIS BOOK tells the story of Mohamed Hassanein Heikal, former editor of the influential *Al-Ahram* (Cairo), in the context of Middle Eastern press and politics. It is not a biography of Heikal. Rather, it is an attempt to represent as thoroughly as possible Heikal as a unique phenomenon in Arab journalism and to discuss in depth his powerful role as alter ego of the late President Gamal Abdul Nasser. Heikal's achievements, personality, thought, and journalistic style are analyzed in detail. His influence on Egyptian and Arab politics and press is emphasized.

The following chapters present Heikal's story as he told it. During the month of July 1976, I conducted taped interviews with Heikal at his Nile-side residence in Cairo. Some may see in these pages a one-sided story reflecting only Heikal's version of the truth. This may be so. But it is doubtful whether there is anybody more qualified to tell Heikal's story than Heikal himself. He might not have told everything he knew, and it is not claimed here that this is the complete story of Heikal the man.

An attempt has been made, however, to balance Heikal's version by presenting his opponent's views in a separate chapter. Private interviews were conducted with a number of prominent Egyptian and Arab journalists who have pro and con views on Heikal's controversial role and personality. Material on Heikal and *Al-Ahram* has been collected from *Al-Ahram*'s headquarters in Cairo, and I was allowed access to *Al-Ahram*'s facilities and archives.

Much effort and attention have been directed toward producing a work that is fair, accurate, and complete. My own conclusions and evaluations appear in the last chapter.

In telling his story, Heikal touched upon the events, the men, and the issues that have made the Middle East what it is today. He revealed information that has never been published. Much of this work, therefore, should be helpful for readers interested in the Middle East conflict because it provides information usually not available to Westerners.

Stockton, California
September 1978

MUNIR K. NASSER

ACKNOWLEDGMENTS

TELLING the story of Mohamed Hassanein Heikal was not possible without the assistance of many fine scholars and journalists. I take this opportunity to reward them the only way I can, with my deepest gratitude and with formal acknowledgment: to my teacher and adviser, Professor John C. Merrill, for providing invaluable guidance and encouragement during the course of my doctoral program at the University of Missouri School of Journalism, and to the members of my doctoral committee at Missouri.

I am indebted to the School of Journalism at the University of Missouri—Columbia for awarding me the Walter Williams Memorial Fellowship in International Press Problems, which partly financed my trip to Egypt in 1976, and for providing me with a teaching assistantship during the three years I spent at Missouri. I am also indebted to the University of the Pacific in Stockton for providing me with a faculty research grant that partly financed the manuscript preparation.

This book could not have been completed without the assistance of Mohamed Hassanein Heikal who spent long hours with me in Cairo answering my questions as honestly and frankly as possible. My deepest gratitude goes also to the editorial staff of *Al-Ahram* for the long chats and discussions in their offices during the summer of 1976.

Thanks also go to Pamela Brown of the University of Iowa for editing the manuscript of this book and to the University of Iowa School of Journalism for its encouragement and support during my year as a faculty member there. This list would not be complete without the recognition of my wife and two daughters for their encouragement and tolerance during the course of my doctoral program.

Press, Politics, and Power

Egypt's Heikal and *Al-Ahram*

دار الأهرام
الأهرام
Al-Ahram
١٤ صفحة
رئيس مجلس الإدارة: يوسف السباعي
رئيس التحرير: علي حمدي الجمال

السادات: مصر فخورة بأن يصل «الأهرام» بكفاحه وأدائه إلى عمر ١٠٠ عام

الرئيس يتحدث عن أخطر قضايا الساعة خلال لقائه بأسرة تحرير الأهرام في افتتاح احتفالات العيد المئوى

■ **لبنان:** كان في وسع فرنجية أن يطوع الأزمة ولكن انحيازه إلى طرف كان مصيبة لبنان

■ **الشرق الأوسط:** آن الأوان لأن يتوقف رسم خريطة المنطقة من خارجها فنحن أصحاب الأرض والقرار

■ **مصر:** أقول لكل مواطن إن قواتنا المسلحة تملك أسلحة أكثر مما كانت تملك في أكتوبر

الرئيس في جولة بالمعرض

الرئيس والسيدة جيهان السادات في جولة حول الأهرام

محادثات الرئيس والأشـاه تبدأ في طهران الأربعاء

فكر عربي جديد بعد ٦ أكتوبر

السادات يفتتح معرض مصر في ١٠٠ عام

٢٠ وزير قطر والسعودية

وطهران تستعد لاستقباله

معرض «الأهرام» مفتوح اليوم للدعوات الخاصة

السفن السورية تتحرك لمحاصرة سواحل لبنان

منظمة تحرير فلسطين الرئيسية

مجلس الوزراء: توفير السلع التموينية في القرى والأحياء الشعبية

The Egyptian Press: Struggle for Freedom

WHEN Mohamed Hassanein Heikal was removed from the editorship of *Al-Ahram* in February 1974, a significant chapter in the history of the Egyptian press had come to an end. For almost twenty years, Heikal had played a leading role in shaping and influencing the development of the press in Egypt. From his office at *Al-Ahram,* he moved the currents of Egyptian politics and helped the late President Gamal Abdul Nasser in shaping events of the greatest magnitude during a boiling period of modern Arab history. Few men knew Nasser better and few retained his confidence firmly to the end. Never in the history of any country has a journalist wielded so much influence and power, and for so long. Heikal's role as Nasser's adviser and friend far exceeded his role as journalist. This accorded him a privileged position through which he freely criticized the ills of Egyptian society.

Heikal's journalistic talents were reflected in *Al-Ahram,* which became under him a household name in world journalism. He was able to create from a dying newspaper a journalistic empire that is generally regarded as one of the half-dozen most advanced newspaper organizations in the world. Under Heikal, *Al-Ahram* became one of the most authoritative and dependable sources for understanding what was happening in the Middle East. To understand Heikal's influence on the press, however, and to place the discussion in proper perspective, a historical review of the Egyptian press is necessary.

When Napoleon invaded Egypt in 1789 he brought with him the first Arabic printing press and used it to print government leaflets and to publish the first newspaper in Egypt, *Al-Hawadeth el-Yawmiyah* (The Daily Events). Through this newspaper he attempted to educate his Egyptian readers in the freedoms of the French Revolution. His liberal ideas produced a cultural shock in the Egyptian society. By the time Napoleon was expelled from Egypt by the Ottomans in 1801, the French imprint on the Egyptian culture was permanent.

No attempt was made to publish a second newspaper until Mohamed Ali was appointed governor of Egypt by the Ottoman Sultan in 1805. The governor started a modernizing program for the country and took a personal interest in establishing a new publication, *Al-Waqa'i el-Masriyah* (The Official Gazette). He exercised full control over the newspaper, and in 1824 he issued a decree prohibiting

3

print shops from publishing any newspapers without his permission. This decree marked the first official press control in Egypt.[1]

A new phase in the development of the press started with the arrival of a new governor, Khedive Ismail, in 1863. He was educated in Paris and encouraged privately owned newspapers. Ismail's liberal policies attracted many intellectuals from Syria and Lebanon among whom were the Taqla brothers who emigrated from Lebanon and established *Al-Ahram* (The Pyramids) in Alexandria in 1876.

The British occupation of Egypt in 1881 led to the emergence of the party press. This press was founded by Western educated intellectuals to serve as a medium of political agitation against the British and to create in the Egyptians a sense of national identity. The party press was able to mobilize the Egyptian people behind its demands for independence and this strong expression of national sentiment led to the popular revolt of 1919.

In 1922 the British granted Egypt limited independence under their domination. The country became a monarchy with a parliament and a multi-party system. The new constitution declared that the press was free within the law and that no censorship would be imposed and no newspapers would be confiscated by the government. The same constitution provided that such measures might be invoked "in the interest of the social system."[2] The constitution of 1936, however, lifted many of these restrictive measures and the party press became more open in criticizing official public policies and government corruption. This limited press freedom continued until 1952, when a group of army officers deposed the king and declared a new revolutionary regime.

Several factors combined to prompt the overthrow of monarchy and bring about a republican regime in Egypt. Mounting social ills, such as unchecked population growth, increasing unemployment, and spiraling inflation, contributed to the unrest among the predominantly illiterate lower classes. The gap between the privileged and the unprivileged groups was vast, with fifty percent of the Gross National Product owned by only five percent of the population and the per capita income averaging about $25. Corruption of the political parties and spread of the black market during World War II added to the economic burden of the country.

The 1940s were marked by organized military resistance to British occupation forces in the Suez Canal zone. The streets of Cairo witnessed bomb throwings and attempts to assassinate cabinet ministers. Public defiance culminated in the Cairo fire in 1952 in which several downtown stores were set on fire by angry crowds.

During this upheaval, three rival political forces were predominant: the Palace with its political parties, the Wafd party of the nationalist movement, and the British who exerted pressure on the other two. Each force had its own newspapers to propagate its ideas and many independent papers solicited funds from political groups due to the low literacy rate and insufficient advertising revenues.[3]

However, the press did not play a serious role in influencing events at that time. Newspaper columns were filled mainly with high society gossip and sensational news about social and political corruption and did not concern themselves with nationalist or ideological issues. The press reflected the political struggle on the surface and at the same time *was aware* of two basic underground movements. At the extreme right was the Muslim Brotherhood, a radical religious group calling for the enforcement of Islamic law in society, and at the extreme left was the Egyptian Communist party. These movements were unable to effect any change in the political structure and resorted to violence as a means of making their voices heard.

Nasser Takes Over

When army officers led by Gamal Abdul Nasser took over on July 23, 1952, they deposed King Farouk, abrogated the constitution, and established a republican regime. Faced with mounting criticism of the military takeover, the new regime promptly dissolved political parties and imposed press censorship.

From the outset, the new regime faced the dilemma of choosing the right political structure for Egypt, including a framework for the press. According to Heikal, the options were limited as there was no distinct ideological movement for Nasser to follow. Arab nationalism was not clearly defined at that early stage, and existing social and economic conditions limited Nasser's options. At the same time in the cold war the superpowers struggled to fill the void caused by declining empires. Egypt, as well as other Arab countries, was still under British occupation and the two major superpowers competed fiercely for political influence in the Middle East. The Soviet Union used Communism to appeal to a wide spectrum of young Egyptians who were suffering under an ailing economy. The United States, with its rising economy following its victory in World War II, painted a lively image of affluent American society and created among poor Arabs a revolution of expectations. The Middle East airwaves were filled with propaganda broadcasts in Arabic from Washington, Moscow, and Peking, each fighting for listeners' attention.

For Nasser, the choice was a hard one. Capitalism was not the real answer to solving Egypt's economic problems since the country lacked enough accumulation of wealth. Capital resources were in the form of exhausted agricultural land and an unskilled labor force. Still, the secular element of Communism might antagonize large segments of Egypt's Islamic society.

In his search for a way out, Nasser chose to follow the path of other developing nations, such as India. Egypt had to develop under several pressures from the superpowers, the cold war, the revolution of mass communications and of expectations. Nasser believed that Egypt needed planned development and some sort of control over its internal affairs. As Heikal put it, Nasser was aware of cold war tactics and American and Soviet plans to invade developing nations from within via coups d'etat. Nasser, therefore, decided to impose political, social, and economic controls to safeguard the regime against external threats and to make his people realize that the affluent society portrayed by the mass media was out of reach for a time.

Following the dissolution of political parties, the new regime created a single political organization called the Liberation Rally, and declared Mohamed Nagib, an army general, president. Shortly thereafter, a feud erupted between Nasser and Nagib over the political future of Egypt. Nagib favored parliamentary rule, while Nasser opposed it. In 1954 Nagib resigned and Nasser became absolute ruler of Egypt for the sixteen years that followed.

Confrontation with the Press

In the first few years after military takeover, the new regime rejected existing Egyptian social and economic structures but failed to offer new alternatives. According to Heikal, "their only thinking was to carry out their adventure, remove the king, and thereafter things should improve."[4]

As soon as the new regime was declared, most newspapers dramatically shifted their support from the king to Nasser and his group and repeated the slogans of the regime: "socialism, revolution and unity." The king came under severe press attacks and was blamed for all the ills of Egypt. Sensational stories about the king and his reportedly corrupt life filled long columns of the press. One exception to this campaign was Heikal, then one of three editors of the daily *Al-Akhbar* (The News), who argued that the whole system had to be held responsible for the ills of Egyptian society. Heikal called on his colleagues to abandon sensational stories about the king and instead to help the new regime in the search for solutions.

The press took Heikal's advice and launched a huge debate about Egypt's political future. Some writers suggested Marxism as an ideology while others, such as the Muslim Brotherhood, saw Islamic law as the only solution. Still others, such as Mahmoud Abul-Fatah, publisher of *Al-Masri* (The Egyptian), called for a return to parliamentary rule and political parties. The twin brothers, Mustafa and Ali Amin, owners and editors of *Al-Akhbar,* gave full support to the new regime without offering any substantial ideas. Heikal himself was unable to take a clear-cut position in the ongoing debate since he felt detached from the political and economic realities in Egypt because he was traveling abroad as a correspondent.

Nasser was following this debate but was unhappy with the new suggestions. While he believed that Islamic law can be a major source for legislation, he disagreed with the Muslim Brotherhood that it was the only source. He also disagreed with Abul-Fatah's ideas about democratic institutions, arguing that "at this stage democracy can create social and economic problems."[5] This led to the first confrontation between Nasser and the press. In March 1954 Nasser briefly lifted press censorship which had been in effect since the British imposed martial law on Egypt in September 1939. Critics of Nasser, particularly Abul-Fatah, took advantage of this opportunity and attacked him fiercely. This prompted the government to reimpose censorship one month later and to warn journalists against spreading suspicion and doubts against the revolution.

Abul-Fatah was charged with committing harmful acts against the national interest and fostering propaganda abroad against the regime. Later he was tried in absentia while in Europe, sentenced to ten years imprisonment, and the license of his paper *Al-Masri* was revoked. According to Heikal, the dispute between Nasser and Abul-Fatah erupted when the latter was denied two government contracts to import arms for the army and to run the public transport system in Cairo. The government claimed he was trying to get hold of these contracts for his own benefit and was disregarding the country's interest.[6]

Confrontation with the press reached a new climax when the government ordered the dissolution of the Press Syndicate (Association), charging that its members had received bribes from old politicians in return for favorable press treatment. They were publicly accused of participating in the corruption and failing to expose the evils of the old political system. In May 1955, however, the government revived the Press Syndicate and among its new objectives were to increase the efficiency of the press, to raise the ethical standards of its members, and to improve their economic conditions. Meanwhile, press censorship was eased slightly as the country prepared for a political transformation. A new plan prohibited political parties and established a new political organization, the National Union, composed of peasants, workers, and professionals. In 1956 a new constitution was enacted and Nasser was proclaimed president. Article 45 of the new constitution stated that "freedom of the press, publication, and copyright is safeguarded in the interest of public welfare and within the limits prescribed by the law." Claiming a desire to mobilize the press in the service of the public, the government started three newspapers of its own and Anwar Sadat, who later succeeded Nasser as president, was named editor of *Al-Gumhouriya* (The Republic).

Nasser Nationalizes the Press

Despite press censorship and the publication of government newspapers, Nasser remained unhappy with press performance in general. In the late 1950s, Nasser was embarking on his plan of nationalizing private and foreign banks and corporations. He started with the Suez Canal and soon thereafter a series of decrees confiscated all British, French, and Belgian interests that controlled banking, trade, tourism, and real estate businesses. At this time Nasser said that the press must be organized to take part in the process of social and economic transformation and to liquidate the interests of privileged groups "who were exploiting Egypt at a time when per capita income did not exceed $25."[7]

On several occasions, Nasser himself publicly expressed discontent with the press for devoting more space to sensational accounts of crime, divorce, and sex than to government development programs. At one meeting with newsmen, he urged that they offer constructive criticism and devote more space to serious articles.

Using state-controlled media, particularly radio, Nasser was able to communicate directly with the masses, arousing their passions and motivating them to strive for the national goals. The press, however, was still in private hands and could not be as effectively mobilized. To solve this problem Nasser issued on May 24, 1960, a presidential decree of thirteen articles nationalizing the press. Under this decree, termed "The Press Organization Law," five major publishing houses had to surrender their private ownership to the National Union, now known as the Arab Socialist Union. The decree stated that owners were to be compensated for their properties in government bonds yielding three percent interest over twenty years. Working journalists or those aspiring to become journalists would have to obtain a license from the National Union, which would also establish press institutes and designate boards of directors to manage the publishing houses.[8]

The decree was accompanied by an explanatory note written by Heikal. Then editor of *Al-Ahram* and a close friend of Nasser, Heikal played a significant role in influencing Nasser's thinking on the press. The note said "organization of the press" was necessary to stop capitalists from controlling the press and "restore ownership of the media of social and political guidance to the people." The note went on to say that "the press is part of the whole popular structure and not controlled by the executive branch of the government." The press, according to the note, "is an authority whose function is to guide the people to actively participate in building their society, exactly as does the People's Assembly (the Parliament)."[9]

Attitudes of the press toward nationalization were generally favorable. Heikal strongly supported the decision and advocated it in his columns. In the discussion that preceded the decree, Heikal spent long hours arguing with Nasser to influence his thinking on certain aspects of the nationalization. Nasser told Heikal that it was not only a matter of nationalizing the press but a matter of transforming the whole of Egyptian society. Heikal argued strongly against ownership of the press by a state or government apparatus. He agreed, however, that the press be owned by the people, represented by their only political organization, The National Union, but he warned that this organization might be dominated by bureaucrats who would turn it into a government agency. Heikal finally presented a plan of his own to Nasser. The plan suggested that the National Union would hold the right to license newspapers in the form of long-term leases. According to Heikal's plan, newspapers would become cooperative organizations that would pay an annual rent to the National Union large enough to compensate owners of the confiscated newspapers. The plan also suggested the cooperative organization in each newspaper would elect its own board of directors who in turn would elect the newspaper editorial board.[10]

Nasser initially did not accept Heikal's plan because he thought it was an attempt by the press to avoid nationalization. However, Nasser was willing to compromise. The new "Press Organization Law" emerged as a blend of Nasser's and Heikal's ideas. According to this law, licensing power would remain with the National Union, which would also designate boards of directors, which in turn would appoint newspaper editors. As far as profits were concerned, the press was given a special status. The law stipulated that the press be a nonprofit institution whose income or profit (if any) would be divided into two equal parts. People working on a newspaper would be entitled to fifty percent of the profits; the other fifty percent would go to upgrading newspaper facilities. This was a drastic departure from policies applied to other nationalized institutions, such as factories and corporations, whose income went to the state treasury.

Initially, the impact of nationalization was not felt in the press because little change in editorial and management positions was made. A committee representing the National Union was formed of former editors and owners to run the nationalized press. Editors and columnists had to abide by the new directives and guidelines of the National Union and promote themes such as Arab socialism, Arab unity, and revolutionary spirit, while attacking themes such as imperialism, Zionism, and "reactionary elements." In 1964 a number of Marxist and socialist writers were given important editorial positions in the press to help sell the Arab socialism concept to the masses. Criticism of Nasser and the regime, however, remained a taboo, and the Egyptian press acquired a reputation for being uniform in handling domestic issues.

One important exception to this uniformity was Heikal's column which, due to his closeness to Nasser, dealt with sensitive issues more openly. On several occasions he refused to abide by the Arab Socialist Union (formerly National Union) directives and even attacked the Union for its tight press controls. Following Egypt's disastrous defeat in the 1967 war with Israel, Heikal urged his colleagues to abandon self-censorship and speak out. He began a series of articles in *Al-Ahram* criticizing the mediocrity of army generals, the secret police, and Egyptian diplomats.

Reaction of other journalists to nationalization was mixed, but most of them accepted the official justification that the press was socialized, not nationalized. They practiced self-censorship because they feared government reprisal or because the new system was more financially rewarding. Profit bonuses made it possible for many journalists to receive salaries high enough to support a life of luxury.[11]

Commenting on foreign affairs, however, journalists had a freer hand than in domestic affairs. Criticism of governments unfriendly to Egypt was uninhibited. The left-wing newspaper *Al-Gumhouriya* was noted for its attacks on foreign governments, whereas *Al-Ahram* took a more moderate stand, and *Al-Akhbar* generally took a conservative line.

Nationalization also had some positive effects on the press. A host of new periodicals was published by the government in a variety of fields. Circulation figures went up as education was expanded and new schools opened.

Among the few journalists who expressed discontent with nationalization of the press were the twin brothers Mustafa and Ali Amin. Often credited with the rise of popular journalism in Egypt, they started their careers in 1944 publishing the weekly *Akhbar el-Yom* (The Daily News). They introduced telegraphic writing style (inverted pyramid structure) and the use of political caricature to the Egyptian press. Educated in the West, the Amin brothers were known for their sympathy with liberalism and free enterprise. When the government decided in 1960 to take over their publishing empire, they opposed the move and shortly thereafter were transferred to another publishing house, Dar el-Hilal. Mustafa Amin, however, was indicted on charges of spying for the United States and was sentenced to life imprisonment in 1965. His brother Ali was in London at the time and decided to stay in exile. He did not return to Egypt until 1974 when Sadat released Mustafa from prison and appointed him editor of *Al-Akhbar*. Ali was immediately appointed managing editor of *Al-Ahram* to replace Heikal.

Sadat's "Free Era"

The stable press-government relationship from 1960 until Nasser's death in 1970 was interrupted only by occasional shuffling in editorial or management positions. The scene was not ready for any drastic changes in the press until 1973, when the whole Egyptian society underwent a series of shocking events as a result of the fourth Arab-Israeli war.

When Sadat succeeded Nasser in 1970, he made it clear that he wanted to run the country by institutions. He stressed the significance of the press and the positive role it must play in the new era. As a veteran journalist himself, Sadat was familiar with the problems facing the press. For several years, he was editor of government newspapers and periodicals, and at one time was in charge of *Akhbar el-Yom*. As early as 1952, he was supervising the Egyptian broadcasting system and his voice was heard on Cairo radio in the early hours of July 24, 1952, announcing the first communique of the military takeover.

In 1971 Sadat was planning a major shake-up in the press with the aim of dismissing extreme leftists. The opportunity came in May when he was the target of a plot by his cabinet members led by Vice-President Ali Sabri. A mass resignation of cabinet members had been planned to create an impression of a collapse of the Sadat regime. But top army officers stood behind Sadat, refusing to follow the minister of war who was among the plot leaders. Soon after the crisis was over, a purge of communists and leftist elements took place in the government, the Arab Socialist Union, the broadcasting service, and the press.

By mid-1972 Sadat began to relax press controls by opening up news sources to reporters. He issued new directives to cabinet members asking them to facilitate news flow from government agencies to the public. At the same time, he tried to be fair to all top editors by giving them access to significant news. Consequently, Heikal started to lose the privileged position he had enjoyed with Nasser.

Government censorship of the press continued, however, and all newspapers had resident censors to whom all copy was submitted. These censors were civilian officials responsible to the Ministry of Information. In 1972 the Egyptian Press Syndicate appealed to the government for the immediate lifting of censorship on newspapers except in military matters involving national security. The syndicate recalled in a statement that Sadat had promised to lift censorship as soon as the journalists adopted a code of ethics. The code was adopted unanimously by the syndicate's general assembly in February 1973. *Al-Ahram* joined the syndicate in its appeal for lifting press censorship.

Instead of fulfilling his promise, Sadat took drastic actions against the press. He charged in February 1973 that several Egyptian journalists were making contacts with foreign correspondents "with the aim of spreading unrest and tarnishing Egypt's reputation by supplying foreign mass media with false information."[12] As a result, sixty-four intellectuals were dismissed from the Arab Socialist Union and automatically lost their jobs in newspapers, radio, television, and the theatre. Clearly the purge was primarily directed at people working in the mass media or otherwise capable of influencing public opinion at home and abroad. Twenty-seven of them were journalists working for daily newspapers and among these were four top editors of *Al-Ahram*.

As Sadat was planning to go to war with Israel, Heikal advised him not to act without the press, intellectuals, and students backing him. Sadat was convinced, and in a decisive move one week before the war started in October 1973, he announced clemency measures for more than 200 dissident journalists and students. All charges against them were dropped and the journalists were permitted to return to their positions.

Sadat's thinking with regard to the press started to change as a result of the October war of 1973. In the first days of the war the Egyptian forces astonished the world by crossing the Suez Canal, storming the Barlev Line, the well-fortified front Israeli line, and pushing the Israeli troops back into Sinai. For the first time in its recent history, Israel was on the defensive. Sadat emerged as a hero who was able to destroy the "myth of Israeli invincibility" created by Israel's stunning victory over three Arab states in 1967. Armed with the confidence the war gave him, Sadat asked the Egyptian mass media to follow an "open information policy." Unlike the sensational and exaggerated press reports in 1967, Egypt's official statements were stripped of much of their emotionalism and the information policies became more realistic.[13] The new style of war reporting in the Egyptian press was planned by Dr. Ashraf Ghorbal, a genial expert on diplomacy who holds a doctorate from Harvard, who was then Sadat's press adviser.

Heikal was the most energetic proponent of the new information policy and *Al-Ahram* played a leading part in advocating it. In fact, Heikal was the first in Egypt to publish information about the Israeli infiltration to the west of the Suez Canal, which tipped the balance to Israel's favor. He insisted on telling the public the truth about this "military setback" and challenged official statements that the Israeli infiltration was only a minor crossing.

Although Heikal moved close to Sadat during the war, he has since become critical of what he regards as Sadat's excessive dependence on the Americans in seeking a settlement to the Arab-Israeli conflict. Under Sadat, Heikal regarded himself as the true exponent of the spirit of Nasserism. Prior to the expulsion of the Soviet advisers from Egypt in 1972 he was very critical of excessive Egyptian dependence on the Soviet Union and came under Soviet attack. This gave him the reputation of being among the more pro-Western of Egyptian leaders. But as the deadlock with Israel continued, he became critical of Sadat's hesitant policy and turned toward Libya's Colonel Mu'ammar Qaddafi, whose uncompromising stand against Israel seemed more in the tradition of Nasser.

In the months following the October war, Heikal kept up a continuous sniping at Sadat. He opposed the first cease-fire arranged by Henry Kissinger, former secretary of state, and the swift resumption of relations with the United States. He warned Sadat that he was falling into Kissinger's insidious negotiation trap and insisted that there had been no basic change in America's pro-Israel policy.

In his long columns, Heikal criticized Arab oil policies as too moderate and timid and accused some oil-producing states of seeking economic advantage through higher prices rather than using the oil for political purposes. He also cautioned against dropping Colonel Qaddafi of Libya and getting too close to King Feisal of Saudi Arabia, the exponent of Arab conservatism. The Saudi government informed Cairo of its discontent with the Heikal columns.

This apparently was more than Sadat could stand. On February 2, 1974, armed with that self-confidence the war gave him, Sadat abruptly relieved Heikal of his post as chief editor and chairman of the board of *Al-Ahram*. The same presidential decree that dismissed Heikal named him "presidential press adviser," a post he never accepted. The following day a government spokesman provided the official reasons for Heikal's fall. He said Heikal had created "a power center, tantamount to a state within a state" at *Al-Ahram*. Heikal was further, but vaguely, charged with some sort of involvement in student demonstrations. More explicitly, he was accused of meddling with upcoming cabinet changes that were in the air in January 1974.

To everyone's surprise, Sadat appointed Ali Amin managing editor of *Al-Ahram;* and Dr. Abdul Qader Hatem, minister of information, was designated chairman of the board of directors. Shortly thereafter, Sadat issued a decree abolishing censorship except for military matters. The dismissal of Heikal and lifting of censorship marked a new era in the history of the Egyptian press. Sadat finally gave editors a green light to "press freedom" and made them responsible for what they published. This new "freedom of expression" was welcomed in Egypt as a symptom of a trend toward a greater freedom.

The winter of 1975 marked a new era of public discontent in Egypt. On New Year's Day, Cairo streets witnessed angry riots by thousands of rampaging workers and students in protest of the intolerable economic burden and the daily problems of the mass of the public. Food prices were continuously rising and the gap between rich and poor was widening steadily. The riots were followed by the arrest of about 250 leftists ranging from Nasserites to Communists, and a promise by the government that the economic problems would be dealt with immediately. Sadat's critics on the Left said the regime must overhaul the structure of the country, establish a list of priorities that take into account the ninety-five percent of poor Egyptians, and deal with corruption in high places.

De-Nasserization of Egypt

The lifting of censorship sparked a stormy debate in the press about what is called in Egypt "de-Nasserization"—the slow but continuous process by which the Sadat government has been debunking what it calls the "negative aspects" of Nasserism while retaining what it regards as the "positive aspects." After a silence that lasted for over two decades, most prominent writers and thinkers started revealing the atrocities committed by the past regime on political opponents. Such criticism had come mainly from journalists and functionaries who were themselves personally affected by Nasser's regime, such as the Amin brothers. The campaign started in March 1974 with a book by Ibrahim Abdo, a Cairo University professor, in which he chronicled the Nasser era in terms that shocked many Egyptians. Abdo described Nasser as the "prince of tyranny who brought Egypt a dark era of terror and torture on a scale unprecedented except in Nazi, Fascist, and Stalinist times."[14] Two days after the book was published, it suddenly disappeared from Cairo's bookstalls following government orders to have it withdrawn.

The real outcry, however, came from Tawfiq el-Hakim, the grand old man of Egyptian letters, who published in late 1974 a short book in which he boldly criticized Nasser for the "disasters that he brought down on the heads of the Egyptians from the moment he assumed power until his death."[15] El-Hakim's book was condemned by hard-core Nasserites as the work of a coward and a political opportunist. One of the first to come to Nasser's defense was Heikal who pointed out in a Lebanese magazine that those who criticized Nasser had been alive and well during the leader's lifetime but apparently lacked the courage to say what they thought was right. They were, he asserted, "weak, frightened ghosts."[16]

Many of the attacks against Nasser involved his repression of political dissent within Egypt. An increasing number of books, articles, and speeches judged Nasser guilty of misrule and injustices. The Amin brothers led the campaign and utilized *Al-Akhbar* to regularly print their broadsides against the late president. Ali Amin, back from exile in London, used *Al-Ahram* columns to attack some aspects of the Nasser era daily. His brother Mustafa, reinstated editor of *Al-Akhbar* after nine years in prison, published detailed stories recounting how thousands were tortured and many killed by Nasser's secret police. Some voices in the press, however, came to Nasser's defense. Editor of the government daily *Al-Gumhouriya* accused the press of becoming carried away in their attacks on Nasser. "We are all against injustice, oppression, and tyranny," he wrote, "but in all sincerity I say that I admire many of Nasser's courageous national achievements and socialist gains. We believe it is a great injustice to stamp out the past twenty years and annul them from history."[17] The campaign reached a climax, however, when Galal el-Din Hamamsy, an *Al-Akhbar* editor and a former professor of journalism, alleged in a new book that Nasser had embezzled $15 million.[18] An official statement by the government denied these allegations and Hamamsy was reprimanded by the attorney general. The Press Syndicate prepared a statement protesting these "serious accusations" and condemning *Al-Akhbar* for this "planned campaign" against Nasser. However, under official government orders, the press refused to publish the statement. An article defending Nasserism by Ahmed Baha' el-Din, a highly respected journalist and a former editor of *Al-Ahram,* was also rejected for the same reason.

This has led many observers to believe that Sadat and his government stood behind the campaign against Nasser and his legacy. Initially Sadat refrained from joining the chorus of anti-Nasser abuse, but he also did not take steps to supress it. It is no secret in Cairo that Sadat has long felt that Nasser's particular brand of socialism and costly foreign policy adventures blocked Egypt's economic progress. Sadat gradually embarked on a systematic process of liberalizing Egypt's political and economic institutions.

To Sadat, the freedom he granted the press seemed to have gotten out of hand. While addressing the People's Assembly in March 1976, he rebuked the press for what he called "a conspiracy and a campaign of unfounded criticism, rumors about nonexistent corruption, and even defamation." In emotional tones, he rejected as shameful and absurd the allegations made by Hamamsy against Nasser. He said he did not want to restore press censorship, but it was clear that the press had to be reorganized and that individual editors should no longer have the power to launch harmful campaigns for personal reasons.[19]

This was a clear reference to Ali and Mustafa Amin, and in a new press reshuffle the twin brothers lost their positions as chairmen of *Al-Akhbar,* the newspaper they had founded thirty years before. They remained contributors to the paper, however, and Moussa Sabri, a staunch supporter of Sadat was appointed as new chairman. Two weeks after his removal, Ali Amin died at the age of 62.

According to Mustafa Amin, he and his brother were removed from the helm of *Al-Akhbar* because their campaign against corruption and misuse of public funds led oil-rich Arab states to halt financial backing of Egypt. He believes that Sadat had to sacrifice the brothers to keep the oil money flowing into Egypt. He sees Sadat's move as a setback to freedom of the press. "Many people thought that we attacked Nasser at Sadat's orders," Amin said in a private interview in Cairo. "President Sadat himself asked me to stop the campaign against Nasserism but I refused because he gave me a license to criticize freely, and I shall insist on using this freedom until he removes me completely," he asserted. To Mustafa Amin, democracy meant that the press had the right to differ with the ruler, who should not have the final word.[20]

Like Mustafa Amin, many Egyptian editors still believe that they are free to criticize and comment without official guidance. According to Ali Hamdi el-Gammal, fourth chief editor of *Al-Ahram* after Heikal, the press has regained its freedom since Sadat lifted censorship in 1974. "Today we are free to write whatever we like without interference from anybody," he said. He also said he believed he could criticize government policies if he did not agree with them.[21]

Sadat, however, made it clear that he did not like anyone to disagree with his policies. Since he rebuked the press in March 1976, an ominous conformity became the rule. Many issues, including Sadat's policies, remained taboo, and freedom to criticize or debate assumed the character of campaigns against unfriendly Arab countries but in favor of everything that sprang from the Sadat administration.

The Supreme Press Council

In a meeting with journalists in August 1974, Sadat appointed a commission to study the formation of a supreme press council and to recommend plans for regulating the press professionally. Commission members, headed by the secretary of the Arab Socialist Union, held a series of meetings with journalists and made several recommendations among which were the establishment of a supreme press council and a journalistic code of ethics. On March 11, 1975, Sadat issued a decree setting up the first press council in Egypt with powers to approve the publication of newspapers and licensing of journalists. Under the decree, the council would draw up a code of ethics to insure "freedom of the press, to plan for press expansion, and to arbitrate disputes." The first article of the decree announced that the press in Egypt "is an independent national institution whose function is to represent the people in watching over their government through free writing and constructive criticism." The second article provided that forty-nine percent of the press institutions be owned by persons working in them and that special bylaws be set up in each newspaper to regulate professional rules and salary scales. The decree also granted the new council a right to investigate any violations of the journalistic code of ethics and to refer these violations to the Press Syndicate which would decide on any legal action to be taken.[22]

Soon thereafter, the Supreme Press Council adopted a journalistic code of ethics that called upon all practicing journalists to commit themselves to the following general principles: 1) to liberate Egyptian soil from foreign occupation, 2) to respect religious and spiritual values of Egyptian society, and 3) to protect freedom, democracy, socialism, and national unity. Article VIII of the code made the following demands of the press:

1. To protect national security, state secrets should not be disclosed.

2. Information and facts should not be obtained by illegal means, and the press should publish only verifiable facts.

3. Journalists should not take advantage of their status for personal benefits.

4. The press should avoid sensationalism and exaggeration in crime news and should refrain from interfering in court procedures.

5. The press should have respect for individual privacy and should not expose private family life.

6. The press must firmly commit itself to the principles of objectivity, particularly when commenting on public figures.

7. Professional secrets must be protected and confidential news sources must not be revealed.

8. Advertisements in the press must not disagree with the values and principles of the society; there should be complete separation between editorial and advertising departments.

9. The press must ensure that paid political advertising by foreign agencies does not harm Egypt's national interests and that fees paid for these ads do not come as indirect foreign subsidies.[23]

The Supreme Press Council is composed of nineteen members under the chairmanship of the first secretary of the Arab Socialist Union. The decree stipulated that council members be appointed by the president in his capacity as chairman of the Arab Socialist Union. Nine members come from the press and Press Syndicate. Other members include the minister of information, secretary of ideology in the Arab Socialist Union, secretary of the People's Assembly, dean of the School of Journalism at Cairo University, a judge from the Appeals Court, and three public figures.

At the council's first meeting in May 1975, Sadat told the members that "from the first moment I assumed responsibility, I insisted that the word should regain its freedom." He said the press should develop into a state institution, but first had to reform itself by adopting a code of ethics "because everything in this world, even freedom, should be controlled." Concluding, Sadat said the press should deepen, confirm, and consolidate state institutions and "should point out mistakes without exaggeration and avoid focusing our lenses only on negative aspects."[24]

In a courageous article which appeared in *Akhbar el-Yom,* Maitre Mustafa Mar'ie, a lawyer who was a cabinet minister during the Farouk regime, sharply criticized the Supreme Press Council. He claimed the council, "which is invested with fearful powers," restricts freedom of the press. Mar'ie announced he would continue to express this opinion until a new, different document was produced and until he saw convincing evidence of liberalization.[25]

Emergence of the Party Press

Since assuming power, Sadat has contemplated reorganizing the Egyptian political structure, including the Arab Socialist Union and its relation to the press. He was eager to liberalize the system but was cautious to keep disruption at a minimum. He said publicly that an abrupt return to the multi-party system after nearly a generation of one-party rule would cause unpredictable strains. During the People's Assembly debate on this topic, a consensus developed against parties and in favor of three "platforms," one representing the right, one the left, and one the center.

On November 11, 1976, Sadat surprised the world by announcing the emergence of a multi-party system in Egypt. Appearing before the People's Assembly, he said the three political platforms of the Arab Socialist Union—right, left, and centrist—would form the basis of three separate political organizations. He indicated they would be the only parties permitted for the time being. The new organizations would be allowed to operate freely except that the Arab Socialist Union would remain the dominant political force, controlling their budgets and retaining ownership of the press "so that these important organs will be kept away from private ownership." Sadat also called on the press to allow the three political organizations to express their views in print.[26]

To keep Sadat's "democratic experiment" under control, the 1953 ban on political parties remained in effect. Each "platform," however, was allowed to lobby for its ideas, to disseminate its views through the media, and to prepare a program and a slate of candidates for elections under the umbrella of the Arab Socialist Union. Sadat's hope was to deflect the pressure for a multi-party system and to encourage the People's Assembly to function as a representative body capable of constructive criticism.

Elections were held in October 1976 for 350 members of the People's Assembly in what was described as the most liberal elections since the 1952 overthrow of the monarchy. The Sadat regime, however, seemed to have engineered the result for its centrist platform, the Egyptian Arab Socialist Organization. Led by Prime Minister Mamdouh Salem, the centrist platform won an overwhelming majority of 310 seats. At the same time, the right platform won 12 seats, and the left platform won 2 seats.

The three platforms represented different sectors of the Egyptian political scene. The left platform—the National Progressive Unionist party—was led by Khaled Mohieddin, a devout Muslim Marxist, who was a member of Nasser's original Revolutionary Command Council. He advocated closer ties with the Soviet Union, a stress on public sector investment, and reliance on class struggle. The center platform supported current government's policy of gradual guided democracy. Adherents of the center favored a mixed economy, with private sector investment and closer relations with the West. The right platform, known as the Socialist Liberals, favored a return to capitalism, greater emphasis on private enterprise, and a reliance on market forces to solve Egypt's economic problems.

In early 1978 an old party was reinstated in the political arena. The Wafd party, banned since 1953, was formally recognized by the government and renamed the New Wafd to parry the prohibition against the old parties. The New Wafd won twenty-four supporters in the People's Assembly. It backed Sadat's peace initiative in the Middle East and favored extensive social and domestic changes in Egypt.

Opposition to Sadat outside the confines of these recognized platforms came from the right and left. The Muslin Brotherhood, which seeks to impose orthodox Islamic concepts in Egypt, was showing signs of a comeback in 1977. The real challenge, however, came from the ideological left, a group of Communists, Marxists, and Nasserites who did not join the left platform of the Arab Socialist Union. They criticized the deteriorating economic situation and the growing disparities in wealth which they believed were the results of Sadat's "open door policy." Another strong brand of criticism came from a group called Nasserites. They accused the Sadat government of trying quietly to dismantle the achievements of the Nasser era. Generally included in this group is Heikal who has been a vocal critic of Sadat and his policies since he left *Al-Ahram* in 1974. His columns, though they continue to be published in Arab capitals and are widely read throughout the Arab world, are banned in Egypt.

Following the emergence of political parties, a similar rough division of opinion developed in the Egyptian press. The principal rightest publications, *Al-Akhbar* and *Al-Mussawar,* called for unbridled free enterprise and a break with the ideology and restraints that prevailed under Nasser. On the left were the weekly *Rose el-Yousef* and the political monthly *Al-Talia',* which is written at a high intellectual level but has a minority readership. In the center is *Al-Ahram,* which remains the most influential Egyptian newspaper though it has lost much of the power it enjoyed under Heikal. The left-wing intellectuals who controlled the political pages of *Al-Ahram* have been handicapped by the new editors.

Meanwhile, a lively debate ensued in the press about its relationship with the new political parties. Many columnists seized this opportunity and called for the liberation of the press from the grip of the Arab Socialist Union. In his regular column in *Akhbar el-Yom,* Mustafa Amin wrote that no journalist would like to see the press owned by the state or the Arab Socialist Union. "Press freedom must not be granted by the government, and the press must be owned by shareholders from among its readers, reporters, editors and workers," he wrote.[27]

Other columnists suggested that the press be owned by the new political parties, but this idea was immediately rejected by both the press and political parties. Other voices called for keeping the existing newspapers and periodicals as independent media of expression and allowing the parties to establish newspapers of their own. Sadat expressed his willingness to permit the parties to publish their own papers and offered that the Arab Socialist Union would support these papers financially. Initially the parties rejected this suggestion to avoid falling under the influence of the government.

The three political parties agreed, however, that the Supreme Press Council must be abolished because it had not proven useful in defending press freedom or journalists' rights and was nothing more than a "parents council" which found fault with the press and threatened action against journalists. Some party members have officially requested that the existing press organizations be taken away from the Arab Socialist Union and turned into private corporations whose shares would be publicly owned and whose editorial boards would be elected by shareholders.

In mid-1977, however, the center platform launched *Garidat Masr* (Journal of Egypt) to speak for the ruling party, the Egyptian

Arab Socialist Organization. The secretary general of the party said the newspaper would be financed by membership dues. Soon after, the right platform issued its newspaper *Al-Ahrar* (The Liberals) which supported many government policies.

Al-Ahaly

In February 1978 the left platform launched its party organ *Al-Ahaly* (The People). Fifteen weeks later, however, this weekly newspaper ceased publication under government pressure for its attacks on Sadat and his policies. Khaled Mohieddin, leader of the National Progressive Unionist party, was in charge of the paper. Incapable of supporting full-time editors and reporters, *Al-Ahaly* had to depend on contributors from the ranks of the left party, including 64 journalists who worked for the government-controlled press. Another problem facing *Al-Ahaly* was the lack of a strong financial base. Revenues came largely from contributions of party members and supporters. To cut production expenses, *Al-Ahaly* did without permanent offices, telephones, and printing and circulation facilities. Arrangements were made to print the newspaper at Dar el-Ma'aref, a government publishing house, and to distribute it through Al-Ahram Publishing Institute.

From the outset, *Al-Ahaly* took a highly critical position on Sadat and his "open door" economic policies. In its weekly editorials, the paper attacked the ruling party on issues ranging from Sadat's peace initiative to Egypt's economic ailments and official ineptitude along with insinuations of corruption and nepotism. *Al-Ahaly* reportedly increased its circulation from 50,000 to 135,000 in its fifteen weeks of existence. According to the *Times* of London, *Al-Ahaly* built up a readership estimated at around half a million.[28]

From the first, *Al-Ahaly* was under fire from the government. State-controlled press organizations gave orders to their members not to work for the party press. To escape official retaliation, most contributors to *Al-Ahaly* submitted unsigned articles. Another form of avoiding government penalty was to publish personal interviews with noted writers and journalists. This was demonstrated when *Al-Ahaly* invited Mohamed Hassanein Heikal to contribute to its columns. It was the first time since he left *Al-Ahram* that Heikal broke a long silence on internal affairs and wrote for an Egyptian newspaper. In a pair of articles framed as an interview to avoid the writing ban, Heikal charged that the Sadat regime had misrepresented the Nasser era and said that Sadat's peace initiative had failed. Soon Heikal became the target of the state-controlled press, and *Garidat Masr* promptly accused him of speaking on behalf of what it described as "his masters in the Kremlin."

Sadat's "Year of Crisis"

The year 1977 was marked by what was described as the most serious civil disturbances since Egypt had become a republic in 1953.[29] Late in January, violent disturbances erupted in all major cities following the government's announcement of immediate increases in prices of basic commodities. The violent attacks on Sadat's regime led to the damage of many public buildings, the death of at least 79 persons, and the arrest of some 2,000 people. In the wake of the riots, Sadat suspended the proposed price increase and announced a cabinet reshuffle in which Dr. Gamal el-Otaifi, minister of information, was dismissed from his post. Otaifi, regarded as a liberal, was accused of opening Egypt's television to political debate and making it possible for Marxist views to be broadcast.

In a formal television broadcast to the nation, Sadat said the disturbances had been caused by Communists under orders from Moscow and "posing as Nasserites." He declared that "for the first time in its history, Egypt was faced with carefully planned sabotage exploiting every mistake by the government and exploiting democracy in order to seize power." One of the main objectives of the Communists, he said, was to destroy Egypt's liberalization policy.[30]

Meanwhile, Sadat signed a decree containing stringent new security laws to prevent a recurrence of the disturbances. Under the decree, which was approved in a national referendum, a number of activities were made punishable by hard labor for life. These included inciting the people or impeding the government, or acquiescing in such activity, taking part in a premeditated strike, and participating in a sit-in.[31] Sadat's decree was strongly opposed by the National Progressive Unionist party in a public statement that described the president's action as unconstitutional. Khaled Mohieddin, leader of the party, declared that the Left had nothing to do with the unrest, adding that the government's policy had failed and the gulf between rich and poor was growing. If President Sadat did not learn the lesson of the January riots, he said, the consequences for Egypt's future would be "very bad."

The decree was also criticized by Kamal Eddin Hussein, an independent member of the People's Assembly and a former vice-president under Nasser. In an open letter in *Al-Akhbar,* Hussein said the new measures "were an insult to the intelligence of the Egyptian people," and that the riots were due to the government's "short sightedness."[32] Ten days later, the People's Assembly voted 281 to 28 to approve a recommendation to expel Hussein from the assembly for "aggression against the constitution and the president at a time of crisis."[33]

During the January unrest Sadat gave the press every opportunity to report on the riots in hopes of arousing other Arab countries to discuss aiding Egypt's economy. Tawfiq el-Hakim, a man of letters who is close to Sadat, wrote in *Al-Ahram* that the lesson of the riots was that "our crushed people cannot bear more than they have borne already." In an implied reference to the wealthy Arab states, he added that any conflagration in Egypt "will lead those who sit on wells of gold to sit on wells of flame, and will expose the whole world to grave dangers."[34]

Despite the generally liberal attitude toward foreign journalists in Egypt, reporting on the riots to the outside world was curbed somewhat by Egyptian authorities. On January 28 *The Guardian* correspondent in the Middle East, David Hirst, was expelled from Cairo on charges that he had been misinforming his readers about the riots. A government statement said that Hirst was guilty of "downright libel" in his reports on the riots, that the sending of "misinformation" about Egypt and in particular about its president was a very serious matter and that something had to be done when it "reached the stage of personalities—not facts."[35]

Meanwhile, the Egyptian press was instructed to launch a strong attack on the Soviet Union for its alleged role in the riots. *Al-Ahram* accused the Russians of "wanting to see Cairo drowned in a bloodbath" and of trying to inflame feelings against the Egyptian government.[36] Following the publication of Sadat's memoirs in Egypt, the Soviet daily *Pravda* retaliated with a strong attack on the Egyptian president. *Pravda* accused Sadat of "lies about the Soviet Union's policy in the Middle East and falsification of the history of the heroic struggle of the Egyptian people, under the leadership of President Nasser and after his death, for their freedom and independence."[37]

Sadat's Crackdown on Critics

In November 1977 Sadat stunned the world by going to Jerusalem in search of a peaceful settlement with Israel. The initial popular reaction to this initiative was enthusiastic. Many Egyptians believed that the Sadat trip to Israel would bring peace and lead to a solution of

Egypt's economic problems. But when Sadat abruptly discontinued negotiations with Israel in January 1978 over what he termed Israeli Prime Minister Menachem Begin's "intransigent position," hopes for a peaceful settlement dwindled rapidly. Complaints among ordinary Egyptians about a steadily deteriorating domestic situation were mushrooming in various forums, including the People's Assembly and the party press.

Critics of the Sadat move, however, were not allowed to express their views in the state-controlled press, but some were able to air their views in foreign news media. One of those was Mohamed Hassanein Heikal who warned in the *Times* of London that the Sadat initiative would lead to a deep and lasting rift between Egypt and the rest of the Arab world. He said that peace reached under such circumstances would be "a weak fabric, a cardboard peace."[38]

Opposition to Sadat's peace initiative in Egypt was largely confined to left-wing intellectuals who expressed their views in *Al-Ahaly*. The Sadat government was attacked for failing to help solve the problem of food supplies and prices. In May 1978, stung by growing criticism, Sadat began a set of procedures to purge his most troublesome critics from the press and political life. Speaking at the People's Assembly, he complained that the country was "full of rumors" and blamed opponents in the assembly and the press for trying to exploit Egypt's domestic difficulties to their political ends. He said he was determined to crush his opponents of the left and the right "by using democratic means" and announced that he would hold a referendum to ask the people if these critics should be banned from the political process.

The referendum, set for May 21, asked Egyptian voters to endorse the banning from politics and journalism of anyone with "atheist and corrupt ideologies," code words in Egypt for Communists and some politicians active both before and after the 1952 revolution. A few days before the referendum, *Al-Ahaly* carried a front-page editorial urging readers to vote no on the referendum. The newspaper was confiscated by police just as it was going to press, though a few copies reached the streets. The seizure was upheld by a court on the ground that *Al-Ahaly* was inciting a boycott of the referendum. Khaled Mohieddin said in a news conference that *Al-Ahaly* was only asking its readers to vote against the referendum, not to disrupt or boycott it. He added that the seizure violated Egyptian law because each party had a legislative, constitutional right to express its viewpoint on the referendum.

As expected, Sadat won an overwhelming majority (98.2%) in the referendum, which gave him a mandate to curtail political dissent and criticism in the press. He said in a press conference that he would use the strong endorsement he received in the referendum to drive his critics out of political parties. Sadat also condemned *Al-Ahaly* as "full of anti-government poison, hate, and bitterness." He called on the press to observe vague patriotic government guidelines and to function as a "fourth authority," along with the executive, legislative, and judicial branches.

Sadat's clampdown on his critics began with an order to thirty Egyptian journalists working in foreign countries to return home immediately to face unspecified charges of "defaming their country abroad." According to *Al-Ahram,* the accused journalists worked for Arabic language newspapers in Lebanon, Iraq, Britain, and France. Copies of their articles and tape recordings of their broadcasts critical of Sadat were referred to Egypt's socialist prosecutor, who is empowered to investigate political offenses. These journalists were requested to report to the nearest Egyptian embassy or be tried in absentia.

Sadat's purge against his critics at home gathered momentum when five leading journalists, including Heikal, were barred from leaving the country pending investigation of charges of defaming Egypt in the foreign media. The four writers named besides Heikal were Mohamed Sayed Ahmad of *Al-Ahram,* Ahmad Hamroush of *Rose el-Yousef,* Salah Eissa of *Al-Gumhouriya,* and Fuad Negm, a poet. The five had been accused of persistently writing defamatory articles against Egypt abroad and of writing articles in the domestic press aimed at "dissension and threatening social peace." All leftists, with the exception of Heikal, these writers had been prevented from writing for publication in Egypt and had turned to markets abroad. Heikal was included on the list for criticizing Sadat in his interviews with *Al-Ahaly* and two other interviews with the *Times* of London and the *New York Times.* On May 22, 1978, he told the *Times* of London that Sadat was overreacting to criticism and risking the loss of his most important political achievements. He urged Sadat to tackle the problems rather than simply to try to get to those who were willing to discuss them in public. A week later he told the *New York Times* that "the whole thing is bizarre," because "Sadat wanted a sort of democracy and I think that what he got was more than he wanted."[39]

Angered with the foreign news media coverage of his drive against his critics, Sadat summoned foreign correspondents in Egypt to a country residence outside Cairo and rebuked them. "I am not happy with what I have read in your papers," he told them, "because you are supposed to be the link between us and your people"[40] He singled out the *Times* of London and the British Broadcasting Corporation (BBC) for particular criticism. Addressing correspondent Christopher Walker of the *Times* of London, he said: "I am not happy with what you have written. . . . I advise you seriously, whenever you want to get a story I am ready to meet you."[41] Sadat said he was not curtailing free expression but was moving only against those Egyptians, particularly the leftists, who sought to exploit the liberalization policies for their ends. The *Times* of London and the BBC were rebuked for their long interviews with Heikal. Without naming him, Sadat denounced Heikal, likening him to the notorious Lord Haw Haw (William Joyce) who broadcast Nazi propaganda to Britain from Berlin during World War II. The next day, attacks on Heikal in the state-controlled press gathered momentum. *Al-Gumhouriya* carried a front-page photograph of Heikal and a short account of Lord Haw Haw's career, including his execution for treason when captured at the end of the war.

Responding to Sadat's critical remarks, the *Times* of London launched a sharp attack on his drive to silence his critics. In an editorial published on May 29, 1978, the *Times* wrote:

. . . Many of [Sadat's] friends in the West will be distressed by the developments of the last fortnight which clearly suggest he is now trying to set stricter limits on freedom both of expression and of political activity. It is hard to believe that such measures are necessary, for no evidence has yet been produced to suggest that the opposition groups and individuals against which they are aimed constitute any serious threat to the regime.

Mr. Sadat must know that by taking action against such well-known figures he does much greater damage to his regime's international reputation than their own criticism ever could. . . . The foreign press was in fact a loophole through which opposition journalists banned from contributing to government-owned media were allowed to go on writing. Another loophole, more recently opened, was the newspaper of the left-wing opposition party, *Al-Ahali*. That, too, it seems, is in the process of being closed.

Ten days later, Sadat threatened to expel foreign journalists who wrote incorrect stories about Egypt. Speaking to units of the Egyptian army at Suez, he said that correspondents who continue casting doubt will be told: "Thank you, we don't need you with us . . . we don't need propaganda."

On June 2, 1978, the People's Assembly, after long hours of debate, passed by an overwhelming majority the internal security law proposed by Sadat. Among those who spoke against it were members of the rightest New Wafd party and the left-wing coalition who warned that this law could put an end to party life and political activities in Egypt. Less than 24 hours after the passing of the law, the New Wafd party voted unanimously at a meeting in Cairo to disband itself in protest against the measure. In a statement issued to the press, the party declared itself "unable to practice its functions under these measures and legislation which sanction a clampdown on the citizens and render any existing political party a mere facade too crippled to undertake its patriotic duties."[42]

The left-wing alliance followed suit on June 5 and announced a freeze on all its activities and the closure of its newspaper *Al-Ahaly*. In a bitterly worded statement handed to foreign correspondents in Cairo, the National Progressive Unionist party said that it would keep its activities suspended until the new law is revoked. The statement accused the Center party of liquidating Egypt's democratic experiment while it was still in its infancy. The statement also said the new law breached the article in the Constitution guaranteeing equality irrespective of race, religion, or political beliefs.

Meeting in Beirut, Lebanon, on June 21, the Union of Arab Journalists condemned Sadat's moves to purge the Egyptian press of his critics. The union, which represents press organizations throughout the Arab world, announced that it was moving its headquarters from Cairo to Baghdad, Iraq. The Iraqi representative at the meeting said his government was ready to grant Iraqi citizenship to any Egyptian journalist or writer who might be deprived of his Egyptian citizenship as a result of the Sadat crackdown.

At this writing, the fate of Sadat's critics is uncertain. In July 1978, there was no indication that the Egyptian journalists living abroad were returning to Egypt to face charges against them. Heikal and Sayed Ahmad, however, both told foreign correspondents they fear the crackdown could lead to imprisonment of dissidents or sequestration of their property.[43]

CHAPTER 2

Heikal: The Rise To Power

CONTRARY to the beliefs of some writers,[1] Heikal does not come from a background of poverty. According to Heikal himself, his father Hassanein Ali Heikal was a middle-class landowner and cotton merchant who lived between the Egyptian countryside and Cairo. He represented the "semi-rich" peasants who often traveled to the city and could afford to send their children to schools in the capital. Later, Heikal's father left his village to live in Cairo to be close to his business. He married a Cairo woman who gave him two sons and six daughters. Mohamed, the eldest of the boys, was born in Cairo on September 23, 1923.

The Heikal family was raised in a middle-class home influenced by village morals and religious traditions. Heikal still recalls "Sheik Qassem," the old man who came to their home and taught them verses from the Koran. Heikal attended Cairo schools and was graduated from high school with a diploma in commerce. Later he studied economics at Cairo University and journalism at the American University at Cairo. Through private study he obtained diplomas in law, advertising, and journalism and acquired a better than average command of English.

Early Journalistic Experience

Heikal's interest in journalism started at an early age. While in high school, he demonstrated excellent style in Arabic composition and feature writing. He was encouraged to expand this talent and later wrote short stories and poetry. His actual introduction to the press, however, came in 1942 when he attended a lecture by Scott Watson, a Briton working for Cairo's English daily, *The Egyptian Gazette.* Watson announced that he was recruiting young journalism students to be trainees at the *Gazette.* Heikal went for an interview and was among three students selected. He worked under Watson as a trainee without pay; then he worked for Phillip Henein, an Egyptian editor in charge of local news at the *Gazette,* who assigned to Heikal the job of crime reporter—also without pay.

At the age of 19, Heikal found himself covering the battle of El-Alamein in North Africa. His reporting attracted the attention of

Harold Earle, editor of the *Gazette,* who advised him to work for the local Arabic press in Cairo. He gave him a letter of recommendation to Mohamed el-Tab'i, editor of the weekly magazine, *Akher Sa'a* (Stop Press). There Heikal worked as layout man without pay for a long time.[2]

According to Fat'hi Ghanem, one of Heikal's close friends at the time, Heikal lived in a small room in one of the poorest sections of Cairo. Ghanem remembers clearly his first visit to Heikal in the early 1940s: "Heikal's uncurtained room had an iron bedstead, a cheap desk, two shelves of books, nails to hang up pajamas and spare clothes—these were its furnishings. Yet outside, in Groppi's, at the Gezira Club, Heikal was already fastidious in his tastes for the material best."[3]

A turning point in Heikal's career came in 1946 when *Akhbar el-Yom* bought *Akher Sa'a* and retained Heikal. He preferred to work for the Amin brothers and turned down an offer to join Dar el-Hilal. At *Akhbar el-Yom* he wrote an unsigned column, "Crime of the Week," but shortly thereafter began to emphasize investigative political journalism, which led to his eventual success.

Heikal Meets Nasser

Heikal's opportunity came with the outbreak of the first Arab-Israeli war in 1948. He urged his editors to send him to Palestine to cover the war from the front lines rather than to depend on official communiques. He knew the battlefield well since he had accompanied Arab resistance units on military operations inside Palestine prior to the war. He flew from Cairo to Amman and conducted a series of interviews with King Abdallah of Transjordan, who was in charge of Arab forces in Palestine. Then he went to Jerusalem and from there joined the Egyptian troops on their way to Al-Magdal in southern Palestine. There he met for the first time Major Gamal Abdul Nasser, commander of the Sixth Battalion in the Negev Desert, whose name was destined to affect Middle Eastern history. Details of that meeting are still fresh in Heikal's memory:

It was one hot afternoon of June 1948. I was riding an Army jeep on my way from Bethlehem to Al-Magdal. Suddenly fighting erupted between the Egyptians and the Israelis at Iraq-Sweidan. The driver could go no further and I had to walk to the nearest Egyptian post at Iraq-el-Manshiyah. When I arrived at the police station, which was turned into a military headquarters, I met many officers and soldiers who were talking about defeating an Israeli attack on their positions. They told me that Gamal Abdul Nasser led the counterattack and won the battle. When I was taken to see him, I met a tall man whose face was clearly marked with exhaustion. He was spreading a blanket on the room's floor and was about to go to sleep. An officer introduced me as a journalist interested in covering the news of the war. He said simply: "I've read your articles. I expected to meet an older man." Nasser refused to give any information about the fighting. He was angry about what was published in the Egyptian press and was dismayed with the way the press handled the war in Palestine. I had to leave him then so he could get some rest following his five days of fighting without any sleep.[4]

When he returned to Palestine to continue coverage of the war, Heikal saw Nasser a second time. They met for the third time after the first United Nations cease-fire in Palestine. Nasser showed interest in a series that Heikal had written from Paris about the UN Security Council's special session on Palestine. While other Arab publicists dismissed the Israelis as disorganized Jewish gangs, Heikal tried vainly to alert the Egyptian army and government to the toughness and determination of the Israeli troops. Then came the siege of Falouja, the small Negeb fort held by Nasser and his troops against superior Israeli forces until the Armistice of 1949. The armistice ended the first Arab-Israeli war and led to the establishment of Israel as an independent state. In a series of articles in *Akhbar el-Yom,* Heikal described the siege under the title: "The Wounded Who Wrote with Their Blood the Story of Falouja." The siege of Falouja, where Nasser was wounded, proved to be the seedbed of the Egyptian revolution.

"Legendary" Reputation

Heikal spent the spring of 1949 in Ankara reporting on the Turkish elections. From there he went to Greece to cover the Communist guerrilla war and spent some time at the borders between Bulgaria, Yugoslavia, and Albania. Then he flew to Damascus to write about the series of military coups d'etat in Syria. Shortly after arriving in Cairo, he was visited in his office at *Akhbar el-Yom* by Gamal Abdul Nasser and Salah Salem, one of the Free Officers who led the coup against King Farouk. "I have been reading your articles ever since you warned us about Palestine," Nasser reportedly said. "Too bad no one took your advice!" Nasser requested detailed information about the military uprisings in Syria and about the reaction of the people to them.

In 1952 Heikal covered the American presidential elections after accepting a State Department Leader Grant to visit the United States, a country that was glamorous to the young journalist. This grant sparked rumors that he was an "American agent," a charge he was never able to live down.[5] He returned to Egypt via Korea where he wrote his impressions of the Korean War. Shortly thereafter, he shifted his interest to the Iranian crises of the 1950s. In Teheran he wrote about the rise and fall of Prime Minister Mohamed Mossadeq. He implicitly condemned the anti-Western movement of Mossadeq for its dependence on Russian support. He included his impressions of Iran in an Arabic book titled *Iran Fawqa Burkan* (Iran on Top of a Volcano). Soon after publication of the book, Heikal was charged with violating what was known as the "Law of Kings' Protection," designed to prevent attack or comment on the reputation of kings friendly to Egypt. He was charged with tarnishing the royal reputation of the Shah of Iran by including a chapter in his book about an Iranian House of Representatives debate in which the Shah was attacked. He was released later on bail. Heikal admitted later that he changed some parts of the debate to make criticisms of the Shah applicable to King Farouk.[6]

Heikal became the star reporter of the Egyptian press and attracted the attention of many observers, including the Farouk government and the army officers planning to overthrow his regime. For three successive years, Heikal won the Farouk Prize for Excellence in Journalism for his reporting on Palestine, Greece, and the cholera epidemic that swept Egypt and claimed 17,000 lives. The committee organizing the competition asked Heikal not to enter for the fourth year to allow other journalists the opportunity to win.[7] Heikal ascribes his success to the challenge of risk and adventure:

I was fortunate to build up my journalistic career outside Egypt. I was not willing to go after government news and wait behind closed doors to ask for official favor. I chose the difficult track of covering foreign news and faced the challenge of death. Finally my name was associated with the dramatic events that claimed public attention.[8]

At the time, Heikal was the only Arab journalist to cover foreign news. The Egyptian press exploited Heikal's scoops and proclaimed his name above the news he covered. Some front-page headlines read in large-size type:

HEIKAL COVERS FRONT LINES FROM PALESTINE

HEIKAL ENTERS KOREA

HEIKAL WRITES FROM IRAN

HEIKAL ON THE COUP D'ETAT IN SYRIA

By the time Heikal settled in Egypt in 1951, his journalistic adventures abroad had become nearly legendary. "The whole Egyptian underground movement was in contact with me," he recalled in conversation. "Everybody was fascinated by my foreign experience and my knowledge of coups d'etat." Many politicans tried to pull him into the political arena and Nagib el-Hilaly, last prime minister under King Farouk, asked Heikal to be director of his prime ministry. Heikal turned down all political offers because he preferred to work as a journalist.[9]

The Message Conveyor

For a second time, Nasser surprised Heikal in his office at *Akhbar el-Yom* following Heikal's return from Iran. Nasser asked to borrow a copy of Heikal's book about Iran to read. Although they chatted for a while about Iran among other things, Heikal was unaware that Nasser was leading a secret movement in the army. It was not until July 18, 1952, four days before the coup took place, that Heikal was taken into Nasser's confidence. On that day he met Nasser and Abdul-Hakim Amer, Nasser's closest friend, at General Mohamed Nagib's house. They discussed the crisis that erupted between the king and the army following the king's orders to dissolve the Officers Club. General Nagib was among a group of officers who won election to the club's executive committee with the support of Nasser and his group. In the discussion Heikal told Nasser: "If the army failed to defend the country in 1948, at least it should defend its honor now." Nasser responded by asking Heikal: "What do you expect the army to do—a coup d'etat like what happened in Syria?" Heikal, though he would later regret it, was against the idea of overthrowing the regime. He admitted later that he offered Nasser a naive idea. He suggested that a group of 1,000 officers meet with the king in his palace, tell him that things were getting worse, and demand that he do something to improve the situation. But Nasser dismissed the idea as impractical. They continued their discussion as Heikal drove Nasser and Amer to downtown Cairo. Nasser asked Heikal: "Do you think the British would intervene if the army were to overthrow the king?" Heikal said that was a remote possibility because the British did not have enough troops to control all Egyptian cities. Nasser was interested in Heikal's analysis and asked that they meet again to talk further. The next morning Nasser called on Heikal and asked him to expand on his belief that the British could not intervene in an army coup. Heikal gave a long list of reasons while Nasser listened attentively. When the meeting ended, Heikal felt that the army was about to embark on a great adventure.[10]

That day Heikal left for Alexandria to meet with Nagib el-Hilaly, whom Heikal admired as a friend and experienced politician. Hilaly was designated the premier following a series of cabinet changes by the king. Hilaly was in the process of selecting his cabinet members when he asked Heikal to join him in Alexandria, where the king was spending the summer. At Hilaly's request Heikal recommended a number of persons whom he knew personally for the cabinet and returned to Cairo that same night. On arrival he found a message that Nasser wanted to see him within the next two days. On July 22, Hilaly contacted Heikal and told him that the king had received information about some kind of movement in the army. Hilaly knew that Heikal was a close friend of General Nagib and suspected that he might know something. Heikal told him he knew nothing about the matter and rushed to army headquarters with the help of an army officer. By the time he arrived, the revolt was over and Nasser and his group were in complete control. It was in the early hours of July 23 that he finally met Nasser. Nasser's first words to Heikal were: "You claimed that the army failed to defend the country in 1948. Are you satisfied with what the army did now?"[11]

With Nasser's permission, Heikal called his newspaper and left his phone number at the headquarters. Mustafa Amin, who was in Alexandria, passed the number on to Premier Hilaly. A few minutes later Hilaly was on the line from Alexandria talking to Heikal. He asked him to find out from the leaders of the coup what they wanted. Nasser was listening to the conversation and said: "Tell him to listen to our communique which will be broadcast over Cairo radio at 7:00 A.M." Heikal conveyed the message but Hilaly insisted that Heikal tell the officers there was no need for such a "noise." Hilaly offered to have the king appoint General Nagib as commander-in-chief of the army and Nagib welcomed the idea instantly. But Nasser said firmly: "No" and asked Heikal to tell Hilaly that his demands were rejected. Heikal closed the line and tried to explain to Nasser that Hilaly was a straight and honorable man who was in a difficult situation. Nasser said: "I don't care what he is; I want the cabinet to resign so people will know that we are in full control of the situation." At that moment

Heikal realized that Nasser, who stayed in the background most of the time, was the real brains of the plot. He published this in a momentous scoop. Their conversations that week started a friendship and a dialogue that continued until Nasser's death in 1970, with no small consequence for Egypt.

CHAPTER 3

Al-Ahram: Heikal's Journalistic Empire

UNDER Heikal, *Al-Ahram* became required reading for any student of Middle Eastern politics. Through its columns Heikal echoed Nasser's thoughts, aspirations, and reflections. For seventeen continuous years *Al-Ahram* was read, digested, and dissected by diplomats and academics and it formed much of the intelligence upon which important decisions were based in cabinet rooms around the world.

In June 1976 *Al-Ahram* celebrated its 100th birthday by opening a centenary exhibition on the newspaper premises in Cairo. The occasion commemorated the establishment of *Al-Ahram* as a cornerstone of the Egyptian press.

Al-Ahram, like many things in nineteenth-century Egypt, had a Lebanese origin. In 1876 two Lebanese brothers, Salim and Bishara Taqla, left Ottoman-controlled Beirut seeking freedom in Egypt. After arriving in Alexandria they started a four-page weekly paper which they called *Al-Ahram* (The Pyramids). In 1900, however, the Taqlas moved their paper to Cairo at a time when much of the commercial, cultural, and political activities shifted from Alexandria to the capital.

The Taqlas became part of the Franco-Turkish-Christian establishment which held the reins of authority in Egypt. In its early days, *Al-Ahram* supported French interests. Later it adopted a more nationalist viewpoint, usually backing the nationalist Wafd party against both the king and the British, though never becoming a definite party organ.

From the start, *Al-Ahram* was a pioneer in journalistic innovations. It was the first newspaper in the Arab world to use interviews as news-gathering tools and the first newspaper to print a photograph (1881). It was also the first Egyptian paper to send correspondents to foreign countries and to open press offices in foreign capitals. In 1917 it introduced the first Linotype typesetter to Egypt.[1]

Unless otherwise noted, this chapter is based on a private interview with Mohamed Hassanein Heikal, Cairo, July 12, 1976.

Al-Ahram Retreats

In the early 1940s *Al-Ahram* suffered a decline in its reputation and circulation. Those were years of agitation, tension, and political unrest followed by the anti-British movement, the Arab-Israeli conflict in Palestine, corruption of the Farouk regime, the Cairo fire, and civil disorders that culminated in the revolution of 1952. *Al-Ahram* was forced out of the picture by other newspapers. It could not compete with *Al-Masri,* which adopted an extreme policy of political agitation, nor with *Al-Akhbar,* which emphasized sensational news and appealed to the young. Under pressure of competition and political unrest, *Al-Ahram* failed to set a definite editorial policy. This proved disastrous for *Al-Ahram,* as readers began to abandon it, feeling they were missing much important news.

Faced with mounting difficulties, *Al-Ahram* tried to survive on its old reputation. Its problems were complicated further by the death of its publisher Gubrael Taqla (son of Bishara Taqla) in 1946 and by the death of its capable editor Antone el-Gumayyel in 1949. *Al-Ahram*'s circulation dropped from 100,000 to 68,000 daily copies and its losses between 1945 and 1955 reached one and a half million Egyptian pounds ($3.5 million). The Taqla family began to worry that, sooner or later, they had to face the inevitable death of *Al-Ahram.* They noticed at the time that their subscription list included only faithful readers from the old generation. As their number decreased there was a proportionate increase in the names of dead people on the obituary page of *Al-Ahram.* This correlation between the subscription list and obituary page was a clear sign that *Al-Ahram* was dying slowly along with its faithful readers.

Heikal's Conflict with the Amins

In an attempt to have a voice of his own, Nasser started a "regime newspaper" *(Al-Gumhouriya)* in 1953 and made Anwar el-Sadat its first editor. That position was previously refused by Heikal who was unconvinced that the regime should have its own newspaper. Heikal instead suggested that the regime have its own political party. He preferred to continue to work for the Amin brothers at *Akhbar el-Yom.* Nasser apparently had genuine fears about the potential power of the privately owned press. Aware of the troubles facing *Al-Ahram,* he waited for the right opportunity to control it.

As early as 1951 *Al-Ahram* approached Heikal and asked him to be manager of both the news and feature sections. He declined the offer because he preferred to stay with *Akhbar el-Yom* and to continue his travels abroad as a correspondent. It was not until 1955, however, that the *Al-Ahram* board of directors offered Heikal the editorship, hoping his experience and name would help *Al-Ahram* overcome its increasing problems. Heikal accepted the offer this time because he was bored and unhappy with the way the Amin brothers were running *Akhbar el-Yom*. His unhappiness stemmed from the paper's handling of the killing of Amin Osman Pasha, one of the prominent political figures in Egypt, who cooperated with the British and was labeled "traitor" by the nationalist movement. At Anwar el-Sadat's orders, Hussein Tawfiq, a young nationalist, shot and killed Osman. But instead of arresting Tawfiq, the king ordered him to flee. *Al-Akhbar's* editorials praised Tawfiq as a "hero" who killed Osman "the traitor." Heikal disagreed with the Amins on this policy and argued against praising a killer, especially one who was given the king's protection. On another occasion, Heikal clashed with the Amins openly in the press. In his weekly column in *Akhbar el-Yom,* Mustafa Amin supported the British-Egyptian treaty and called on the government to sign it. Heikal, now promoted to editor of *Akher Sa'a,* answered Amin's article and argued against the signing of the treaty.

When the editorship of *Al-Ahram* was offered to Heikal, he decided to leave the Amins without consulting them. He went directly to Bishara Taqla and signed an initial contract. When news of the agreement reached the Amins, they sent for Heikal, locked the office, and argued for hours against his leaving them. Heikal told them that he had no personal feelings against them but thought he had a better opportunity at *Al-Ahram* where he might be able to save a "dying" newspaper. But the Amins persisted and promised him a few changes in the administration and policies of *Akhbar el-Yom.* Finally Heikal surrendered and signed a letter to Bishara Taqla stating that, for personal reasons, he was turning down editorship of *Al-Ahram.*

Heikal continued to work for the Amins throughout 1956 and 1957 but remained discontented at *Akhbar el-Yom.* In early 1957, however, Sadat sent for Heikal at his home in Zamalek and told him dramatically: "We have decided to buy *Al-Ahram,* and you will be in charge." Heikal said he was unwilling to work for a government newspaper but Sadat urged him to accept, saying these were the president's orders. Heikal refused and went to see Nasser. He told him that he was not convinced that the government should buy "a dying newspaper." "Before you buy *Al-Ahram,*" Heikal told Nasser, "you better make out of *Al-Gumhouriya* a successful newspaper; if you really buy *Al-Ahram,* it will inevitably die and I am not willing to be the one who marches in its funeral and sends it to its grave.''

Heikal Goes to *Al-Ahram*

By June 1957 Heikal had come to feel that *Akhbar el-Yom* was turning into a marketplace rather than a jornalistic institution. At this time, the *Al-Ahram* board of directors contacted Heikal and again offered him the editorship. This time Heikal made up his mind and went to *Al-Ahram* and signed a new contract. The Taqlas were cautious not to give Heikal a free hand in changing the personality and tradition of the newspaper. They included several strings in the contract which read in part as follows:

Mr. Heikal has to take into consideration the following policies and principles of *Al-Ahram:*
Al-Ahram is a nationalist and independent newspaper which stands for respect of public order, state authority, laws, religion, and ethical standards. It does not believe in attacking religions and stands against atheism. In its support of social justice, *Al-Ahram* resists Communism as an ideology. It is committed to the principles of truth, moderation, sympathy, politeness and independence in opinion with respect for opposing views. . . .
It is taken for granted, however, that any change in the existing policies of *Al-Ahram* cannot be made without the approval of the board of directors.[2]

Before signing the contract, Heikal spent some time arguing with the board that some of the items were meaningless and would tend to limit his activities as editor. The board finally agreed to ease some items and eliminate others completely. The contract gave Heikal a handsome monthly salary of 500 Egyptian pounds ($1,500). Later, when Heikal asked for a share in *Al-Ahram* profits, he was told that *Al-Ahram* was losing money. He replied: ''I can wait until *Al-Ahram* makes a profit.'' The board agreed to give him a share of 2.5 percent of *Al-Ahram* profits, when and if that would happen.

Before starting his new job, Heikal took a month's leave and went to Alexandria to study *Al-Ahram*'s budget and circulation. Meanwhile, the two editors of *Al-Ahram,* Ahmad el-Sawy and Aziz Merza, continued to work for the newspaper. On August 5, 1957, at Heikal's first meeting with the staff, he was asked how he wanted the next morning's issue. He said: ''I want it exactly as yesterday's.'' He was worried that, if he were to introduce any changes then, he might lose the 68,000 subscribers who chose to stay with *Al-Ahram.* He also had no idea at that time what sort of changes he wanted to bring about.

In his first tour of the *Al-Ahram* building, he came out with a sad impression. The building, which once belonged to the Italian Consul in Cairo, was located on an old downtown street. When the Taqlas moved *Al-Ahram* to the building in 1900, typesetting and engraving machines were placed in the basement, and upper floors were used for editing. Later an annex for administration was added and connected with the old building by bridges and an underground tunnel. To Heikal, the whole structure was a symbol of backwardness. "I had a feeling that the building was filled with ghosts," Heikal recalled. "I could feel the inhibitions in every corner, but nobody was willing to do something about it; nobody wanted to change; they were scared of development and chose to hide behind their superiority complex."

Plan for Development

For a month Heikal kept *Al-Ahram* going without any change. In September 1957, however, he met with the board of directors under the chairmanship of Madame Taqla, widow of Gubrael Taqla. Like the rest of the Taqla family, Madame Taqla had been educated in French schools and had lost touch with the Arabic language. Ironically, she could not read *Al-Ahram,* the oldest and most celebrated journal of the Arab world. She asked Heikal to prepare a report for the meeting in French, a language he did not know well. As a compromise, she agreed that he could present the report in a mixture of French and English.

From the first moment, Heikal told the board members he was unwilling to accept the status quo at *Al-Ahram* and suggested a three-stage plan for development:

1. A priority plan to change *Al-Ahram* into a real "news" paper. In order to compete with the "sensational" *Al-Akhbar,* and the "official" *Al-Gumhouriya,* Heikal wanted to emphasize true political news and provide readers with quick news service backed by interpretation and background analysis.

2. A short-range plan to allocate a special fund for recruiting new staff members and buying modern press equipment. Heikal said there was a lack of trained reporters in Egypt and he would train his own team.

3. A long-range plan to allocate funds for a new building for *Al-Ahram.* Heikal said progress would be impossible without getting rid of the present facilities and assets.

The board agreed to Heikal's demands with some reservations. They allowed him a budget of 10,000 Egyptian pounds ($28,000) for investment during his first year. This was over and above what he could save from the editorial budget. Later he pared his news budget in two ways. First, he cut an Associated Press special service fee from 2,000 pounds ($6,000) to 300 pounds ($800) every month. Second, he closed down idle *Al-Ahram* offices in foreign capitals but retained them for future use.

Heikal's Unique Experiment

When Heikal started looking for new reporters he found the market acutely short of experienced journalists and the Department of Journalism at Cairo University hardly filling the needs of other newspapers and magazines. In Heikal's opinion "borrowing" veteran journalists from other newspapers would not fit into his plans for a modern newspaper. Finally he decided to embark on a unique experiment that Heikal considers a landmark in the history of *Al-Ahram.* He hired fifty fresh university graduates from different areas and started for them a "small school of journalism." They were given regular college-level courses in news reporting and other fields and were taught the "secrets of the profession" by a group of veteran *Al-Ahram* craftsmen. Bishara Taqla was not enthusiastic about the idea and one time, seeing Heikal lecturing to one class he commented sarcastically: "You are turning *Al-Ahram* into a Kuttab."[3] Heikal was displeased with the comment but told Taqla that that was the only way to train reporters.

To Heikal, the training process was very important. Shortly he was able to create a dependable reporting team out of the young recruits. These were the "striking force" with which he started to build *Al-Ahram*'s new image and reputation. By the end of 1958, *Al-Ahram*'s circulation had jumped to 120,000 and its budget had gone from a deficit to a net profit of 23,000 pounds ($65,000). People who once read Heikal in *Akhbar el-Yom* watched his move to *Al-Ahram* and waited to see what he was going to do. Many of them sensed the new pulse in *Al-Ahram* and began to notice the difference between it and other newspapers. Many news stories in other newspapers turned out to be untrue while *Al-Ahram* offered a more dependable news service. Heikal gave his attention mainly to the front page and emphasized significant news in big headlines. Foreign news was stressed in a special daily corner on the second page, and a complete "op-ed" page, including letters to the editor and other articles of opinion and comment, appeared in a daily corner. One month later, Heikal began to increase the number and size of photographs on the front and last pages.

Heikal's first scoop in *Al-Ahram* was an exclusive interview in

Moscow with Soviet Premier Nikita Khrushchev in September 1957. Heikal accompanied an Egyptian delegation to Moscow to celebrate the fortieth anniversary of the Soviet revolution. He published a long debate with Khruschev and commented on the events in the Kremlin that led to the fall of the antiparty group in the Soviet Union. These events were significant to the Egyptian reader in the aftermath of the 1956 Suez war and the backing of Egypt by the Soviet Union.

Heikal's well-known column "Bisaraha" (Frankly Speaking), begun at *Akhbar el-Yom,* was moved to *Al-Ahram* where it appeared irregularly. It did not become a regular weekly item until 1960 when the press was nationalized and Heikal was given a free hand at *Al-Ahram.* He started a week-end supplement in which he included his long column "Bisaraha" which consumed more than a full page. The supplement also featured news analysis, foreign affairs, literature, art, science, and sports, among other things. Heikal also recruited "big names" from the literary world to write for the supplement. He wanted to create prestige for *Al-Ahram* by associating it with Egyptian household names such as Tawfiq el-Hakim, Nagib Mahfouz, Yousef Idris, Lewis Awad, and Bint el-Shati'. In an attempt to keep the reputation of *Al-Ahram* as a dignified institution, he announced that he would refuse to meet with anybody outside his office, short of the president and foreign heads of state.

Al-Ahram's New Face

Heikal was careful, however, to introduce editorial changes gradually. But in early 1964 he surprised his readers with a total shake-up in *Al-Ahram's* personality and editorial content. Heikal, who had prepared for a full year for this major step in the development of the newspaper, increased the number of pages from 10 to 12 and gave more space and attention to foreign news, activities of mass organizations, and cultural events. He assigned special correspondents to *Al-Ahram* offices in foreign capitals and signed new contracts with press associations and syndicated services of large newspapers around the world. Thus he could offer two full pages of foreign news every day.

On the cultural level, Heikal came out with a unique idea. In a series titled "Da'irat Ma'aref *Al-Ahram*" (Encyclopedia of *Al-Ahram*), he started a daily corner covering all sorts of knowledge alphabetically with a different topic each day. For this project Heikal assigned a committee of three university professors to coordinate the works of more than one hundred specialists in humanities and social and natural sciences.

In his efforts to compete with radio and television, Heikal created a team of specialized news reporters and emphasized news coverage in depth. He selected a group of young reporters and trained them to become investigative reporters. Then he embarked on another ambitious project. He set up three study centers at *Al-Ahram* for journalistic, historical, and political and economic studies. From these centers, he created a joint center for strategic studies for which he recruited a group of researchers to deal with highly complicated subjects such as conflict analysis and conflict resolution. The purpose of these centers was to guarantee for *Al-Ahram* a dependable and accurate source of news analysis and background material and to prepare young reporters for future control of the editorial and opinion pages in an attempt to raise the general editorial quality of the newspaper.

It took Heikal about five years to make *Al-Ahram* a household word in the world press. *Al-Ahram* started gradually to grasp readers' attention on the local level and then began to build rapidly a worldwide reputation. Its circulation climbed to 650,000 copies on weekdays and nearly a million copies on Fridays, the Moslem sabbath. In the late fifties and during the sixties, *Al-Ahram* became one of the most important sources for understanding the Middle East. It was quoted daily around the world as one of the most authoritative and dependable sources of information about Arab life. In a book on quality journalism around the world, Professor John Merrill of the University of Missouri, in 1968, ranked *Al-Ahram* as an elite newspaper among the top newspapers; this ranking was based on opinions of an assortment of international opinion leaders. The book also contained a profile of *Al-Ahram.*[4]

What made *Al-Ahram* significant in world circles, according to Heikal, were three major factors:

1. Heikal's emphasis on "news" as a major selling point for *Al-Ahram,* and his creation of a first-class news team headed by a veteran editor.

2. Heikal's closeness to Nasser and to big events in Egypt and the Arab world.

3. World interest in the Middle East as a region of strategic value and natural resources, and the significance of Egypt as an axis for the Arab nationalist movement and a center of events shaping the destiny of the entire region. Through accurate reporting on these events *Al-Ahram* subsequently captured world attention.

Heikal does not believe, however, that his closeness to Nasser was the major factor in building *Al-Ahram's* world reputation. He dismisses as nonsense the accusation of his critics that he had a total monopoly over news because of his friendship to Nasser.

There was no such thing as a news monopoly. I was close to Nasser not only as a friend, but as a newsman who was interested in being close to events and in speaking his mind. . . . Nasser never gave me a single news item, and I had to depend totally on my first-class team of reporters. These were my striking force and the major recruitment that I made at *Al-Ahram.* . . . No doubt, my closeness to Nasser helped me make a quick verification on the news to be sure of its accuracy. At times I had to check major news stories and add to them because I was in a position to see the whole picture. . . . But news gathering at *Al-Ahram* was a collective effort to which I only contributed a minor part.

Heikal thinks of himself as having been a successful reporter even before he came to know Nasser. He believes that what made *Al-Ahram* a significant newspaper was not only his closeness to Nasser but also the significance of Cairo as a center of important events in the Middle East as well as his own journalistic talents. He argues that if Egypt had not had this influential role in Arab affairs, his closeness to Nasser would not have made a difference. He thinks that many journalists were very close to heads of state but were unable to do what he did at *Al-Ahram.* He gives an example of Tareq Aziz, the Iraqi minister of information, who is still close to the Iraqi president. As editor of *Al-Thawra,* organ of the ruling Ba'ath party in Iraq, Tareq Aziz was the mouthpiece of the regime and at one time he considered himself "the Heikal of Iraq" and campaigned against Nasser and Heikal together. According to Heikal, these campaigns were not effective because Iraq did not have the same distinctive role as Egypt. Heikal tells a similar story about President Tito of Yugoslavia:

When I was visiting Yugoslavia with President Nasser, I was summoned to meet President Tito one evening. I entered the room and found Presidents Tito and Nasser talking about *Al-Ahram.* Tito looked at me and said: "I am very pleased with what you are doing at *Al-Ahram;* our journalists here in Yugoslavia write in *Borba* good things but nobody quotes them in the foreign press." He thought for a while and said: "I need to have my own Heikal." I was surprised at this remark, while President Nasser was laughing. Tito continued: "Can I send you a journalist who is close to me to train him at *Al-Ahram?*" I said: "That's fine with me." Later he sent to me in Cairo one of *Borba's* top editors who spent three months with us at *Al-Ahram.* After his leaving, we never heard a word about him.

To Heikal it was not a matter of being close to the top leader as much as it was a matter of being a good journalist who was close to events of news value. He believes that Egypt during the fifties and the sixties was much more significant than Yugoslavia or Iraq in influencing world affairs. Cairo was the spokesman for the Arab world, a region boiling with significant events because of the superpowers' struggle over its strategic value and oil reserves.

Heikal's News Philosophy and Style

Heikal's emphasis on his news team reflects his philosophy with regard to news coverage. He chose to stress significant news and explain it to readers with analysis, interpretation, and comment. He was careful, however, not to mix news with views. He included his own opinion and that of other columnists in *Al-Ahram* editorials and columns and kept straight news in separate columns. He believes, however, that a news story should have its own interpretation and background material within the item itself. Separation of straight facts and personal views, in Heikal's opinion, is a matter of theory.

I don't believe there is such a thing as objectivity in news coverage. In fact, we separate news and views only in appearance; the way in which we present news reflects a certain position that we adhere to. There is no newspaper in the world whose news coverage is not colored by one political position or another. It is humanly impossible for any person to filter views from straight news completely.

However, Heikal used to call the attention of his editors at the central news desk of *Al-Ahram* to the fact that most news stories coming over wire services were colored with certain views and that they should be separate from the straight news. In spite of that effort, Heikal believes he was unable to reach total separation of news and views.

To Heikal, the newspaper business is a highly personal one controlled by the editor. He makes an analogy between a newspaper editor and an orchestra conductor.

A conductor does not play any musical instrument but he is the one that controls the rhythm. Like a newspaper editor, a conductor gives part of himself to his work and that's what makes the difference between one conductor and another, or between one editor or another. Newspapers like the *Times* of London or *Le Monde* of Paris, for example, reflected the character and style of their editors at different times. A newspaper is an instrument of human communication and not a deaf printing machine. The human element is there, whether we recognize that or not.

Heikal believes that the arrangement of facts within a news story and the way a story is displayed are important. He thinks, however, that an editor's major job is to control the balance of his newspaper, deciding how different pages are to be built up and different items emphasized. Heikal believes this balance is what gives every newspaper its own style and character, particularly through front-page balance and display of the major news story of the day.

In editorial writing, Heikal developed his own novel and vivacious style in Arab journalism. In a period of feverish political interest in the Middle East, he ignored the sensationalizing influence of the Amin brothers and gave detailed, serious attention to burning issues. Just as news columns of *Al-Ahram* were the most informative source about Egypt, his long weekly editorial "Frankly Speaking" was read by millions for its reflections on Nasser's thought. A British writer once remarked that "Heikal spoke with an earnestness of a college lecturer who was unusually attentive to the thematic sequence of what he wrote. Subdivision within subdivision became a feature of his style."[5] Edward Sheehan, an American journalist and novelist who is a close observer of Heikal, wrote about his style:

He is always interesting, often funny, and sometimes maddening. He writes as he talks; his favorite subject is himself, and he is so fond of elaborate digressions that he can consume thousands of words before he comes to his point. He is a master of the overwrought purple-patch: "The sultans of the dark have fallen," he wrote of the abortive conspiracy of 1971 against President Sadat, "and the phantoms of fear have vanished. Twice Providence intervened to undo the disaster that would have plunged Egypt into the pit of night, causing her to lose her sweetest and most precious posession. . . ." It reads better in Arabic.[6]

The New "Pyramid"*

When *Al-Ahram* began to make profits under Heikal, the board of directors in 1958 set up a planning committee to study Heikal's proposed new building for *Al-Ahram*. Heikal sent two members of the committee abroad to study major newspaper plants. They toured three technologically advanced newspaper houses: the *Daily Mirror* in

---

* "Heikal's Pyramid," meaning "Ahram of Heikal" in Arabic, is a term used by his critics in reference to the extravagance of the new building of *Al-Ahram* which they compare to the ancient Pyramids of the Pharaohs in Cairo.

London, the *Springer* in Hamburg, and the *Mainichi* in Tokyo. Heikal decided to have a closer look at the *Daily Mirror* house because it had some similarities with what he had in mind for *Al-Ahram*. At the same time, he invited to Cairo a German engineer who specialized in designing newspaper plants. He advised Heikal to prepare a report about *Al-Ahram* needs for the next twenty years instead of ten years, explaining that by the time the new project was completed in ten years, *Al-Ahram* would have fallen behind the anticipated plan. Heikal proceeded accordingly.

When the press nationalization law came in 1960, Heikal's project seemed to have fallen apart. Finally he convinced Nasser to allow newspaper profits to stay within the press institutions rather than go to the state treasury. Theoretically, *Al-Ahram* ownership passed to the Arab Socialist Union, but Heikal outmaneuvered the union and formed a cooperative, giving the real ownership of the newspaper to its employees and satisfying the technicalities of the law by leaving the license in the hands of the Arab Socialist Union. The new law stipulated that fifty percent of *Al-Ahram* profits would go to its employees and the other fifty percent would be used to improve services and facilities.

On the day of press nationalization, Heikal called an urgent meeting at *Al-Ahram* and told his employees that the new situation had imposed on them two choices: "Either we accept and surrender to the bureaucracy which will be imposed upon us or we stand up and fight." The word "fight" was soon traveling on AP wires and finally it reached an angry Nasser. "What do you mean by fight?" Nasser asked Heikal. "You know how I talk to my employees at *Al-Ahram,*" replied Heikal. Nasser calmed down and said: "I thought so myself, and I told the cabinet that you were only pushing the new spirit you have been trying to create at *Al-Ahram.*"

At the end of the year, Heikal met with *Al-Ahram* employees and told them he needed their help in financing the new project. He asked their permission to borrow half of their shares in *Al-Ahram* profits as a loan. "If you agree to this," he told them, "we can proceed with our project rapidly and prove that social ownership can be as creative as private ownership." They agreed with Heikal and granted him twenty-five percent of *Al-Ahram* profits. Under this arrangement, they became entitled to only a twenty-five percent share of the profits, ten percent of which came as an annual cash bonus and fifteen percent in social services, including health and sports facilities.

Heikal then pushed the project into full swing. He hired the British engineer who did pioneering research in designing the *Daily*

Mirror house in London. He designed a complete scheme for the technical part of the newspaper, taking a news story from editing through its final printed form. A leading architect in Egypt designed the structure of the building, and another Egyptian artist was in charge of inside decor. Heikal invited a host of Egyptian painters and sculptors to contribute their art to *Al-Ahram* elegance.

It took Heikal ten full years to complete his new "pyramid." In 1968 *Al-Ahram* moved to its new building. The remarkable process of moving 800 tons of archives to the new building in just six hours testifies to Heikal's managerial talents. Before embarking on the moving process, he sent a film crew to Tokyo where they shot the moving process of the *Mainichi* equipment to its new building. These films served as a guide for moving *Al-Ahram* equipment. On the night of October 31, 1968, the last edition of *Al-Ahram* was printed in the old building, and immediately thereafter, everything was moved to the new building, a few blocks to the west. Complete walls were cut down and huge machinery taken out; tens of trucks carried tons of files and office equipment. By 10 A.M. the next day, the operation was completed and the new building was ready to receive *Al-Ahram* employees.

At the completion, the new building had consumed more than four million Egyptian pounds ($9.2 million) of newspaper profits. "We constructed the building and bought the equipment by depending totally on *Al-Ahram* sales and advertising without borrowing from a single bank," said Heikal. "We relied largely on *Al-Ahram* foreign exchange earnings from abroad to import our new equipment." In fact, Heikal was able to increase his foreign exchange earnings to 250,000 pounds ($600,000) annually by expanding his advertising market abroad and by entering into book publishing.

To pay back his employees, Heikal worked out a plan with Nasser. He issued a limited number of capital bonds to cover what was spent on the building, and these bonds were given to the 4,000 employees who practically became the actual owners of *Al-Ahram*.

Al-Ahram: Museum for Egyptian Art

The new fourteen-story building of *Al-Ahram* stands today as one of the half dozen most advanced newspaper complexes in the world. When A. M. Rosenthal, managing editor of the *New York Times,* visited the building in 1970, he was astonished. "There isn't anything in America to compare with it," he said.[7] A host of top journalists were invited by Heikal to speak at *Al-Ahram* as part of its cultural programs. Lord Roy Thompson; Cecil King, board chairman of the *Daily Mirror* group; and Sir Denis Hamilton, editor-in-chief of the *Times* (London) were impressed by what they saw. On returning to London, Sir Hamilton told his staff in an editorial meeting: "If you want to learn some modesty, you must go and visit *Al-Ahram* in Cairo." Some of them took his advice and went to see *Al-Ahram.* One of them wrote his impressions in an article for the *Times:*

> The point that strikes the visitor about *Al-Ahram,* especially as he leaves the congested urgency of Cairo streets, is the elegance, the decor, the cleanliness, the facilities, the lack of vulgarity, haste or spilled emotions. I am sure there is no more hygienic newspaper in the world for I have never seen one with such a conscious facade of art. A paper with its own doctor in permanent attendance, a rota of medical specialists and its own mosque.[8]

The *Al-Ahram* building is really more than a newspaper house. It is both a communication complex and a way of life. It houses the most sophisticated printing equipment that Western technology can offer. Immense marble reception halls, decorated with paintings and ceramic sculpture, lead to antiseptic rooms where technicians tend electronic perforators, American computers, and British typesetting machines. "Every nook and cranny of the *Al-Ahram* building breathes Heikal's presence," wrote Edward Sheehan in the *New York Times Magazine,* "particularly his obsession with cleanliness."

> The elevator boys . . . in polite English remind you that you must not smoke inside their lifts; the cafeteria on the twelfth floor is the best and cleanest in Cairo, and the same seems so of the free workers' clinic. . . . Any worker who is dirty or who soils a wall with his hands or feet is docked a day's pay.[9]

Heikal believes that architecture can bring dignity to the profession of journalism. Standing guard in the foyer of the *Al-Ahram* building is a black and gold, abstract sculpture showing wheels and a globe. Its subject, "the evolution of journalism," sets the tone for the rest of the building's 200 oil paintings, plus sculptures in ceramics and metal dispersed on every floor like a collector's dream. "My intention was to make of *Al-Ahram* a museum for contemporary Egyptian art," recalls Heikal in conversation. "I invited many artists to contribute to this project, and I assume that *Al-Ahram* is the only newspaper that has its own art consultant, Mr. Salah Taher, the leading painter in Egypt today."

On the top floor there is a calm and insulated boardroom suite with an oil painting of Nasser in one corner overlooking the magnificent surroundings. Next to it there is a VIP suite called The Panorama, which looks more like a setting for a Hollywood movie script. Everywhere in the building there is an impression of order and routine. The heart of the newspaper's editorial operation is the fourth floor. With its rows of neat steel desks, the main editorial room looks more like a computer center than a working newspaper office. Western newsmen visiting *Al-Ahram* are usually struck by the fact that there are no typewriters in the building. Nearly all of *Al-Ahram* writers and reporters prefer the old Arabic way of writing by hand in flowing, calligraphic Arabic script. On the wall there are clocks showing the time in fourteen countries. Next to the editorial room is the electronic typesetting system, with tape connected to Linotype machines. Next door are chattering radio monitors in four booths—English, French, Arabic, and Hebrew.

Most journalists of *Al-Ahram* are university graduates whose salaries range from 25 pounds to 50 pounds ($60 to $120) a month. The range for editorial specialists and editors is 150 to 300 pounds ($350 to $700) a month. Some twenty people in the building earn the maximum the state permits—500 pounds ($1,200) a month.

Al-Ahram: Publishing House

The *Al-Ahram* building is also the seat of the most commercially successful publishing operation in Egypt. It turns out a host of Arabic-language books and magazines. Among the most important of these is the monthly magazine *Al-Talia'* (The Vanguard) which Heikal in 1965 gave to several talented leftist writers "to preach their Marxist views within the framework of Nasserism."[10] Ironically, *Al-Talia'* coexists under the same roof with *Al-Ahram Al-Iqtissadi* (Al-Ahram Economic Review) and *Al-Siyasa Al-Dawliya* (International Politics) which are edited by conservatives with pro-Western, free-enterprise philosophies.

Within the *Al-Ahram* building is the Pyramid Advertising Agency, in charge of placing most of Egypt's advertising in newspapers, posters, and television throughout the world. The electronic data processing center on the eleventh floor is regarded as the "economic egg-beater" of *Al-Ahram*. An IBM System 360 Model 30 computer is fed facts on finances, circulation, and advertising—not only for *Al-Ahram* but for a score of other large companies as well. The rental paid by *Al-Ahram* is 4,000 pounds ($9,600) a month. The new revenue from renting time to outside business was running at 32,000 pounds ($77,000) a month in 1972, an 800 percent profit.[11] Ironically, the *Al-Ahram* building is situated in one of the poorest sections of Cairo. It is surrounded by medieval alleys filled with multitudes of impoverished Egyptians. On the streets, malfunctioning tramlines and buses are loaded to three times their capacity. The scene appears far removed from the mechanical symbolism of *Al-Ahram*. After its completion in 1968, the building was criticized by some Egyptians, particularly Communists, as being too opulent for such a poor country. The matter was even brought up at the Central Committee of the Arab Socialist Union. Defending his position, Heikal told the committee that he would answer his critics by quoting Lenin:

When the Soviet Union embarked on building the Metro underground in Moscow, Lenin insisted that it should be done in the most luxurious way possible, including marble halls, chandeliers, and other luxury items. When asked about the need for that luxury in a socialist country, he said: "Moscow Metro is here to stay for the next 100 years; therefore, I am doing it to fit my vision of Moscow after the success of socialism." I am doing the same thing with *Al-Ahram* which lived in its old building for the last 100 years and will live for the next 100 years in its new building. I conceived a project that portrays my faith in Egypt's future. It is your privilege to think that the future of our country will be less than what *Al-Ahram* represents today.

Heikal wanted to provide for *Al-Ahram* workers the finest conditions and thereby attract the best people. He wanted every writer to see his future in *Al-Ahram*. At the same time, he built in his staff a "team spirit" which distinguished *Al-Ahram* from other newspapers and made other journalists feel a sense of alienation and futility toward what they used to label "the arrogant nobles of journalism at Heikal's Pyramid."

Heikal's faith in Egypt's future, however, exceeded his journalistic ambitions. In an attempt to serve his fellow Egyptians, he planned a series of cultural conferences and adult-education courses for Cairo's new middle-class generations who were restless and hungry for knowledge. He made of *Al-Ahram* a center for significant events. He invited most heads of state who visited Egypt to speak at *Al-Ahram* and pioneered in introducing such high-quality cultural events as musical performances by well-known musicians and conductors who performed and explained classical music to the public.

Heikal's purpose was to create at *Al-Ahram* an outpost for progress. "We wanted to make health 'contagious' so others would imitate us at *Al-Ahram,"* said Heikal. "We hoped that our exemplary project would become a vanguard for advancement in Egypt." According to Heikal, *Al-Ahram's* example was actually followed in many institutions in Egypt such as the Foreign Ministry, Al-Nasr Trading Company, and Egypt Petroleum Institute.

CHAPTER 4

Heikal: Nasser's Privileged Friend

FROM the start of the 1952 revolution, Heikal grew ever closer to Nasser. He told a friend: "I intend to put myself close to the new man in power. He must be made to recognize his need for the services of a professional journalist."[1] Nasser indeed needed to communicate and welcomed the help Heikal was ready to extend. Soon Heikal was as powerful as most cabinet members. It is believed that Nasser's famous pamphlet *The Philosophy of Revolution*[2] resulted from conversations between the two men, and it bears the imprint of Heikal's style. The same influence marked the speeches with which Nasser electrified Egyptian and Arab masses. Heikal fed Nasser ideas and debated politics with him. He passed to him books on politics, philosophy, and art; tutored him on Arabic poetry; entertained him with a stream of funny stories; and urged him to favor a more liberal society.[3] At the same time, Heikal enjoyed immediate access to Nasser. On Nasser's official instructions, he was given copies of all documents of state and access to every file in the president's office.

Heikal and Nassar had more than one thing in common. Both belonged to the same generation, although Nasser was six years older than Heikal, and despite different intellectual backgrounds their evaluations of the Egyptian political and economic situations were similar. Heikal thinks he was fortunate to be close to Nasser from the early days of the revolution. He built up his journalistic career and name while covering foreign news abroad without asking for favors from anybody in Egypt. To Heikal, this was very important because he could speak his mind to the power elite without inhibitions. To Nasser, this was also important because he would try out his ideas on Heikal who had the nerve to volunteer a response. It was Nasser's custom to open a meeting of the cabinet or his close political advisers by asking Heikal what he thought. Nasser liked to keep his own point of view to the end. "I suspect he felt some of the others might conceal their real thoughts until they knew what his were," wrote Heikal, "whereas I was above all a newspaper man and used to speaking my mind as well as writing it."[4]

Unless otherwise noted, this chapter is mainly based on a private interview with Mohamed Hassanein Heikal, Cairo, July 20, 1976.

From the outset, Heikal did his best to avoid mixing politics with journalism. To him, a top reporter must be close to the decision-making process to know what is going on rather than being dependent on secondary sources. He has always kept a dividing line "as sharp as a razor's edge" between his journalistic career and his participation in the decision-making process. "While moving in the decision-making orbit," says Heikal, "I never forgot for a moment that I was there as a journalist whose job was to see the whole picture and select those news stories as judged by my professional ethics." In this process, Heikal believes, there is always a struggle between decision makers, who would want to feed the press with their "views," and newsmen, who would want to get "news" from decision makers. This ebb and flow, he thinks, would lead in the end to a sort of balanced relationship between both sides. Heikal warns, however, that a journalist must keep his independence by not taking advantage of his privileged position to accumulate power, otherwise he would become a mouthpiece for the power elite. In fact, Heikal resisted all pressures from Nasser to join his cabinet. He was offered ministerial posts in 1955, 1958, 1961, and 1967, but he turned them down, telling Nasser that he preferred to be a journalist. In 1970, nevertheless, Nasser appointed Heikal as minister of information without even consulting him.

Later events, however, proved that Heikal was more than a newspaperman watching the decision-making process. He was Nasser's friend, confidant, adviser, propagandist, and diplomatic emissary. "I wasn't employed by Nasser," recalls Heikal, "I just was his friend. In his whole political career, he only trusted and loved two persons: Abdul Hakim Amer, and it proved wrong, and me, and I hope it won't prove wrong."[5] In his long journalistic career, Heikal believes he never breached the confidence of Nasser or any other foreign leader. "In my conversations with many heads of state I printed only those parts that they permitted me to quote. Fortunately, in my whole career my reports were never denied and I was never to retract any statement," he states.

Nasser's Confidant

Heikal's role as Nasser's friend made him closer to the president than any member of the cabinet. Nasser ordered a direct telephone line between his private bedroom and Heikal's office at *Al-Ahram*. The reason for this, according to Heikal, is that Nasser wanted to keep up with what was going on in Egypt and the world. Heikal and his journalistic "empire" at *Al-Ahram* seemed to serve this purpose very well. Heikal used to go to the office at 8:00 A.M. every day. This was unusual for a country where cabinet members and high government officials do not go to their offices before 11:00 A.M. Nasser, however, woke at an early hour and did not want to disturb any of his cabinet members. "The first thing he used to do after getting out of bed in the morning was to call me," says Heikal. "We used to talk for about half an hour about what was going on in the world after I had the chance to look at the wire services in *Al-Ahram*'s newsroom." Heikal insists, however, that this was not a job that he had to do especially for Nasser. It was only a part of his preparation for his daily meeting with *Al-Ahram*'s editorial board.

Heikal's relationship with Nasser was not restricted to reporting the news to the chief. They spent long hours debating certain ideas or issues. Heikal saw the president almost every day at his home in Cairo, particularly during the summer when both sent their families to Alexandria for vacation. They usually spent the evening chatting, dining, walking around the garden, or watching movies at Nasser's house. According to Anthony Nutting, Nasser was a great lover of gossip and it was because of this that Heikal first became one of his close associates. Nutting believes that Nasser formed a considerable liking for Heikal's quick wit, lively mind, and chitchat about the social and political goings-on in Cairo.[6]

Heikal denies, however, that he was a decision maker like Nasser. He believes that he only took part in debating the problems and ideas surrounding a decision, but not in making the decision itself. "When I used to argue with Nasser about an idea," recalls Heikal, "there is no doubt that his thinking in the final decision would be conditioned by my ideas." The influence of their conversations was mutual, however, and Heikal wanted his friendship with Nasser to be deep and lasting. This was one of the reasons Heikal insisted on refusing official government positions. He once told Nasser: "I would like to keep my right to talk to you as a friend; if I become a cabinet member under you I shall be inhibited and you can fire me any time you want, but as a newsman, nobody can dismiss me. You can ask me to leave *Al-Ahram,* but as a journalist I still can express my opinion through other means." Nasser seemed to have accepted Heikal's argument and permitted him to say things in *Al-Ahram* that no other Egyptian journalist would dare to. One of Heikal's talents was in calculating how far he could safely go.

Heikal the Crusader

Following the collapse of the union between Egypt and Syria in what was known as the United Arab Republic (1958–1961), Nasser ordered Heikal to conduct a campaign against the ruling Syrian Ba'ath party. Through his editorials, Heikal denounced the Ba'athists as the wreckers of the union. In a series of articles in *Al-Ahram* entitled "I Accuse," he attacked the Ba'athists for trying to discredit Nasser and blame Egypt for the rupture of 1961. Soon Heikal became a target of press attacks from Damascus. At Nasser's orders, Heikal retaliated by publishing in *Al-Ahram* a verbatim record of the Cairo talks between Syrian and Egyptian leaders to revive the union. Commenting on the conference, Heikal said the minutes showed clearly that Nasser had distinguished between the Syrian Ba'ath whom he could not trust and the Iraqi Ba'ath with whom he had no quarrel. The Syrian government protested Heikal's articles and said the conference minutes were distorted, especially those passages relating to Syria's secession from the union. In another article, Heikal laid down new conditions for the reestablishment of unity. He wrote that the Syrian secession had shown that a different form of Arab unity would be needed. He concluded that unity must be complete in defense, in foreign policy, and in a program of social work based on socialism and democracy. He suggested that a united Arab state should have a central parliament in which national entities were clearly identified and fairly represented.[7]

In a series of *Al-Ahram* campaigns throughout the sixties, Heikal crusaded against Nasser's regime. His main target was the intelligence services and their "arbitrary arrests." When he criticized the head of the General Intelligence Agency in 1967, two bullets were fired at him while leaving *Al-Ahram*'s building. He did not report the incident to the police and told a worried Nasser that though he accused nobody, he thought it was a reaction to what he wrote in *Al-Ahram*. Heikal also ridiculed the bureaucracy for its "pettiness and inefficiency" and campaigned for an open society with more freedom for universities, scholarly research, and respect for court orders. Heikal also encouraged some of the most talented writers in Egypt to criticize freely. In 1967 Nagib Mahfouz, Egypt's most distinguished novelist, published a novel that exposed corruption in the regime. Dr. Lewis Awad, *Al-Ahram*'s literary editor, attacked the errors of the government's educational system, and Tawfiq el-Hakim, Egypt's leading playwright, contributed a satire on the Arab Socialist Union under the title "Souq el-Hameer" (Market of the Donkeys). The sensation caused by these writings encouraged Heikal to continue needling the regime. In one instance, however, he seemed to have faced trouble. At one of *Al-Ahram*'s editorial meetings, Tawfiq el-Hakim passed Heikal a novel called *Bank el-Qalaq* (Bank of Worry) in which he criticized Egyptian intelligence. He asked Heikal to read it and delay its publication.

Heikal told him: "If you have the courage to write, I would certainly have the courage to publish." When the first part of the series was published in *Al-Ahram*, the regime was upset. The press censor ordered the series be stopped, and finally the uproar reached Nasser. He called Heikal and asked for the rest of Hakim's story. After reading it in his office, he told Heikal to go ahead and publish it. "If Hakim could criticize our social problems during the Farouk regime," he said, "he is entitled to the same opportunity now."

Nasser did not, however, back Heikal in all his campaigns. He was sometimes cross with Heikal over what he wrote in his column, but never made any move to censor him. According to Heikal, Nasser did not even read most of his articles, unless somebody called his attention to a specific one. Sometimes Nasser read Heikal's articles but did not talk to him about them because of an agreement the two made in 1957. After arguing over one of Heikal's articles, they agreed to avoid discussing any of his future articles. "He knew that I was very sensitive," says Heikal, "and many times accused me of being 'aleet' (arrogant)." Their agreement stuck and they talked about everything except Heikal's column. At times, however, Nasser could not help but answer Heikal's articles in his public speeches but without mentioning him by name. At other times, Nasser found himself obliged to call Heikal to account. In 1967, for instance, Heikal warned Nasser privately and in print against going to war with Israel. He argued for hours with him against closing the Gulf of Aqaba to Israeli shipping. He warned in writing that Israel must resort to arms. Ten days before the eruption of the 1967 war, Heikal wrote in *Al-Ahram*:

Now this is the first time the Arabs have challenged Israel in an attempt to change an accomplished fact by force and to replace it by force with an alternative accomplished fact consistent with their rights and interests. The opening of the Gulf of Aqaba to Israel was an accomplished fact imposed by the force of imperialist arms. This week the closure of the Gulf of Aqaba to Israel was an alternative accomplished fact imposed and now being protected by the force of Arab arms. To Israel this is the most dangerous aspect of the current situation. . . . Therefore it is not a matter of the Gulf of Aqaba but of something bigger. It is the whole philosophy of Israeli security. It is the philosophy on which Israeli existence has pivoted since its birth and on which it will pivot in the future. Hence I say that Israel must resort to arms. Therefore I say that an armed clash between Egypt and the Israeli enemy is inevitable.[8]

But it was after the defeat that Heikal truly raised his voice for realism. He said the defeat was Egypt's own fault—that not only the army had failed but the entire social and political structure of Egypt.

Many people in Egypt took Heikal's articles about the war as those of a defeatist. Some voices said he shared responsibility with Nasser for the defeat. When General Sidqi Mahmoud, commander-in-chief of the Egyptian air force during the war, was brought to military trial and sentenced to ten years imprisonment, mass demonstrations objected to the "light" court ruling and asked for more severe penalties. Under popular pressure, Nasser ordered a retrial for General Mahmoud who was resentenced to twenty years in prison. Heikal objected to Nasser privately and in print. He wrote in his column that responding to such popular pressure would scare future military leaders. "Any military leader will hesitate to take the right action at the right moment without having a signed political order," argued Heikal. "Every military officer is liable for mistakes during a war because of the risk element involved; his initiative for actions should not be paralyzed by the feelings of angry masses in the street," he said. Angry masses of students, however, answered Heikal by surrounding *Al-Ahram*'s building and shouting for his downfall. Heikal thinks that after the 1967 defeat, people needed a scapegoat and were given one. "I expressed my views in contrast to Nasser's view and the popular view," said Heikal, "and I think that was a proper exercise of freedom of expression which I have always believed in."

Heikal continued to maintain a critical approach toward public affairs and was consistently on the side of liberalization and free expression. Following the student-worker riots of February 1968, he took pains to explain that while the counterrevolution did exist, crushing it by force was not the way to save the revolution. He said the youth and the masses had reason to protest in view of the defeat. When the second wave of student demonstrations occurred in November, some government officials described them as "a world disease." Defending the students, Heikal asserted that Egyptian youth were not "the drug-addicted deviationists" found in other countries and urged a continuing dialogue with them. He argued that the students had a right to differ with their elders at a time when defeat in war "had laid bare the gap between promise and performance."[9]

The real confrontation with Nasser, however, came in 1968 when Heikal wrote, "if the regime cannot change itself, it must be changed." Heikal described Nasser's reaction to his article:

One evening I was in my rest-house in Burqash, where I used to spend every Friday with my family, when the president asked to talk to me on the phone. I felt that something was wrong because he rarely called me on

Fridays. Nasser's voice was different when he started to speak. "You want to know my opinion of your article about change," he said. "I am not pleased with it at all," he continued, "because it is written in Ghassan Tueni's style of attacking Charles Helu. But I am not Charles Helu and I hope you are not Ghassan Tueni." We argued for a long time and finally I told him: "I would rather stop writing because you complicate things for me." Our conversation ended at this point.[10]

Heikal did not stop writing, however, and continued his sniping at Nasser's secret police. In a series entitled "Zuwar el-Fajr" (Visitors of Dawn), he denounced "arbitrary arrests" by intelligence agents and called for an open society. Nasser read the articles but did nothing to stop them. When Heikal finished the series, however, Nasser said sarcastically: "Salasel el-dahab khilset ya sidi?" (Did you finish your "precious" series?) Heikal was surprised but Nasser continued: "I saw your coinage 'visitors of dawn' used by students in their underground leaflets at the universities. The trouble with you is that you create new terms that appeal to you and then other people steal them and instigate against us."

Nasser's tolerance of Heikal's attacks on the secret police intrigued many people in Egypt. Many observers seemed to believe that Nasser wanted assurance that the secret police would never grow so strong as to threaten Nasser himself. Heikal has always justified Nasser's creation of the secret police as protecting the process of social transformation. "He had to do that to cope with all of the internal and external forces that were plotting against him," he said. "Intelligence activities had stretched themselves too far beyond their intended limits." Heikal seemed to believe that many of the most repressive forces in Egypt were unleashed without Nasser's knowledge. He thought that Nasser sometimes didn't know what the intelligence services were doing. Over the years, Heikal says he told Nasser of these abuses as a friend, and Nasser did all he could to correct them.

Confrontation between Heikal and some government agencies caused him and his colleagues more trouble. Several top columnists at *Al-Ahram* were arrested for what they had written. One instance involved Gamal el-Otaifi, a prominent writer who later became minister of information under Sadat. Otaifi was arrested by police for writing a series in which he criticized the Egyptian judicial system. This led to tension between Nasser and Heikal, who insisted that Otaifi be released. Nasser became angry and the two did not speak for a week. Finally Sadat intervened and settled the matter between them and Otaifi was released. Sadat told Heikal on several occasions that he was fortunate to have a direct phone line to Nasser's room, "otherwise the intelligence poeple would have caused you a lot of trouble."

On other occasions, trouble came to Heikal from Nasser's aides. Some of them tried to extend their influence over the press as part of the power struggle in Egypt. At one time, Ali Sabri, vice-president under Nasser, tried to organize a governmental institution similar to a supreme press council that would coordinate various newspaper activities. He nominated Heikal to be its chairman. But Heikal rejected the idea and attacked it in his column. Ali Sabri counterattacked in *Al-Gumhouriya* and the matter became a public issue. Heikal argued that before such a body is set up, its purposes and functions must be specified. "Coordination between newspapers is a meaningless concept," he wrote, "because we already have such a coordination on the commercial level. If the government imposes somebody on top of us, freedom of expression will come to an end." Under pressure from Nasser and others, Sabri was unable to pursue his suggestions.

At still another time, Heikal fought government efforts to control news flow in Egypt. When the different press institutions agreed to establish a news service under the name Middle East News Agency (MENA), the government asked to be a partner in its ownership. The press rejected the idea and Heikal argued against it: "Either we keep it all, or lose it all." The press lost ownership of MENA and the government placed it under its Information Agency. But Heikal had yet another battle ahead. The Information Agency suggested that all foreign news coming through international press associations be centralized, translated, and then transmitted in Arabic to all MENA subscribers. Heikal said that was out of the question because government officials would act as gatekeepers and control the news at the source. The idea was never realized and Heikal won the battle.

Complaints about Heikal

Some of Heikal's articles caused personal embarrassment to Nasser, who received complaints from foreign leaders and close associates. Sometimes he was annoyed because Heikal's criticism embarrassed those who worked closely with him. His real trouble, however, came from complaints by Arab leaders against Heikal. Many of them seemed to believe that Nasser fed Heikal with ideas for his articles. At a meeting in Cairo in 1969, the late King Feisal of Saudi Arabia told Nasser, "Your real problem is that everything that is printed in *Al-Ahram* is believed to come directly from you." Nasser said: "I talked to Heikal yesterday and told him that he was creating a lot of trouble for us in Saudi Arabia. I don't have anything at all to do with *Al-Ahram* myself; Heikal is my friend, but I don't tell him what to write. He wouldn't accept instructions if I gave them to him. As you know, he's much too obstinate for that."[11]

A different kind of complaint about Heikal came from President Numeiri of Sudan. Nasser, Heikal, and Numeiri were on board a plane en route to the 1969 Arab summit conference in Rabat. Heikal was sitting between Nasser and Numeiri who kept looking into a magazine and did not talk to Heikal. Nasser noticed that and asked Numeiri: "Don't you know Mr. Heikal?" Numeiri said: "Heikal neglects the Sudanese revolution and we neglect him because he only writes about his friend Mu'ammer Qaddafi." It took a surprised Heikal the rest of the trip to explain to Numeiri why he was interested in writing about Libya more than the Sudan.

Heikal denies vehemently that Nasser passed to him ideas and news for his articles. "Many people think that I used to go to Nasser every Thursday to get ideas from him for my Friday article," recalls Heikal. "This has caused me a lot of embarrassment, but our agreement that we should avoid discussing my articles stuck to the end." Heikal argues that he admired Nasser as a symbol for a cause and national movement, and that forced him to be sincere and open in his private discussions with him. "I lived in the center of events next to Nasser," says Heikal, "but I never slipped my hand inside his pocket to get out an idea or waited for him to call me and give me an exclusive story." Heikal believes that most decision makers do not distinguish between news and views. "Nasser used to deal with news every day, " says Heikal, "but he never realized which of his actions had news value, because everything to him must be kept in secret." When Heikal became minister of information in 1970, Nasser was talking at a cabinet meeting about a certain topic. On hearing that, Heikal said: "My God, that could make sensational news!" Nasser looked at him with surprise and said: "Mohamed, we are talking serious business, and you are sitting there fishing for news like a cat waiting for a bone to drop from the table."

Heikal, however, did not only fish for news; he also undoubtedly reflected Nasser's thinking. He admits that at times Nasser tried to use him as a vehicle to carry his ideas to the public, but Heikal says he tried to keep his journalistic independence by seeking only Nasser's news and immunizing himself against his views. Sometimes Nasser talked publicly about ideas that Heikal raised in his column. This has led many people to believe that Nasser passed these ideas along to Heikal. But Heikal sees it differently: "If Nasser had to discuss my articles in public, this should mean that he was convinced by the value of my ideas.''

Catalyst for Debate

Heikal's ideas, however, were not only expressed behind the scenes to Nasser. He served as a catalyst for continuing debate on the future of Egyptian society. Many intellectuals in Egypt used to argue that their society could not be radically improved without resolution of the confrontation with Israel. Heikal dumped that argument upside down, insisting in his column that Egypt could never face up to the Israeli challenge unless it discarded its own backwardness. Heikal believes that could be accomplished by creating an open society, dominated by rule of law and democratic institutions and freed of most of the police-state restraints that have burdened the country since 1952. "Unless we allow all ideas to be expressed freely," he asserts, "we will remain a society in a test tube."[12]

The conflict with Israel was one of Heikal's favorite themes in his columns. He believes that Israel does not want peace but territorial expansion to establish a mini-imperialist apparatus to control the Arab world. "If they persist in this," he argues, "they will make the present struggle an intractable one for them or us. For in spite of themselves, they are pushing Egypt to change. They are creating a power that will defeat them."[13]

In 1959 President Nasser openly condemned Communism and imprisoned several Egyptian Communists. This led to a period of strained relations with the Kremlin, followed by a controversy between Cairo and Moscow. Heikal became the center of this controversy in 1961 when *Al-Ahram* published a critical article about Khrushchev who had embarrassed a visiting Egyptian parliamentary delegation headed by Anwar el-Sadat by criticizing Nasser's anti-Communist campaign in Egypt. When diplomatic protests from Cairo had failed to get any retraction from Moscow, Nasser authorized Heikal to publish the full text of Khrushchev's abusive criticism. Heikal also spelled out the major differences between Communism and Arab Socialism. He wrote that Communism has no place in the Arab world because of basic ideological differences and because it does not correspond to the character of the people.[14]

In the early sixties, however, when Nasser proclaimed Arab socialism and nationalized everything in Egypt, Heikal persuaded him to release prominent Communists from jail. As part of this arrangement, the Egyptian Communist party voluntarily dissolved itself, and many of its members entered the Arab Socialist Union and were given jobs in the press.

Diplomatic Companion

Prior access to Nasser's news and views was not Heikal's only advantage. He was also Nasser's diplomatic companion and adviser on trips abroad. In the summer of 1958, Heikal and his wife joined Nasser and his wife and Dr. Mahmoud Fawzi, the foreign minister, and his wife on a yacht trip to Yugoslavia. The first news of the Iraqi coup d'etat of July 1958 reached the Egyptian party while visiting with President Tito on the island of Brioni. The Iraqi coup precipitated a crisis which brought American troops into Lebanon and British troops into Jordan. Nasser decided to pledge support to the revolutionaries and his yacht put to sea that same night for Cairo. Shortly, Tito signaled Nasser not to proceed because his safety could not be assured. Nasser agreed and returned to Yugoslavia. That night he called Dr. Fawzi and Heikal to his cabin on the yacht and told them that Tito was suggesting that they take a Soviet plane to Cairo. "But I have another idea," said Nasser. "I am thinking of going to Moscow and seeing Khrushchev so that I can be sure of the Russians' position and learn what they are proposing to do. . . ."[15] He asked Fawzi and Heikal what they thought of the proposition. Both asked for some time to think. As Heikal writes: "We looked at the president's proposal from all sides, the arguments for it and those against. We gnawed at it but we could not make a decision and so went back to Nasser's office." They told him that their calculations had reached a deadlock and it was for the leader to make a decision. Nasser thought for thirty seconds and said: "All right, we will go."[16] The next day Nasser, Fawzi, and Heikal boarded a Soviet plane secretly and flew to Moscow. For the first two hours of the eight-hour meeting Nasser and Khrushchev talked alone—except for the interpreter. Then Heikal and Fawzi joined in the discussions. They mainly discussed America's intentions. Later the Egyptian party flew to Damascus where Nasser pledged support to Iraq with Soviet backing.

At this point Heikal became known for his diplomatic tact and know-how. In September 1959 he was dispatched to New York with Dr. Fawzi to make arrangements for Nasser's first and only trip to the United Nations. Nasser addressed the General Assembly and proposed a third-force movement between East and West.

Conflict between Nasser and Khrushchev over Nasser's arrest of Communists and rejection of Communist ideology for Egypt ended in

1964. That year Nasser invited Khrushchev to visit Egypt and attend opening ceremonies of the first stage of the Aswan High Dam, which was built with Soviet cooperation. Nasser asked Heikal to travel with the Soviet premier and his family on the ship to Egypt. "It was all very pleasant and easygoing," wrote Heikal. "Khrushchev was keen to learn about Egypt and the Arabs and talked with me for hours, listening with fascination to the ideas of Arab nationalism that he had dismissed before. His old interest in Nasser had returned, but this time with more intellectual curiosity. It was not now curiosity solely about one man, but about a historical movement and its meaning."[17] At one point during the trip Khrushchev received radio reports that the Egyptian government was playing down his reception. He became concerned and asked Heikal about it. "This cannot be true," said Heikal, "you are the guest of Nasser and if you are badly received the insult will be to Nasser, not to you. This is the Arab tradition, which says that the dignity of the guest is part of the dignity of the host."[18] On his arrival at Alexandria, Khrushchev got a tremendous reception and was impressed with Egypt.

After the Aswan Dam celebrations were over, Nasser arranged for a day of fishing on the Red Sea for Khrushchev. They were joined by Heikal, President Ben Bella of Algeria, and President Aref of Iraq. Khrushchev refused to talk to Aref "who was hanging Communists in his country." Ben Bella defended Aref, and Nasser and Heikal joined in the discussion. The heated debate went on for six hours, until it was too late to do any fishing. They talked about Communism and Arab unity and nationalism, and by the end of the discussion Heikal felt that Khrushchev had a better understanding of Arab hopes and ideals.[19]

In diplomatic maneuvers Nasser took Heikal's advice on many occasions. Heikal played a major part in introducing leaders of the Palestine liberation movement to Nasser and in 1968 suggested that these leaders be introduced to the Russians to negotiate for arms and supplies. Nasser agreed and invited Yasser Arafat, chairman of the Palestine Liberation Organization, to travel with him to Moscow. In July 1968 Heikal and Arafat went to Moscow with Nasser, who was under Soviet health treatment. Arafat was introduced to the Soviet leadership and was promised arms deals in the future.[20]

One month after the Moscow visit, Nasser's health started to deteriorate. He had a mild heart attack and his doctors prescribed rest for a month. Heikal was summoned to his room. "I found Nasser sitting in a chair eating some of his favorite white cheese," recalls Heikal in writing. "He was very pale and unshaven, which was unusual."

Nasser asked him to join a committee with Vice-President Sadat and other cabinet members to handle government business in his absence. "But why do you want me to join this committee?" asked Heikal. Nasser said: "You know how I react to things. All others are officials, but you know the way my mind works, and so I want you to be on this committee." Heikal said: "But this is quite different. Talking things over with you is one thing, but talking them over with others is something completely different." "Do it for me," Nasser said. "All right," said Heikal, "for you I do it with pleasure." Heikal then suggested to Sadat that they should get a Soviet doctor to see Nasser. Within a few hours, a top heart specialist had been flown to Cairo in a special Soviet plane from Moscow.[21]

At this time, Heikal took part in one of the most heated negotiating sessions between Nasser and the Soviets over arms sales to Egypt. Despite his illness, on January 22, 1970, Nasser secretly boarded a special Soviet plane to Moscow with Heikal and General Mohamed Fawzi, minister of war, to ask for Soviet air defense missiles. Nasser spoke firmly and tensely about his need for SAM-3 antiaircraft missiles to protect his "naked" country. Then he shocked the Soviets by asking that Russian crews man the missile sites in the interior of Egypt. The Soviet leaders objected, arguing that this would precipitate a crisis between the Soviet Union and the United States. Nasser said:

Let me be quite frank with you. If we do not get what I am asking for, everybody will assume that the only solution is in the hands of the Americans. We have never seen the Americans backward in helping the Israelis. . . . We are not asking you to fight for us . . . but as far as I can see, you are not prepared to help us. . . . I shall go back to Egypt, . . . step down and hand over (the governement) to a pro-American President. . . . That is my final word.[22]

Nasser's words electrified the room and the meeting was adjourned until the evening. The Soviet leaders decided that such a critical decision as sending their own crews to man the SAM-3 sites in Egypt should be put before the whole Soviet Council. By evening, the council had decided to give Nasser what he asked. Secretary Brezhnev made the historic announcement and Nasser thanked him. At one point, Brezhnev left his place at the negotiating table, came all the way around it, and sat beside Heikal. "Gospodin Heikal," he said, "all this is secret." Heikal said he knew of course it was secret. "But it is important," continued Brezhnev, "that it should stay secret for a long time. Of course the Americans and the Israelis are bound to know, but before that happens, we come to your domain. How can we present it to the world? I want you to work out a scheme so that we can face the campaign they are certain to wage against us." Heikal said: "Mr. Secretary, it is up to the statesmen to make the big decisions. We can always find ways and means by which we can present their decisions to the world." Heikal believed that Brezhnev was a showy man who used public relations tools to achieve his ends. "His words and his actions were all those of a man who enjoyed power, enjoyed exercising his authority, and enjoyed showing his strength," Heikal said.[23]

Diplomatic Emissary

As Heikal traveled with Nasser as companion and adviser, he acquired a broad experience in diplomacy that far exceeded his role as journalist. This made him more valuable to Nasser who began to trust him as a diplomatic emissary. As early as 1952, Nasser reportedly asked Heikal to be his contact with the American Embassy in Cairo. According to Edward Sheehan, press officer at the American Embassy in Cairo during 1957–58, Heikal used to come often to see Ambassador Raymond Hare. "Among other purposes," said Sheehan, "Heikal's mission was to persuade Washington, through Hare, to show more sympathy for Nasser's neutralism and his aspiration for hegemony in the Arab world."[24] After the death of John Foster Dulles and his anti-Nasser feelings, Hare was able to improve Egyptian-American relations. The United States resumed aid to Egypt in the form of wheat shipments, long-term loans, and credits that were eventually to amount to over a billion dollars—an achievement that can be largely credited to Heikal.[25]

Reports about Heikal's connections with the American Embassy in Cairo came from another American source. In his book *The Game of Nations,* Miles Copeland, former CIA agent in the Middle East, said Heikal introduced Nasser to the staff of the embassy in Cairo.[26] William Lakeland, the embassy's political officer, became friendly with Nasser's military group through Heikal and, during the months following the coup of 1952, he entertained them frequently in his apartment overlooking the Nile. According to Copeland, the real business between the American and Egyptian governments was conducted through Lakeland and Nasser—or, rather, Lakeland and Heikal and Nasser, "Heykal [sic] getting more and more into the channel of communication because of his developing ability to sugarcoat Nasser's views as he passed them on to the embassy and the embassy's views as he passed them to Nasser."[27]

Similarly Heikal played an active role in improving the Anglo-Egyptian relations after the Suez War of 1956. When diplomatic connections between Cairo and London were partially restored in 1959, Heikal was designated as political contact with the British Embassy. His contact there was Colin Crowe, British charge d'affaires until the restoration of full diplomatic relations between the two countries in 1961. At that time, Crowe had no diplomatic status with Egyptian government officials. Nasser, however, asked Heikal to contact him because he wanted to communicate with London before he agreed to resume relations with Britain.[28]

Heikal formally was Nasser's emissary in the Libyan coup of 1969 which brought Mu'ammar Qaddafi to power. The army officers who carried out the coup contacted Nasser through the Egyptian Consulate in Benghazi and asked him to send Heikal as an emissary. Nasser called Heikal and said: "The people in Benghazi seemed to want you, so you'd better go off tonight." Upon arrival in Benghazi, Heikal was met by a member of the Revolutionary Council who took him to the Egyptian Consulate. At about 2 A.M., Mu'ammar Qaddafi came to see Heikal. "It was quite a shock to me," Heikal wrote later, "to see how young he was and I began to think that perhaps I had been tricked and that this man could not be the leader of a successful revolution. But once he started to talk I revised my views."[29] Qaddafi spoke eloquently on many subjects and suddenly told Heikal that he wanted immediate union with Egypt. "Tell President Nasser," said Qaddafi, "we made this revolution for him. He can take everything of ours and add it to the rest of the Arab world's resources to be used for the battle. Libya represents depth; we have hundreds of miles of Mediterranean coastline; we have the airfields, we have the money; we have everything."[30]

Heikal had taken a photographer to Libya with him because he knew Nasser's habit of studying photographs of new persons he was going to have dealings with. When he returned to Cairo, Heikal, upon request, went directly to Nasser's house and the moment he saw him said: "It's a catastrophe." Nasser asked: "Why? Are they against Egypt?" "Far from it," said Heikal. "The problem is that they are shockingly innocent—scandalously pure. They are your men and they want unity with you."[31] Nasser was astonished by this news and made Heikal go over and over every detail of his journey and his meeting with Qaddafi. From then on Heikal was a close friend of Qaddafi and a supporter of his calls for Arab unity.

Heikal as Cabinet Member

In April 1970 Nasser surprised Heikal by announcing his appointment as minister of information without consulting him. The announcement said also that Heikal would keep his position as board chairman and editor of *Al-Ahram*. Nasser knew very well that Heikal would not accept any government position without practicing journalism. When Heikal heard the news at his rest-house in Burqash, he became upset and returned to his office at *Al-Ahram*. Ironically, he found that two of his colleagues at *Al-Ahram* had been arrested by police. One of them was Lutfi el-Kholi, a leftist writer and editor of a sister publication of *Al-Ahram*. The other was Mrs. Nawal el-Mahallawi, Heikal's personal secretary. This increased the tension between Heikal and Nasser. Heikal sent a letter to Nasser stating that he was unable to accept the post. It was the only letter he ever wrote to Nasser because he preferred to deal with him directly as a friend. This time it was different and Heikal was frustrated by Nasser's action.

The next morning Nasser sent Sadat to Burqash to talk the matter over with Heikal. Sadat spent four hours trying to change Heikal's mind about the post. "The president told me," said Sadat, "that in no way will he accept your reasons for rejecting his offer. He made a decision and that's the end of it." Heikal could not help but go and talk it over with Nasser. "You are behaving in a very strange manner," Nasser told Heikal on seeing him. Heikal said: "I was surprised you did this to me; in the past I begged you to exempt me from serving in the government and you accepted. But how can you do this now by radio?" Nasser told him it was only a specific mission for one year and Heikal agreed but asked, "Can I print that it is only for a year so nobody will think when I leave that I was fired?" Nasser said: "This would be very silly. It would sound as if you accepted the position on your own terms. Aren't you ashamed of the scandal you caused by rejecting my offer? Just forget about it now and later we'll find a way to manage it as you wish." Six months later, however, things went differently. Nasser died unexpectedly, and Heikal resigned his post.

Nasser's insistence on bringing Heikal into the cabinet puzzled many people. One interpretation came from Anthony Nutting. He said by 1970 Nasser became an "extremely lonely man" when most of his close associates had left the government. Except for Heikal, Nasser had hardly anyone around him whom he could call a personal friend. According to Nutting, when Nasser decided to replace Mohamed Faik as minister of guidance in April 1970, he did not want to appoint a newcomer whom he did not know so he insisted on Heikal undertaking the hard task of doubling the new cabinet position with his editorship of *Al-Ahram*.[32]

Another explanation came from Robert Stephens in a book about Nasser. He said the gulf between the government and the critics of the educated class remained largely unbridged. The press remained controlled or careful about criticizing government policies and this had led to public scepticism about the credibility of official statements and of press reporting and comment. According to Stephens, it was partly to try to counter this feeling that Nasser brought Heikal into the cabinet because he advocated more frankness in official news about the war with Israel.[33]

According to Heikal, however, Nasser wanted to entrust the mass media in Egypt to a person who would know his own thinking without referring to him often. This was important in a period of sensitive political and military action. To Nasser, Heikal was the only person he could trust and with whom he could discuss the secrets of his upcoming moves. At the time, Egyptian troops were still fighting a "war of attrition" with the Israelis at the Suez front. In June 1970 U.S. Secretary of State William Rogers announced that his government had undertaken a new political initiative to encourage the Arab states and Israel "to stop shooting and start talking." The American initiative called on all parties to restore the cease-fire for a limited period and subscribe to certain basic principles relating to peace and security. Nasser thought that the Rogers plan would fit in with his overall strategy. He was preparing the army to cross the Suez Canal and needed breathing space to finish building the missile sites that would protect the Egyptian troops after crossing. Also, he needed to give the army a break and cut down civilian casualties. Heikal believes Nasser was unable to explain this complicated plan to anyone, including his cabinet members. He trusted only Heikal and wanted him to carry out this "limited mission" for only one year.

This was a tough job for Heikal to undertake. When Nasser announced acceptance of Rogers' initiative, shock waves immediately went around the Arab world. At this time, Heikal was acting minister of foreign affairs while Mahmoud Riyad was abroad. It fell to Heikal to negotiate the details of the cease-fire. The Americans asked for a standstill cease-fire which had to be completed in a matter of hours. Nasser asked Heikal to gain time for him because he needed six hours to get some dummy missile batteries into position. The Americans were expected to photograph from their satellites the exact position of everything at the moment of cease-fire, and Nasser wanted to be able later to replace these dummy missiles with real ones. Heikal managed to stall the American negotiators and Nasser got his six hours; fake missiles were prepared overnight.[34]

Nasser's acceptance of the cease-fire outraged many Arabs, particularly the extreme Palestinians. They accused him of growing "tired of the struggle and should leave it to the younger generation which was ready to make the necessary sacrifices." The Voice of Palestine radio from Cairo carried similar attacks against Egypt, Nasser, and the Rogers initiative. At Nasser's request Heikal met with the Palestinian leaders in Cairo and told them that they could attack the Rogers initiative as much as they liked but they could not label as traitors those Arabs who had accepted it. Two days later Nasser ordered the radio station closed following interception of a coded message to the station encouraging continuance of attacks on Nasser.[35]

According to Heikal, Nasser understood the bitterness of the Palestinians. He was particularly worried that King Hussein might think his chance had come for a showdown with the Palestinians in Jordan. So he asked both the king and Yasser Arafat to come to Cairo. He told them in separate meetings to refrain from taking action against each other. In September 1970, however, the king began huge military operations against the Palestinian resistance movement in Jordan. Palestinian leaders in Cairo came to see Heikal. They told him that if no word came from Nasser to stop the fighting, the king would take it as a green light to go ahead and liquidate their movement in Jordan. Nasser was on vacation at the time on doctors' orders. When the situation in Jordan deteriorated even more, Heikal decided to contact Nasser. Nasser called for an immediate conference of the Arab heads of state to deal with the situation. The meeting ended with an agreement signed between King Hussein and Arafat which provided for an immediate cease-fire. Heikal was assigned to make arrangements for the cease-fire observation committee.

The Death of Nasser

The next morning Nasser, busy seeing off the Arab delegates at the airport, suddenly felt unable to stand and was taken home immediately. His doctors found that he had had a heart attack. He asked to see Heikal, who hurried to his house. But it was too late for Heikal to talk to him; Nasser was already dead. It was hard for Heikal to realize that he had lost his friend. He kept repeating to himself over and over again: "It can't be true; it can't happen."[36]

A while later Sadat, the vice-president, called for a cabinet meeting at his house to discuss what should be done. Sadat followed Nasser's example and opened the meeting by asking Heikal what he thought should be done. "I have never felt so responsible," wrote Heikal, "as I did at that moment. Everyone in the room except for myself had an official career to think of. . . . But it was only by chance that I was there in an official capacity. . . . I came to the conclusion that my time as minister must be brought to an end." Heikal told Sadat that they ought to call a joint meeting of the cabinet and the Arab Socialist Union. He said he thought they should follow the constitution, which would mean that Sadaι would become acting president until a plebiscite could be arranged to confirm the new president. Nobody objected to these proposals or put forward any alternatives.[37]

Later Heikal drafted a statement announcing Nasser's death and told radio and television stations to stop regular programs and replace them with readings from the Koran. This was an Arab tradition for mourning top leaders of the state. The country immediately realized that something was wrong. At this time, Sadat asked Heikal to broadcast the statement he had prepared. Heikal refused and told Sadat that it was essential that the country be given a sense of continuity and suggested that Sadat tell the nation of Nasser's death. Sadat agreed and went with Heikal to his office in the Ministry of Information, which houses radio and television studios, where he read the prepared statement. Then Heikal took off to his office at *Al-Ahram* to write the story.

Heikal and Sadat: Confrontation

FOLLOWING Nasser's death, Heikal became one of Sadat's close advisers. He had often counseled Sadat on crucial decisions in domestic affairs. At first, the new president and the orphaned favorite needed each other. Heikal's advice helped Sadat foil the conspiracy mounted against him in 1971 by seven of his own cabinet members. But Heikal was to find in Sadat's presidency first a challenge to his established role, then an erosion, and finally a loss of his journalistic and political influence.

The day after Nasser's death, maneuverings began taking place to fill the seat of power. Heikal thought much about his position and determined to leave his cabinet post and go back to *Al-Ahram*. Sadat asked him, however, to form a committee to discuss what should be done about renewing the cease-fire with Israel, due to expire in six weeks. At the recommendation of the minister of war, Heikal suggested the cease-fire be extended for an additional three months. Some committee members protested and said that Egypt should go to war as Nasser had planned. Heikal argued that it would be unfair to expect the new president to go to war shortly after taking the reins of office, and while the country was still distracted by grief. Heikal's suggestion was accepted as nobody was prepared to argue for another position.

Soon after the meeting, three cabinet members (Sami Sharaf, Sha'rawy Guma', and Amin Huwaidi) asked Heikal to join them in a private discussion. They invited him to form with them a Nasserite front against Sadat and his group. Heikal told them: "If you want to coordinate as ministers, don't do it in front of me. I have made up my mind to quit—to leave the cabinet. I'm going to stick to journalism."[1] The group objected to Heikal's decision and asked him to stay. He told them acting together as Nasserites would inevitably provoke reaction and a struggle for power. "If there is going to be a clash of ideas," said Heikal, "I'll play my part in it as a newspaperman, but if there is going to be a struggle for power based on personalities, I will have nothing to do with it."[2]

The next day was Nasser's funeral. Sadat discussed with Heikal a

---

Unless otherwise noted, this chapter is mainly based on a private interview with Mohamed Hassanein Heikal in Cairo, July 20, 1976.

suggestion put to him that, as the crowds might easily get out of hand and set fire to the city, the procession should be canceled. Heikal said he thought this would be a catastrophe because everybody would assume that something had gone terribly wrong. Heikal suggested that the body should be flown by helicopter from Kubba Palace to the center of Cairo on the Nile where the procession could start. Sadat put the suggestion to the military and they agreed. Assigned to escort Soviet Premier Kosygin during the funeral, Heikal got the impression that Kosygin was more than usually gloomy. "He was never a man to display emotion," Heikal wrote. "In public indeed, he presented himself as a walking computer." Kosygin found the funeral scene, with the crowds packed solid in every street, strange and even shocking. He was overwhelmed by the people and their sorrow. "You must try to control things," he told Heikal. "If you allow yourself to surrender to grief, anything may happen. The whole country could collapse."[3]

Shortly after the funeral, Sadat felt tired and went into a room for rest. Elliot Richardson, head of the American delegation to Nasser's funeral, came to see Sadat but Sadat sent him to see Heikal. Richardson met Heikal at *Al-Ahram*'s building and talked to him about American-Egyptian relations. Vladimir Vinogradov, at the time deputy Soviet foreign minister, was another foreign visitor who called on Heikal at *Al-Ahram*. Heikal told Vinogradov that two days before Nasser died he had expressed the wish that the Soviets would send him (Vinogradov) as the new ambassador to Cairo. To Heikal's surprise, Vinogradov said that Moscow had nominated him for the Cairo Embassy.

Heikal Supports Sadat

As things settled down after Nasser's death, Heikal told Sadat that he wanted to give up his ministerial post and go back to *Al-Ahram*. He argued that staying in the cabinet might involve him in disputes with others. "In that case," said Heikal, "I should be nothing but a liability to the new president, whereas from my editorial chair I could give him useful support."[4] Sadat agreed but asked Heikal to stay on until he was confirmed as president. Heikal did that, and a friendly exchange of letters between them was published in the press. "After I stepped down," Heikal said, "I continued to see the president frequently and was happy to maintain with him the informal and confidential relationship which I had enjoyed with his predecessor."[5]

In fact, Heikal had a good personal relationship with the new president. "My dealings with Sadat," said Heikal, "were much easier than my dealings with Nasser." According to Heikal, Sadat was the only member of the Free Officers group, which started the 1952 revolution, with whom he had a social relationship. Their families visited each other quite often and their children were very good friends. Heikal believes that Sadat was willing to give him power ten times more than Nasser. "He was so nice to me and allowed me the same access (as had Nasser) to all information," said Heikal.

When Sadat was nominated for the presidency, Heikal and *Al-Ahram* supported him. In his weekly articles, Heikal said he would support any electoral procedure that was based on constitutional grounds. "Nasser's death was a shock that might have led to the collapse of authority," Heikal argued, "and without constitutional controls a contest will be open for a power struggle." He said the text of the constitution states that in case of the president's death, the vice-president will become acting president for sixty days during which a plebiscite should confirm the nomination of the new president who would be chosen by the Parliament. So Heikal said he would support Sadat because he was the vice-president. These proposals were adopted later in confirming Sadat as president. This annoyed the group seeking the nomination of Ali Sabri for the presidency, and Heikal came under their fire. One report, however, said that Heikal left Nasser's deathbed to launch a brief campaign to support Zakaria Muhyeddin, a close associate of Nasser, in the struggle for the succession.[6]

Soon after the plebiscite confirmed Sadat as president, he asked Heikal to recommend somebody for the premiership. Heikal recommended Dr. Mahmoud Fawzi because he thought he was well known abroad and trusted by people in Egypt. Sadat asked Heikal if he could persuade Fawzi to accept the post. Heikal found Fawzi very reluctant. He feared there was a struggle for power ahead and did not want to get involved. After hours of arguing, Heikal convinced him to accept the post. This made the Ali Sabri group extremely angry and part of their anger was directed against Heikal because of his friendship with Fawzi.

In his articles in *Al-Ahram* Heikal soon began to advocate an end to treating the Americans as the enemy. "The United States was too strong to be opposed head on," he argued. "Egypt needed to work toward the neutralization of the United States as a prerequisite of the battle with Israel which seemed to me inevitable," he said. He concluded that Egypt must deal with the United States, for only then could Washington pressure Israel to evacuate occupied Arab land.

Sadat was reaching similar conclusions. Addressing the National Assembly in February 1971, he announced his new peace initiative. He proposed to agree to extension of the cease-fire for a month and said that work on clearing the Suez Canal should begin, provided Israel made a partial withdrawal in Sinai.[7] Sadat asked Heikal to tell the Americans that this initiative was entirely his own and had nothing to do with the Russians. The Ali Sabri group criticized Sadat's proposals and attacked Heikal in *Al-Gumhouriya,* contending that he was a pro-American defeatest. Heikal replied in his column: "I sometimes find Arab folk strange for the way we are fond of rhetorical disputations, savoring words which lead us nowhere. My comments on neutralizing the United States have been singled out for a civil war of words."[8]

This was the beginning of a conspiracy to depose Sadat and liquidate Heikal. The Ali Sabri group and other members of the Arab Socialist Union thought that Sadat had come too much under Heikal's influence. Heikal came under the surveillance of the secret police and his office at *Al-Ahram* was bugged. "Now my telephone was tapped, my house, the people I met, all my movements were placed under their surveillance," said Heikal. "Taking over *Al-Ahram* was one of their chief objectives.[9]

Heikal started to back Sadat in his battle against "centers of power," a famous coinage of Heikal which means the accumulation of illegal, illegitimate power in the absence of public control. The Ali Sabri group pressured Sadat to go to war against Israel according to Nasser's plan. The plan would have gone into effect in December 1970, had Nasser lived. In a meeting with the Sabri group, Sadat was pinned down to a precise date for the start of war in March 1971. "I knew that Sadat was a cautious man," said Heikal, "and that he was just maneuvering for time." Heikal opposed the decision and wrote in *Al-Ahram* that war was not "a game" to play. "Those advocating war," he said, "had not properly weighed the obstacles in Egypt's path, and it is utterly wrong that a decision regarding so vital an issue as peace and war should be determined by considerations of purely internal politics." This outraged the Sabri group which asked for Heikal's arrest for treason and accused him of being against the idea of fighting Israel. "I admit that I was against the war in 1971," recalls Heikal in conversation. "Under pressures of the power struggle, Sadat was cornered and forced to make such a crucial decision. I was against the group's attempts to embarrass the president and twist his arm." According to Heikal, *Al-Ahram* supported Sadat for two continuous weeks.

Confrontation between Sadat and the dissident Sabri group escalated on the question of proposed union with Libya and Syria.

The group opposed the union on grounds that the experience of the 1958 union with Syria should not be repeated. Heikal thought the group's real reason for opposing the union was fear of losing its monopoly of power. In a stormy meeting of the Higher Executive Committee of the Arab Socialist Union, Sadat spoke in favor of the union and exchanged hard words with the rival faction. It was not long before the news leaked out about the breakdown in the political leadership of the party. In a second meeting, Sadat called on Heikal, who was a member of the Central Committee of the Arab Socialist Union, to tell about the Benghazi agreement in which the idea of a union had first been approved. Heikal had been a member of the Egyptian delegation with Nasser and had taken the minutes of the meeting. Heikal stressed the point that Sadat was merely completing Nasser's work. Heikal was interrupted by one member of the Sabri group who accused him of widening the rift between the two factions instead of healing it.

A few days later the opposition arranged a hostile demonstration against Sadat while he delivered a speech in the industrial town of Helwan. Sadat spoke openly of his determination to liquidate all "centers of power." The next day he relieved Ali Sabri of his post as vice-president. On May 15, 1971, Sadat sent his daughter to Heikal's apartment with a message that he wanted urgently to see him. Heikal was surprised that Sadat had not called him by phone or sent one of his secretaries. He hurried to his house and found him sitting with a tape recorder in front of him. Sadat had a most extraordinary story to tell Heikal. That morning a police officer had brought him two tapes including conversations between members of the Sabri group who were plotting to depose Sadat. Heikal listened to the tapes and said he thought the two key figures in the plot were the commander of the Presidential Guard and the army's chief-of-staff. Two days later, Sadat ordered the dismissal of Minister of the Interior Sha'rawy Guma'. The dissident group reacted by resigning en masse, calculating that their action might cripple Sadat's government and lead to its fall. Heikal was listening to news of the resignations on the radio late one night when Sadat called and asked him to come to his house at once. "I found him in good spirits," said Heikal, "his nerves were holding out well. He had accepted all the resignations."[10] Sadat later ordered the conspirators arrested and put on trial.

The Drift

The first signs of difference in opinion between Heikal and Sadat surfaced in 1971, when Sadat began to talk about what he termed "the year of decision." By that he meant a decision to fight must be made and implemented by the end of that year. In *Al-Ahram,* Heikal argued that there was no such thing as the "year of decision," because the battle with Israel would be a long one. "It was more appropriate to avoid fixing a definite period of time within which action was to be expected," he said. Sadat criticized Heikal's comments while addressing the Arab Socialist Union.

The rift widened as Heikal continued sniping at Sadat. "Unlike Nasser, Sadat argued with me over every paragraph [of my articles]," said Heikal. "When I write," he told Sadat, "I am entitled to express my own opinion, and you are entitled to withhold your news from me." In fact, Sadat did withhold information from Heikal and stopped Nasser's practice of inviting him on foreign trips. When Sadat secretly visited Moscow in March 1971, he left Heikal behind. When he came back, however, he told Heikal what happened in his meetings with Soviet leaders. "I had to make an angry scene," said Sadat, "but in the end I got what I wanted."

At this time, Heikal's role as presidential adviser was diminishing gradually. Sadat kept Heikal out of meetings with foreign leaders who visited Cairo. He did brief him occasionally on specific issues. When Soviet President Podgorny arrived in Cairo after the fall of Ali Sabri and his group, Sadat assured him that the move was not directed against the Soviet Union. Heikal was not present, but Sadat gave him an account of his talks with the Soviet leader. Among other things, Podgorny told Sadat: "Now is the time to get rid of Heikal." According to Heikal, the Soviet leadership misunderstood many of the things he said and wrote. More than once, earlier, the Soviets had insisted that Nasser would be wise to dismiss Heikal.[11]

As a result of their talks, Sadat and Podgorny agreed to sign a twenty-year friendship treaty between their countries. Heikal was against such a treaty and told Sadat it was no different from the 1936 Anglo-Egyptian treaty that tied Egypt to Britain for twenty years. Heikal used *Al-Ahram* and even national television to express his reservations about the Egyptian-Soviet treaty. He argued against the whole idea of treaties between small and large nations, particularly after the experience of the Anglo-Egyptian treaty. Sadat was irritated by Heikal's comments and sent his foreign minister, Mahmoud Riyad, to talk to him. Riyad suggested, as a compromise, to reduce the treaty's duration from twenty to fifteen years. Later Sadat signed the treaty for fifteen years.

Another conflict between the two involved Sadat's interference in Heikal's journalistic autonomy. Unlike Nasser, Sadat insisted on telling Heikal what to write or not to write. An example of this interference happened in early 1971 when President Numeiri of Sudan was visiting Egypt. One morning Sadat called Heikal and said: "What made you upset Numeiri?" Heikal said: "Why? I didn't write anything about him." "This is the problem," said Sadat, "he is upset because you don't write about him. I suggest, therefore, that your article this week should be about Numeiri." Heikal did not like Sadat's tone and said: "That's impossible because Numeiri didn't do anything significant that deserves comment." Sadat said: "I've already promised him that your article this week would be about him; I need no further argument." On Friday, Heikal's article dealt with a topic that had nothing to do with Numeiri. Heikal felt that it was impossible for him to accept this outright interference in his journalistic independence.[12]

The year 1972 marked another period of confrontation between Heikal and Sadat. The year started with disturbances among students, frustrated by Sadat's lack of action. The war between India and Pakistan provided him with an excuse for not carrying out the promised "year of decision." All newspapers supported Sadat except *Al-Ahram*. The press generally condemned students and described their demonstrations as part of a "Communist plot" against Egypt. *Al-Ahram* took a more sympathetic attitude toward the students. Sadat was outraged and in a public speech accused *Al-Ahram* of "walking a tightrope." When he saw Heikal, he told him: "You are not supporting me any more; why do you allow students to come to *Al-Ahram*'s offices and meet with editors?" Heikal said: "They come to argue with us, and sometimes they attack us, but we cannot shut the doors in their faces." Heikal told Sadat that when the regime quarrels with this young generation, it is disputing its own future.

At this time, the Soviets were insisting that Egypt give them navy facilities on the Red Sea. The Egyptian army and navy opposed the idea. Heikal disliked the proposal and told Sadat it would commit Egypt too deeply to the naval strategy of the Soviet Union. Heikal then launched a celebrated series of articles in *Al-Ahram* titled "No Peace: No War" in which he argued that the Soviet Union might have a vested interest in preserving the status quo in the Middle East. Sadat told Heikal: "You are causing me embarrassment with your articles." Heikal said he could stop writing if Sadat wished. Sadat said he should continue but without causing trouble for him. Heikal, however, did not accept that and continued his critical writing. Sadat was infuriated and did not talk to Heikal for three weeks.

Another point of conflict between the two resulted from Sadat's decision to end the Soviet military presence in Egypt. In July 1972 he expelled all the 20,000 Soviet military personnel because of the Russians' refusal to provide offensive weapons to Egypt. The continuing state of no peace, no war had become so frustrating that he was obliged to make a momentous gesture of this kind to appease public opinion. Before announcing the decision Sadat called Heikal in Alexandria, where he was spending a summer vacation, and asked him to come to Cairo. On arriving, Heikal told Sadat he feared his articles must be causing him a lot of embarrassment. "I see that our relations are becoming tense," said Heikal, "and therefore I suggest I stop writing or you dismiss me from *Al-Ahram* if you see fit. I could write nothing except what I believe in, and that seems to cause you trouble with the Soviets." Sadat said: "It seems you don't know what's going on; we have broken with the Soviets." Heikal was stunned. He had felt for some time that such a decision was possible, but he was surprised at the timing and the way the expulsion was carried out. Heikal told Sadat that short of their delay in arms deliveries, the Soviets actually did nothing serious to hurt Egypt. "In the final analysis," said Heikal, "we have to depend on Soviet arms, and therefore we have to 'manage' our relations with the Soviets in a way that is not humiliating to them." Later, in his articles, Heikal expressed his reservations about Sadat's move.

Heikal had often thought of the Soviet Union as a friend of Egypt, but he had some reservations about its role as a superpower. "The Soviet Union had to think in global terms," he wrote, "and these sometimes came into conflict with its role as a helper and protector of countries like Egypt. I had the greatest admiration for what the Soviet Union had done for Egypt, which had proved it Egypt's most reliable friend . . . but the fact remained that the Soviet Union was deeply concerned with *detente* and with the development of its naval strategy."[13]

After announcing the expulsion, Sadat held a confidential meeting with a small group of Cairo editors including Heikal. Sadat gave the editors a full account of what led to his action. He told them the main reason was the Soviets' evasion and delay over the deliveries of arms to Egypt. He read them a message he received earlier from the Soviet leaders about their meeting with President Richard Nixon in Moscow. The message was written in three pages, two of which attacked Heikal and what he had been writing about the no peace, no war situation. It referred to "saboteurs like Heikal."[14] While Sadat read the message, Heikal listened without comment.

After the Soviets overcame their initial shock, Brezhnev sent Sadat a message that warned about "the efforts being made by rightist elements to halt Egypt's progress and turn it back.'' Sadat thought this was insulting and amounted to interference in Egypt's internal affairs. He asked Heikal to publish an item which he dictated as follows: ''We have learned from well-informed sources that the message from Brezhnev is of no significance and is not expected to lead to any new contacts between Egypt and the Soviet Union in the near future.'' After some discussion with Heikal, Sadat agreed that this should not be published but he told Heikal to play down the importance of the message. Another news item published at Sadat's orders was that the Egyptian ambassador in Moscow had been called home on leave.[15]

Meanwhile, Sadat was receiving indirect messages from the United States to the effect that the key to the Middle East conflict was in American hands. By 1972 Sadat became convinced that the Nixon administration's State Department was doing only routine diplomatic business, and that the really big issues of foreign policy were dealt with by Henry Kissinger in the White House. Sadat made new attempts to open channels of communication between Egypt and the United States. One of the contacts involved Heikal, whose name was circulating in American news reports as a possible contact man with Presidential Adviser Henry Kissinger. In 1972 Donald Kendall, chairman of the Pepsi-Cola Company and a personal friend of Nixon, came to Cairo and contacted Heikal. He suggested that Heikal meet Kissinger and offered his ranch in Connecticut for a long weekend of private talks. When Kendall returned to the United States, he pursued the idea with the Egyptian ambassador and Egypt's permanent representative at the United Nations. A date for the meeting was suggested and a report was sent to Cairo. Sadat then discussed it with Heikal who said he was not enthusiastic about the idea. He thought Egypt should strengthen its internal position before starting any serious talks with the Americans. Heikal sent a cable to Kendall calling off the meeting and apologizing.

Heikal and Qaddafi

Then another incident widened the gap between Heikal and Sadat—the proposed union between Egypt and Libya. Following the withdrawal of Soviet military personnel from Egypt, Qaddafi feared the Soviets might try to take revenge. He offered assistance by proposing a complete merger between Egypt and Libya. He had been a strong advocate of Arab unity and wanted to implement his idea as soon as possible. Sadat told him a union needed careful preparation.

According to Heikal, Qaddafi could display a terrifying innocence of how things worked in the modern world. Many of his friends, including Heikal, were annoyed at the way he interfered in countries like Ireland. Heikal tried in vain to convince him that the IRA was not a revolutionary movement in the sense that he understood the term. Another time, Heikal tried to explain to him that the Bangladesh problem was one of self-determination and that the new state deserved recognition from Libya. Qaddafi could not see this, however, and insisted that Bangladesh was a separatist movement from the big Muslim country, Pakistan.

Qaddafi's strong religious feelings made him refuse to deal with the Soviet Union which he regarded as a land of atheists. Heikal tried to persuade him that Marxism was an essential ingredient of modern political thought. Whenever Qaddafi came to Cairo, Heikal would invite him to come to *Al-Ahram* where he arranged for some of the best brains in Egypt to meet him and discuss every conceivable topic. On one occasion when the discussion became interesting to him, Qaddafi asked for a notebook and started making notes. Heikal noticed that he had filled three complete notebooks and offered to make a transcript for him, but he preferred to take it all down himself.

Qaddafi was very upset by the death of Nasser, but he still believed in Egypt's key role in the Arab world. He thought that the vacuum left by Nasser should be filled by a collective leadership of Egypt, Syria, and Libya. Heikal supported Qaddafi because he had always been a believer in a union between Egypt and Libya. "I thought then that both countries had a unique opportunity to pool their resources, to combine their lands, peoples, and economies into one country," said Heikal. He still believes that a union could solve a lot of problems for the two countries. Without such a union, he thinks, the Libyan oil wealth will be spent on building an infrastructure at a time when the Egyptian infrastructure could be utilized for both countries.

Sadat disagreed with Heikal on the grounds that Qaddafi might cause trouble for them. Such trouble came when a Libyan Airlines plane enroute to Cairo lost its way over Sinai and was shot down by Israeli fighters, killing 108 passengers. Qaddafi was outraged and proposed to send fighters to bomb the Israeli town of Haifa. Sadat calmed him down and convinced him that the Israelis were likely to retaliate and bomb Libyan airfields. The situation was complicated further when Qaddafi gave orders to a commander of an Egyptian submarine working with the Libyan navy in Tripoli to torpedo the *Queen Elizabeth II*. The British ship was on its way to Israel with a full load of Jewish passengers. When Sadat learned the news, he ordered the submarine back to its base in Alexandria and informed Heikal: "It seems that Qaddafi wants to put us on the spot. He is trying to sink the *Queen Elizabeth II*."[16] As a result of this incident, Egyptian-Libyan relations deteriorated even further, and Qaddafi's frustration mounted. He took the extraordinary step of printing leaflets announcing his resignation and tried to distribute them on the streets of Tripoli to the passersby. When attempts by fellow officers to stop him from resigning failed, he took his family to Cairo where he settled in a self-imposed exile. To Sadat, Qaddafi was not an easy guest, and he arranged for him to go around the country and listen to what people had to say about unity with Libya. Heikal was opposed to this and thought it gave some elements the opportunity to air complaints about irrelevant issues. When Qaddafi started expounding his ideas about strict Islamic punishment and women's liberation, he encountered stiff opposition from Egyptian audiences. He was shocked and decided to go back to his country.

Meanwhile, one of Qaddafi's colleagues suggested sending 40,000 Libyans on a 1,500-mile march to Cairo to demonstrate to Sadat that the union idea was supported by the mass of the Libyan people. Sadat looked at the Libyan march not as a political event but purely as a problem of security. Some of his advisers thought the Libyans would be armed and that they planned to smash nightclubs and restaurants. Sadat gave orders to block the border road between Libya and Egypt to stop the march from reaching Cairo.

At this time, Heikal, on a trip to Paris, heard about the Libyan march and saw it as a healthy sign and a real demonstration of political consciousness. The next morning Heikal held a press conference and stated he was against stopping the Libyan march. *Le Figaro* quoted him as saying that the march should proceed to Cairo, and once there, 400,000 or more Egyptians could join them and all would go to Sadat and ask for unity. Heikal said the impact of this demonstration would have been irresistible. Heikal's statements in Paris reached Sadat in a slightly different form. He understood Heikal to have said that if he were in Egypt, he would have permitted the march to come. When Heikal returned to Cairo, Sadat told him angrily: "Egypt has only one president; how dare you give such statements in Paris?" Heikal denied he said such a thing and showed him his statement in *Le Figaro* as proof. Sadat was still unconvinced and said to Heikal: "Your problem is becoming too difficult for me, and I have three propositions concerning your future. You have to choose one of the following: (1) either you stay at *Al-Ahram* and commit yourself to the government line, or (2) you leave *Al-Ahram* and join the cabinet or my staff at the presidency, or (3) you leave *Al-Ahram* and go to your home." Heikal said: "I agree to your third proposal." Sadat said: "But I don't accept it because I still believe you are a national entity that should be utilized for the good of Egypt." Heikal then tried to explain to Sadat how it was impossible for him to commit himself to a policy that he did not believe in. He told Sadat that he had always fought against political commitment in journalism. "When the regime wanted journalists to commit themselves to the political line of the state," he said, "it was forcing them to commit themselves to the regime itself and to the head of state." To Heikal, the real commitment of a journalist was to believe in an ideology and a higher strategy for the country. Their argument continued for hours but no conclusion was reached.

Heikal believes that Sadat has an erroneous concept about the press-government relationship. He told Heikal more than once that journalism is a "dirty profession." Heikal's reply was: "Journalism to me is a good profession, despite the fact that some journalists might give it a bad name." When Heikal refused to join Sadat's cabinet, many people thought he was crazy to prefer journalism to government. He insisted, however, that a job he is fond of is much more important to him than a ministerial post.[17]

Trip to the Far East

Heikal's love for journalism took him on a month's trip to five Asian countries in the Far East. In early 1973 he visited China, Japan, India, Bangladesh, and Pakistan. The purpose of the trip was to get a fresh look at these countries which for a decade had made big headlines in the world press. His articles about those countries contained several unfavorable references to the Egyptian regime. The leaders of the countries, however, received Heikal as a celebrity and he was treated as a visiting official. Heikal accompanied a group of young journalists from *Al-Ahram* as part of his plan to encourage his team of reporters to travel abroad and see events and people for themselves.

Heikal's first stop was in Peking, where he met with Chou En-lai, the Chinese premier. Chou started the meeting by asking about Nasser's family and told Heikal how surprised he was to see Nasser die at the age of 52. "You couldn't protect him well and allowed for pressures to kill him," he said.[18] Then he criticized Heikal for not visiting China more often. "This is your first visit to China," he said, "but you have visited the Soviet Union fifteen times. We counted them for you and you have to make up for the difference." Their interview that evening went on for nearly four hours. Most of their talks concentrated on the Middle East and the Sino-Soviet conflicts. Heikal admired Chou En-lai greatly and wanted to learn from him how the Chinese system works and thinks. A special program was arranged for Heikal to visit many places including universities, newspaper plants, hospitals, and underground shelters.[19]

Heikal then flew to Tokyo where he had a long interview with Prime Minister Tanaka of Japan. From there he went to Dacca to meet Sheikh Mujeeb el-Rahman, prime minister of Bangladesh. In Delhi he met with Indira Ghandi, the Indian premier, and Field Marshal Manishko, commander of the Indian army during the war with Pakistan. During his 48-hour stay in Delhi, Heikal was invited to run a seminar in the Institute of Political and Strategic Studies at Nehru University about Egyptian-Indian relations, and to participate in a panel on Indian-Arab relations on television. In his statements to reporters, Heikal supported Bangladesh in her conflict with Pakistan and urged Arab countries to recognize the new state. He also revealed for the first time that some Soviet arms were shipped to India through Egypt.

These statements were to cause Heikal some embarrassment in his next stop at Karachi. The Pakistani press widely publicized Heikal's statements and angry editorials asked him to explain his "antagonistic views." One newspaper's front page headline read: "Mass Anger in City Against Heikal." On arriving at Karachi airport, Heikal, surrounded by newsmen and television cameras said he had not had the chance to read what the Pakistani press had said and promised to clarify his views at a lunch meeting with Pakistani editors. The official position was more cordial to Heikal than that of the press. President Ali Bhutto gave orders to treat Heikal as a guest of honor and a special helicopter was put at his disposal to take him around during his visit. In his press conference, however, Heikal defended his position and said he would stick to his statements and would not change them under pressure from the press. He insisted that he did not want to become involved in the cold war between the mass media in India and Pakistan. In the meantime, the Pakistani Embassy in Cairo filed a formal protest against Heikal in the Egyptian Foreign Ministry.[20]

Sadat became furious about the dissidence and diplomatic disarray that Heikal created for him abroad. Returning to Cairo, Heikal learned that Sadat had dismissed a number of *Al-Ahram*'s journalists, including top columnists Ahmad Baha' el-Din and Dr. Lewis Awad. Heikal refused to abide by Sadat's orders and told the suspended journalists to continue their work at *Al-Ahram*. He went to see Sadat and told him that his journalistic conscience could not accept the suspension of journalists whose professional integrity he believed in. "I agree that you can suspend these journalists," he told Sadat, "but on several conditions: (1) that they know why they were suspended, (2) that they have the right to defend themselves, and (3) that they have the right to appeal any ruling against them to you." Sadat refused and said he did not want to be involved in such things. Heikal said: "There is only one solution left; either I have to submit my resignation from *Al-Ahram*, or you have to ask me to resign." Sadat did not accept Heikal's proposal and a long argument ensued without reaching a settlement.

Heikal and the October War

It was not until early September 1973 that Sadat took Heikal into his confidence about his plans for war against Israel. Heikal had often expressed the need to fight a limited war for a long period of time during which Israel would suffer in casualties and equipment. Sadat felt that Heikal never believed his sincere intentions to fight. On September 10 Sadat asked Heikal to come to his house near Alexandria and join him in a car ride. As the president drove along the desert road that leads to Alamein, he started talking about the war. "I suppose there must be a great many people who think we are never going to fight," said Sadat. "I think it is our destiny to fight," said Heikal. "But there are others in the Arab world," said Sadat, "who have lost hope of our ever fighting." Then he turned to Heikal and said: "By God, we are going to surprise them. I think you are going to be surprised too. I'll tell you a secret. Have you got strong nerves? Our battle will start one month from now." Heikal said: "Mr. President, why are you telling me this? Now I shan't be able to sleep." Sadat said, "I don't want you to sleep."[21]

By this time they had reached the president's rest-house in King Mairut where Sadat gave Heikal a complete exposition of the coming operation. For an hour he outlined the thinking behind it, as well as the problems yet to be solved. Then he talked about Egypt's internal problems and Heikal suggested that Sadat encourage a climate of reconciliation by improving his relations with students and intellectuals. Sadat was convinced and decided to drop outstanding charges in the courts against students involved in demonstrations and to reinstate the writers and journalists who had been expelled from their jobs earlier that year.

From then on, Heikal worked with Sadat putting the finishing touches to the political and information plans. Heikal helped Sadat decide what should be the trigger for hostilities. They would claim that the Israelis had launched an attack on an Egyptian military base on the Red Sea. Normal programs on Cairo radio had to be interrupted to announce the "claimed Israeli attack," and news items about the Egyptian counterattack had to follow. Radio announcements had been prepared by Heikal in advance. He also planted news stories in *Al-Ahram*. The commander of the army passed him a fabricated news item that a group of army officers had been allowed to go to Mecca for a small pilgrimage. The intention was to camouflage Egypt's war plans. When Heikal saw the item he called the commander and said: "All right, that means we are going to be liars, but for your sake I will accept it." Later Heikal allowed for two more "claimed stories" to be printed in *Al-Ahram* in an effort to create an atmosphere of normality that might help in deceiving the Israelis. It was the Israelis' custom to get an early copy of *Al-Ahram* via Cyprus and study it carefully.[22]

During the war, Heikal stayed close to Sadat. He helped in drafting communiques and memoranda along with Dr. Ashraf Ghorbal, press adviser to the president. The first signs of conflict between Heikal and Sadat about the war came on the fourth day of fighting. The initial Egyptian thrust after crossing the Suez Canal had stopped at 10–12 kilometers east of the canal. Heikal thought that the impetus of the attack was lost and Egyptian troops missed the opportunity to break out toward the passes that control the center of Sinai. He told Sadat if the Egyptian troops were left in the open country between the canal and the passes they would be exposed to Israeli attack. Sadat said that territory was not important and the purpose was to exhaust the enemy. "I don't want to make the mistake of pushing forward too fast for the sake of occupying more territory," he said, "we must make the enemy bleed."[23]

After the canal crossing, Heikal became critical of the army information services which printed leaflets and distributed them to all serving soldiers. One leaflet said the victory came as a result of help from God and His Prophet Mohamed. "I felt this sort of exhortation to be inappropriate," said Heikal. "By implying that the success of the crossing was due to a miracle, it diminished the part played by the troops who had been engaged in the battle," he said. Heikal became worried that Egypt might lose its information war. He felt that military reports underestimated Egypt's achievements and "the information services seemed to have suffered a sort of heart attack. Almost nothing came out of them. People lost confidence and went back to their habit of listening to foreign broadcasts." When the

Israelis counterattacked and crossed the canal to the west, the Egyptian information services tried to hide it from the public. Heikal insisted on publishing news about this "military setback" and said people had a right to know what was happening in the battle.

Another conflict between Heikal and Sadat came on October 22 when the Americans and the Soviets arranged for a cease-fire. Sadat agreed to the cease-fire on the grounds that during the last ten days of the battle he was not fighting Israel alone but the United States as well through the arms it had been sending to Israel. Heikal disagreed and told Sadat that it was not advisable to accept cease-fire before pinpointing the date and the hour. Heikal's point was that the Egyptian troops should continue fighting for at least six hours after the cease-fire went into effect. As Heikal expected, the Israelis did not respect the cease-fire agreement and continued to expand their bridgehead west of the canal. Heikal blamed the Egyptian command for allowing this to happen.

Heikal Meets Kissinger

The situation exploded between Heikal and Sadat when Kissinger came to Cairo to negotiate a "disengagement" of the armies along the Suez Canal. Heikal suspected that Kissinger might trick Sadat if they met alone. Heikal told Sadat to take to the negotiating table at least one of three persons: Vice-President Mahmoud Fawzi, Foreign Minister Ismael Fahmi, or Hafez Ismael, adviser for national security. Sadat refused Heikal's proposal and decided to meet with Kissinger tête-à-tête. Sadat was under intense pressure in his own camp to rescue the city of Suez and the Third Egyptian Army from Israeli siege. According to Edward Sheehan, Sadat had to submit to Kissinger's implied threat that he would unleash the Israelis on the Third Army if Sadat did not defer to his suggestions.[24] After his first meeting with Kissinger, Sadat accepted his six-point proposal which provided for a relief corridor to the city of Suez and the Third Army, to be followed by a full exchange of prisoners and resumption of diplomatic relations between their countries, suspended since 1967. That crucial meeting started a friendship between Sadat and Kissinger and laid the foundation for a new American foreign policy in the Middle East.

Heikal was shocked at the six-point agreement because he was not consulted about it in advance. The government gave orders to the press not to publish anything about the six points, but Heikal defied these orders and published them in full. Sadat asked Heikal to meeet with Kissinger and assess his position on American intentions. That evening Heikal met with Kissinger at a dinner party at Ismael Fahmi's residence overlooking the Nile. They chatted for a while, then Kissinger took Heikal back to his suite at the Nile Hilton where they talked for another ninety minutes.[25] Heikal had recorded their conversation on sixty-one index cards and later that night he composed a long account of the conversation for his column in *Al-Ahram*. The next morning, he took his note cards and went to see Sadat at Tahra Palace. He said he wanted to tell him his sincere and honest feelings about his meeting with Kissinger. "My conclusion is that the United States policy in the Middle East has not changed," said Heikal. "Kissinger has no strategy except to reduce the Arab-Israeli conflict into fragments, to stop Soviet influence in the area, and to break OPEC to safeguard the flow of cheap Arab oil to the United States," he said. Heikal had a number of other impressions to share with Sadat:

1. The Arab future could not be allowed to depend on the efforts of one man in America, nor should the Arabs let themselves be dazzled by Kissinger's success in other crises.
2. Heikal was not convinced that Nixon was in a position to exert effective pressure on Israel.
3. World balances of power were major factors in Kissinger's estimates; Egypt therefore had to recognize the importance of the Soviet role in the crisis.
4. He did not believe that there was a definite and detailed Soviet-American agreement that could be relied on. Nor did he believe that there was an American guarantee that Egypt could accept against Israel.[26]

Sadat disagreed with Heikal and said he was just aiming at "neutralizing" the United States and carrying out a disengagement agreement with Israel. Unlike his previous arguments with Sadat, Heikal was vehement this time. He felt that Sadat was gambling with a strategic and significant issue. "I am not trying to stand against the United States," he told Sadat, "but I am for normalizing our relations with the Americans without being forced to expose all our cards at once." The two argued but could not reach any conclusion.

At this point Heikal sensed that his fall from *Al-Ahram*'s editorship was imminent and decided to launch a series of articles that radically changed his reputation in the Arab world. He started by interviewing Marshal Ahmad Ismael, minister of war, who gave Heikal fascinating military revelations about the war. Heikal left his readers with a concealed question whether the crossing of the canal was planned, not as a war of liberation, but as a limited operation with a political purpose. Heikal questioned Sadat's reliance on the Americans for peace at a time when Sadat was publicly referring to Kissinger as his "friend and brother." Heikal continued needling Sadat, openly charging that Kissinger was unable to deliver a satisfactory settlement to the Arabs.

Then came the Sinai disengagement agreement, and the dispute between Heikal and Sadat seemed to have reached a deadlock. In a well-argued and candid article titled "The Israeli Style of Negotiation," Heikal said that whatever Kissinger might intend to do, the Zionist influence in the United States combined with internal problems in Israel insured that Kissinger could never produce a solution satisfactory to the Arabs. He said the Israelis insisted on a concession for each movement of their own and, as an example, cited Kissinger's promise to the Israelis of $2.3 billion in exchange for acceptance of the cease-fire. Between the lines was Heikal's message that if Sadat had to put all the cards on the table he would soon find himself without any cards to play.[27]

Sadat's expected reaction to the article was outrage and soon after he ordered Heikal to stop writing. Heikal's final article showed him at the height of his polemical powers. In "The Shadows and the Glitter,"[28] he referred to the troubles of President Nixon and the charisma of Henry Kissinger. He predicted that Nixon would resign his presidency after six months, in spite of the fact that Kissinger told Heikal that that was a remote possibility.[29] Heikal questioned whether a troubled president could actually modify American aims in the Middle East. Heikal listed these United States aims as he saw them:

1. Safeguarding the security of Israel.
2. Ensuring a free flow of oil at acceptable prices.
3. Expelling Soviet influence.
4. Regaining United States influence in the Middle East.
5. Preventing the emergence of a strong Arab power centered in Egypt, and to divide the Arabs.

The Fall

Sadat was waiting for the right moment to dismiss Heikal, whose articles had become a burden that he could carry no longer. He wanted, however, to give him one last chance to change his position. When they met one afternoon at the Rimaya Club, Sadat told Heikal that his articles had become intolerable and that he must choose between joining the cabinet or serving as presidential press adviser. Heikal insisted that he wanted neither, but Sadat asked him to think it over. Two days later, Heikal came to see Sadat at his house and brought with him Francois Mitterrand, leader of the French Socialist party, who was invited by Heikal to speak at *Al-Ahram*. The three chatted cordially for two hours and on their way out, Sadat called Heikal aside and asked: "What is your final decision?" Heikal said: "About what?" "Do you prefer to join my staff at the presidency, or to join the cabinet?" asked Sadat. Heikal said: "Neither one." Sadat insisted: "Is this your final decision?" Heikal said: "Yes, it is final." Sadat hummed but said nothing. Two days later, Heikal heard of his dismissal from *Al-Ahram* by a presidential decree broadcast over Cairo radio. The same decree named him press adviser to the president.

The next morning, a government spokesman, Ahmad Anis, met with foreign correspondents to explain Heikal's suspension. (Ironically, the spokesman's statement was not published in the Egyptian press.) The government said Heikal had been relieved of his post because he turned *Al-Ahram* into a "power center that was tantamount to a state within a state."[30] He also said that the motive behind Sadat's decision to appoint Heikal as his press adviser was to liquidate this "power center" rather than punish the man. Anis went on to say that it was no longer admissible or acceptable to have a state within a state, nor was it tolerable that *Al-Ahram*'s building should turn into the headquarters of a new power center—"a practice that President Sadat put an end to once and for all in May 1971." This was a reference to the Ali Sabri group who were accused of forming a power center and were tried for plotting against Sadat. The spokesman then cited the following reasons for Heikal's removal from *Al-Ahram*:

1. While Mr. Sadat was preparing for last October's war against Israel, "some elements closely related to *Al-Ahram* and Mr. Heikal personally started to cast doubts about the president's intentions regarding the launching of the battle."

2. Some of these elements were involved in instigating anti-government student strikes and demonstrations from October 1972 to January 1973.

3. While Mr. Sadat was contemplating a cabinet shake-up early last month, Mr. Heikal tried to convey the impression, in private conversations and in front-page reports in *Al-Ahram,* that he was instrumental in the choice of the new cabinet lineup.

4. In some of his recent articles, Mr. Heikal expressed views and voiced criticisms that were "at variance with state policy." These are crucial times, and now is not the time for fault-finding.[31]

Soon after removing Heikal, Sadat assigned Dr. Abdul Qader Hatem, a deputy prime minister, to be in charge of *Al-Ahram* as chairman of its board, and Ali Amin, a former editor of *Al-Akhbar,* was appointed managing editor. Amin had just returned from exile following Sadat's release of his twin brother Mustafa, who was serving a life term on charges of spying for the United States. The day after his removal, Heikal went to *Al-Ahram's* building where he met with Dr. Hatem and handed over to him a record of *Al-Ahram's* budget, including its profits and circulation figures. Then he left for his home. Later in the day the minister for presidential affairs called him and said they had prepared an office and five rooms for him and asked how many secretaries and cars he wanted. Heikal told the minister he had no wish to take up his new job and that he would talk to the president about it later.

Heikal's friends, particularly Dr. Mahmoud Fawzi, tried in vain to convince him to work with Sadat. They told him that he could not defy the president's decree and that the president would not see him unless he was ready to take up his job. Heikal said: "I told President Sadat not to look for a job for me because this is my own decision. He only had the right to tell me not to work at *Al-Ahram,* but I have the right to decide what to do with my future."

Although Heikal is generally undefensive, he was anxious to refute the charge made by the official spokesman that *Al-Ahram* had become a "power center." He was annoyed by the application of his own term to himself. He coined the term which had become an accepted phrase in Egyptian political life. To Heikal, many people, including Sadat, had misused or misinterpreted the phrase. Heikal believed a "center of power" had to be based on a power source, such as an army, a police force, or a youth movement of a party organization. "A newspaper," he said, "is only a newspaper. Its power is limited to its ability to persuade, either through its columns or its editor's contacts with those in power." Heikal recalls that Sadat once told him that *Al-Ahram* was turning into a "center of power" that decided foreign policy for Egypt. "Politics is none of your business," he told Heikal, "because a journalist has to conform to state policy." Heikal disagreed with him and said: "The essence of journalistic freedom is that I express my opinion to persuade public opinion or the head of state. I don't have any militia forces to use against the state. The only power I have is to influence public opinion by what I write to make your political movement difficult." Heikal believes that one of the major duties of the press is not to cheer for any government decision but to criticize and give options for policymakers.[32]

Heikal: Post *Al-Ahram* (1974–1978)

As a result of Heikal's removal, tension began to build at *Al-Ahram* among the editorial staff who regarded him as their protector. Even those who opposed his ideas admired his courage. The new editor, Ali Amin, subscribed to a different journalistic school and wanted to impose his own stamp on *Al-Ahram*. To many people, his popular style of journalism was out of place in the traditionally serious *Al-Ahram*. At his first meeting with the editorial staff he said: "I started a revolution in the press in 1944 when I founded *Akhbar el-Yom*. Heikal carried this on. Now a new revolution is required away from the 'crumbs' of my generation and away from the political meddling of the recent past, to responsibility and free comment." One editor asked Amin whether they really could write freely. Amin said: "I have myself seen the president's decree abolishing censorship. Except for military matters, we may henceforth publish what we choose." Another editor interrupted and said: "Some of us have prepared a brief tribute to the man who built not only this building but its spirit, making of *Al-Ahram* an island of differing opinions and free discussion in a uniform sea. Have we your permission to publish it tomorrow?" Amin said: "I shall have to ask." The next morning the tribute to Heikal was not published in *Al-Ahram*.[1]

The tension between Ali Amin and his staff surfaced a week later when he made some remarks about *Al-Ahram* which his staff regarded as offensive. Asked by a television interviewer what he had done in the week since he took over the editorship, Amin said he had only had time to give the paper "underclothes." Later, he said, he would dress it in its "bridal gown."[2] *Al-Ahram*'s editorial staff were indignant and took his reference to underclothes to mean that the paper had been indulging in smutty journalism before he arrived. They maintained that, with its worldwide reputation as a newspaper of high political standing, this was unjustified slander. The staff members held a meeting in the newsroom and decided to call on Amin to issue a retraction and an apology. Amin declared that under no circumstances would his staff dictate to him. He offered to allow the staff a defense of the Heikal era in *Al-Ahram* but this was turned down as inadequate. Finally Dr. Hatem, the new chairman of the board, intervened as a mediator. It was decided that Amin would appear on television again to put the record straight and retract his statement.[3]

Reaction to Heikal's Fall

Although Heikal's dismissal from *Al-Ahram* sent shock waves through the Egyptian establishment, not a word of protest was murmured in the Egyptian press. Ironically, most comments about his fall came from the foreign press. The *Times* of London wrote an editorial praising Heikal under the title "The Fall of a Great Editor":[4]

Short of resigning himself, President Sadat could not have made any change in his team more spectacular than the sudden removal of Mr. Muhammad Hassanein Heykal [sic] from the editorship of *Al-Ahram*. . . . Mr. Heykal is an institution in himself. . . . By moving now to replace Mr. Heykal, President Sadat shows that he is sensitive to [his] criticisms, but unwilling to bow to them. He has in effect staked his whole reputation on the success of the Kissinger policy. That might be right, but dismissing Mr. Heykal is a discouragement for Egypt. *Al-Ahram* under Mr. Heykal has been the nearest thing to an island of free thought and free speech that "revolutionary" Egypt has known.

Similar praise was broadcast over the BBC airwaves by a commentator for the external broadcasting services: "It is hard to imagine Mohamed Heikal apart from his empire in *Al-Ahram* and still harder to believe that this very able, energetic, and ambitious man will fade into obscurity."[5]

The *Guardian* said Heikal was the great pillar of Nasserism to fall from Sadat's favor. "It should be said in fairness," wrote the *Guardian,* "that Heikal is greater in his downfall than he was in his days of glory. It was widely expected that, when Nasser died, Heikal would quickly fall from favor. But his position weakened only slowly. . . . From Nasser, he got the inside information that furnished the substance of his great scoops and revelations, the advance knowledge for his predictions . . . that could make heads of state tremble."[6]

The *Neue Zuercher Zeitung* of Zurich said that the removal of Heikal by Sadat was a political event of the first magnitude. "Heikal and 'his' newspaper had become a political and cultural institution rivaling the Foreign Ministry in importance and exceeding that of the Ministry of Information."[7]

After Heikal left *Al-Ahram*, many attempts were made to convince him to accept the post of presidential press adviser but Heikal persisted in rejecting the post. Press reports circulating in Beirut said Heikal was offered a ministerial post in the Libyan government by his friend Qaddafi.[8] Heikal later denied these reports and told the *Sunday Times* of London that he would never accept an offer to leave Egypt or work abroad. "I am too committed to Egypt for that," he said. "I have had many offers, both journalistic and others, but I do not intend to accept any of them."[9]

Meanwhile, Heikal occupied himself with writing projects. A book that included his insights on the period between the Six-Day War of 1967 and the October War of 1973 was finished then and published in London in 1975.[10] He spent most of his time at his rest-house near the Pyramids. "I had the time to read more, think more, and debate more," he wrote.[11] He also had the time to travel and visit countries that he had wished to visit before. At home, he enjoyed family life and practiced some of his hobbies. According to Heikal his favorite hobby is work, although he finds some time to play golf at the Gezira Club or listen to some favorite Western classical music. "Our family enjoys listening to classical music, and we consider it part of our culture," said Heikal. Reading also fills much of Heikal's leisure time. Book shelves fill almost all parts of his and his wife's apartment. Though the titles cover a wide range of interests, most of their home library consists of books on politics, history, and Islamic art. He and his wife occupy one apartment and their Jesuit-educated sons another on the same floor of a tower building overlooking the Nile. His wife, Hidayat Taymur, comes from a wealthy family famed for its mango groves. Before marrying Heikal, she earned a college degree in the French language. After marriage, she returned to college and obtained two degrees in Arabic language and Islamic antiquities from Cairo University, where she still works as a teaching assistant.[12]

During this period, relations between Heikal and Sadat remained cool. Heikal continued to ignore the post to which he was assigned by a presidential decree, and Sadat did nothing to cancel that decree. Heikal did not want, however, to "burn all his bridges with Sadat" and kept occasional social contacts with the president and his family. When Sadat's second daughter was married during the summer of 1974, Heikal and his wife were among the wedding guests. Their invitation was addressed to the "Adviser to the President." During the wedding, Sadat hinted that television cameramen take a close shot of Heikal and his wife. This was seen by many observers as a gesture of goodwill from Sadat who was still trying to bring Heikal back to his camp. On another occasion, when Heikal's eldest son, Ali, a medical student at Cairo University, fell sick and was taken to London for treatment, the Sadats contacted the Heikals and wished their son a speedy recovery.

While in London, Heikal was approached by several publishers urging him to write a book about changes in the modern Arab world. Before leaving London he signed a five-year contract with the *Sunday Times* to write a number of books about the Arab countries and the superpowers' struggle over the Middle East.

Sadat's Rapprochement

In November 1974 Sadat started his rapprochement with Heikal by inviting him to his house. There Sadat asked Heikal what his plans were for the future. Heikal said that he was writing articles for newspapers in Beirut and had book contracts through 1979. Sadat said: "I don't mean your private plans, but your plans to serve your country." Then Sadat offered Heikal a position as his political adviser. But Heikal asked Sadat to withhold any formal position and just keep him as a friend.[13] Some press reports said Sadat was trying to fill the political gap left by Heikal's departure from *Al-Ahram*. According to one press report from Beirut, Sadat needed Heikal as his adviser for national security affairs to eventually plan state policies and give the president options to choose from, a role similar to that of Henry Kissinger under Richard Nixon.[14]

Soon after meeting with Sadat, Heikal went on a long trip to the Arab countries to collect material for his forthcoming book. During the trip, in statements and press interviews, he criticized Sadat and the disengagement agreement with Israel. Heikal told a Syrian newspaper in Damascus that Israel would not give up all or even some of the occupied Arab territory unless forced to do so. "The fifth war is almost the only solution left now," he said.[15] At the same time, in an article in the *New York Times* Heikal said Kissinger was wrong in his approach to the Middle East problem.

Kissinger wanted to end the war because he wanted to avoid confrontation between the superpowers. But he did not look at the root of the problem. This led him to a policy of pacification instead of a policy of seeking a solution. This was wrong because pacification is at best a passing phase. You cannot pacify forever. Having been within reach of a controlled solution, we are now slipping back into an uncontrolled situation in which the local parties try to finish the unfinished business. That's the real danger.[16]

In a *Newsweek* interview, Heikal said Kissinger's big mistake was to divide the problem into three Arab fronts—Egypt, Syria, and Jordan—and then each front into several subdivisions. "That can only lead to each one outbidding the other," Heikal said. "Divided they will ask for more than they would settle for together."[17]

On returning to Cairo, Heikal found Sadat very upset about his statements abroad. They argued for eleven hours and Heikal told Sadat he was just repeating views they had discussed before. "You've punished me once for expressing my opinion," said Heikal. "Are you going to punish me again for expressing the same opinion?" Sadat tried to change Heikal's opinion, but in vain. Their relationship, however, started to improve.

Soon Mamdouh Salem was designated prime minister and started forming his cabinet. He offered Heikal the title of deputy premier for information and Arab affairs but Heikal turned it down, still arguing that he did not want to get involved in politics. Sadat then told Heikal: "I agree that you go back to journalism provided you commit yourself to the state policy." He refused and told Sadat he was still against political commitment in journalism.

During the summer of 1975 Heikal resumed writing his column "Frankly Speaking" outside Egypt. He made arrangements with *Al-Anwar* of Beirut to syndicate his articles in other Arab countries. In his first article, Heikal tried to explain why he was resuming his column eighteen months after leaving *Al-Ahram*. He said his wish as a journalist had always been to comment on current affairs. He thought he might have some views to express and share with readers outside Egypt. Heikal wrote: "Maybe I am not forbidden to publish in Egypt, but I have chosen to publish in other Arab countries to avoid causing embarrassment to others or to myself."[18]

He said he had chosen the Lebanese press because he needed a forum from which he could address his readers. Then he explained his views about the difference between "voluntary" commitment and "imposed" commitment for a journalist. "I am committed to the thoughts and ideologies of the 'Arab Revolution' as expressed by Gamal Abdul Nasser," he said, "but I don't consider myself a protector of what Nasser has said. This is the responsibility of one man: Anwar el-Sadat." Heikal said his commitment to Nasser's principles did not mean that the Nasserite "experiment" should not be criticized for faults that occurred in the course of its progress. He listed the faults that he openly criticized under Nasser and said he had willingly accepted the whips that had fallen on his back as a result of his articles. Heikal said he had twice thought of quitting writing forever— once after Egypt's defeat in 1967 and again after Nasser's death in 1970—"but I decided to continue writing until our land was liberated."[19]

Heikal's next trip took him to Teheran, where he had a long interview with the Shah. They talked for three hours about oil politics and the Iranian role in the Middle East conflict. A full account of the interview was published in his column in Beirut.[20] Meanwhile, the *Sunday Times* of London started serializing extracts from Heikal's book *The Road to Ramadan*. Sadat, unhappy with what Heikal had written in the book, accused him of "faking Egypt's history." Heikal thought that Sadat reached unfair judgments of his views by reading badly translated second-hand excerpts from his book. When he returned to Cairo, Heikal tried to straighten the record with Sadat. He argued that he had no interest in "faking history." "I might have made some errors in judgment," said Heikal, "but I've always warned in my articles that I've only written what I've seen; I don't claim, however, that I've seen everything." Heikal insisted that making errors in reporting historical events is not the same thing as "faking history."[21]

In his syndicated column, Heikal continued sniping at Sadat and the second Sinai accord with Israel. In a series about the accord, Heikal attacked United States policy in the Middle East, saying the only winner in the accord was Henry Kissinger who had succeeded in "dividing the Arabs and guaranteeing Israel's security."[22] Heikal emphasized that he was not trying to be antagonistic toward the United States as such. "I greatly admire the American nation," he wrote, "because it has led humanity to wide horizons of progress. When many people saw in Watergate a sign of decline in the American society, I thought it was a sign of health and ascendancy, because nowhere in any modern society can democratic institutions bring the head of state to account and ensure his fall as it happened to Richard Nixon." Heikal distinguished, however, between the American people and the American foreign policy power elite who "use their power foolishly and create terrible human miseries in many parts of the world."[23] At this point, Sadat thought there was no use in attempting to lure Heikal to his camp and decided to relieve him of his post as press adviser to the president. This also stopped Heikal's monthly salary of 500 Egyptian pounds ($700) which he had continued to draw since his dismissal from *Al-Ahram*.

Heikal Visits the United States

On the eve of Sadat's visit to the United States in October 1975, Heikal flew to Chicago at the invitation of the Association of Arab-American University Graduates, a community of professionals, academics, and businessmen of Arab origin. On October 18 Heikal addressed the association's general convention in Chicago and got an eight-minute standing ovation from the audience.[24] The thrust of his speech was an attack on Sadat for signing the Sinai accords and

Kissinger for dividing the Arabs. He told the convention that he doubted whether Kissinger's efforts would achieve anything meaningful. "Look at what Dr. Kissinger is doing," he said. "We must admit at once that he is the most accomplished player of the game. The objectives of Washington are clear and immediate. Kissinger knows how to manipulate people and events to achieve what he wants. And if we look at the Middle East now, it is clear that he is succeeding."[25]

Heikal then expressed his views to the press in Washington. He told the *New York Times* that Sadat's agreement with Israel was a tragic mistake. He said these agreements were "nothing, worse than nothing. They divided the Arab world, which is a horrible thing, and made the Soviet Union more mischievous."[26] He criticized Sadat for trying to silence him; "I am ready to admit it is Sadat's right not to have any other voices although I differ with that; as a newspaperman I don't like it, as a patriot I don't like it."[27]

Heikal felt later that these were strong statements to be aired in the United States a few days before Sadat's arrival in Washington. In a letter to the *New York Times* Heikal explained the purpose of his visit:

In an interview that was published in the *New York Times,* it was made to appear that I was coming to the United States to undermine the visit of President Sadat of Egypt. Nothing was further from my intentions. President Sadat is the leader of my country and my people, and I only wish him every success in his mission to the United States. . . . It was a mere accident that my visit to the United States coincided with that of President Sadat. . . . If some of my observations have been seen as critical of the Sinai accord, those observations were not directed against President Sadat. They were intended to be solely an objective assessment of the agreement and its possible consequences.[28]

Anti-Heikal Campaign

Upon Heikal's return to Cairo, Arab press reports circulated that he had been put under house arrest. One newspaper said President Sadat ordered Heikal's arrest because of the Beirut articles and Washington statements.[29] These reports proved to be based on rumors, and Heikal was still moving freely. However, he had to face a well-orchestrated campaign against him in Egypt. At Cairo airport, he was received by eight journalists from *Al-Ahram* as a gesture of goodwill to their former editor. Following this, a member of the Arab Socialist Union called for punishing Heikal "and his group of journalists who back him against President Sadat by burning them alive without trial."[30] This statement created waves of protests in the press

and prompted the Press Syndicate to investigate and send a memorandum to Sadat protesting such threats against Heikal and journalists.

The campaign against Heikal escalated when some press reports
accused him of involvement in the imprisonment of Mustafa Amin in
1965 on a charge of spying for the United States. Other news stories
speculated that Heikal might be put on trial for contributing to the
1967 defeat by Israel when he helped Nasser "misguide" the Arab
masses by his writings.[31]

News of these charges reached Heikal while on a visit to Kuwait.
He refuted the charges in a statement to the press. "I am going back to
face a vehement, widespread, and concentrated campaign against
me," he said. "Shall I answer only part of what is being said or shall I
ignore it as I did in the past, confident that, in the end, only what is
right will be upheld." Heikal added that what had been said against
him amounted to three things: "(1) Slander, which I shall definitely
not reply to because without any modesty or pretensions I know how
to conduct myself and it is not my business how others behave; (2)
tales and stories, some of which are attributed to history, and which I
have enjoyed reading; and (3) political allegations, some authors of
which went so far as to demand my trial. Perhaps they know that I do
not object to a public political trial in which all the records are opened
and all chapters are reviewed."[32]

Another incident involved United States Senator Adlai
Stevenson III. A press report accused Heikal of having predicted to
Senator Stevenson during his trip to Cairo in 1975 that there would be
a "coup against Sadat within six weeks." At Heikal's request, the
senator confirmed in a letter that nothing like that had passed between
them. Heikal sent a copy of the letter to Sadat.[33] Some Arab regimes
opposed to Sadat's agreements with Israel came to Heikal's defense in
the campaign against him. The Syrian mass media defended Heikal
and attacked Sadat for "selling out to Israel." A commentator on
Damascus radio said:

... the Egyptian regime can no longer tolerate any criticism of the Sinai
agreement. The regime attempted to level various accusations against any
Arab attempting to expose the real dangers consequent upon the treasonous
[Sinai] agreement. However, when criticism emanates from an Egyptian Arab
citizen like Heikal, the Egyptian regime loses its head and attempts to suppress the citizen with every possible means and false pretense which the
authorities allow their officials to fabricate.

All that Heikal did was to write a series of articles about the Sinai agreement.
He explained that the agreement was in favor of Israel and Washington and
against the Arab nation. . . . This was all Heikal did. They are now calling

for his trial after dismissing him from a post which he neither accepted nor assumed. This poses a new question. If this was the action of the Egyptian regime regarding a patriotic journalist like Heikal, despite all President Sadat's talk about freedom of the press, what is to be the fate of the Egyptian Arab masses who reject and condemn the agreement?[34]

Heikal Defends Nasser

While the anti-Heikal campaign was going on, the campaign against the late President Nasser was escalating. After a silence lasting more than twenty years, the press started a stormy debate about the "negative aspects" of Nasserism. Such criticism came mainly from journalists who were affected by Nasser's regime such as the Amin brothers. The attacks against Nasser involved his repression of political dissent within Egypt. Newspaper articles attacked both Nasser's police apparatus and the socialism that was the very foundation of his regime.

Initially, Heikal refrained from answering the anti-Nasser campaign. But when a report alleged that Nasser had embezzled $15 million,[35] Heikal came to the defense of his late friend. In a series of articles published in Beirut, he said that Sadat shared responsibility with Nasser for all decisions he had made. "There can be no de-Nasserization without de-Sadatization," he said. "Sadat was with Nasser all the way from 1952 to 1970." To Heikal, the anti-Nasser campaign was launched to "assassinate the revolutionary symbol" that Nasser represented in an attempt to "cut the tree from its deep roots." Heikal admitted, however, that Nasserism had some "negative aspects" and faults, but this did not justify concentrated attacks on Nasserism and its positive achievements. To him, this required serious study and deep analysis to help Egypt avoid such mistakes in the future.[36]

Early in 1976 Heikal found himself defending Nasser again. He said he regretted that his articles could not reach people inside Egypt, but he could not keep silent any more. Heikal explained that since he started writing outside Egypt, he tried to avoid writing about internal matters in Egypt. "We in the Arab world have not yet learned how to argue well," he wrote. "We are good at making hate campaigns and wars of words without allowing any opposing view to be expressed freely." Heikal said that the time had not come for him to write the full story of Nasser, with all his achievements and failures, because he was still emotionally involved with Nasser's memory. He wanted to wait a few years more to put the story in historical perspective. "The campaign against Nasser today," he wrote, "is only part of a continuous effort by the CIA to 'assassinate' his reputation and what he stood for."[37] He supported this by quoting John Marks, a former CIA agent, who said the CIA had tried to assassinate Nasser three times during the late fifties.

At this point, the relationship between Heikal and Sadat deteriorated further and they stopped seeing each other. When *Al-Ahram* celebrated its 100th birthday in June 1976, Heikal was not invited to the opening ceremonies of the centenary exhibition. Members of the *Al-Ahram* staff were indignant that out of the vast collection of articles on show, only one was by Heikal. Organizers also kept his photograph out of the gallery of pictures of *Al-Ahram*'s former editors and chairmen. When Sadat inaugurated the exhibition on June 13, the chairman of the board of *Al-Ahram* announced that 100,000 Egyptian pounds ($130,000) would be distributed as a gift to editors and workers. Sadat himself was presented with the first issue of *Al-Ahram,* dated 1876 and engraved on a silver plate.[38] Some of Heikal's supporters had been sent into limbo—where they were given a desk, a salary, and orders not to write. The most recent victims were some of the paper's leading writers including Mohamed Sayed Ahmad and Lutfi el-Kholi.

Following the riots of January 1977, in which students and workers demonstrated against the government for raising food prices, Heikal became more vocal in his criticism of Sadat. In an interview on Hungarian television in March, Heikal called for a return to Nasser's strategy and said the Soviet Union still had a role to play in the Middle East. He charged that the food riots in January "were a popular uprising and that the Communists had nothing to do with them."[39]

Speaking in Cairo to a group of Egyptian students studying in West Germany, Sadat attacked Heikal without naming him. He said that just before going to the meeting he was informed that a "malicious" Egyptian journalist—one that had been an editor of a Cairo newspaper—had told the Hungarian television that what happened on January 18 and 19 was a popular uprising. This journalist, Sadat said, had always been an agent of the United Sates and had been used by Nasser to contact the Americans. But today, he continued, it is the fashion to contact the Soviet Union.[40]

Late in 1977 the smear campaign against Heikal mounted following a series of twelve articles he wrote about Nasser. The articles, giving what he felt was a fair evaluation of Nasser, were printed as a book. According to Heikal, the sixteen editions of the book were selling "like hashish under the counter" in Egypt. When he visited London in October to work on the English drafts of his two books, he told newsmen about the campaign against him at home. "When there are daily accusations against me by officials from the highest to the lowest levels, and when the president repeats, in practically every speech he makes, attacks against me, then I know there is trouble." Heikal insisted, however, that he did not intend to live outside Egypt. "I don't like the profession of political refugee," he said. "My place is in Egypt, in my office or in prison."[41]

Sadat's Peace Initiative

Sadat's visit to Israel in November 1977 stunned Egyptians at all levels, including Heikal. Initially, Heikal refrained from attacking Sadat's initiative in his articles but he was willing to criticize it in interviews with foreign newsmen. On November 14 he spoke for the first time against the initiative with John Snider, ABC Middle East correspondent. The interview was aired on ABC television network via satellite from Cairo. Heikal told his American viewers that he was confused about the visit and said that peace cannot be made because it is the wish of one man. "It needs the conviction of the people in Egypt and other Arab states because it is not only our problem," he said. Heikal recalled that when Sadat visited the United States in 1977 he said he was not going to see peace in his lifetime and all he was ready to give was an end to the state of belligerency with Israel. "So what happened?" asked Heikal. "Something must have happened which Sadat alone knows—I must confess my ignorance."[42]

On November 17 Heikal was facing the cameras of BBC television to answer questions on Sadat's initiative. But as Sadat was getting ready to go to Jerusalem November 19, Heikal stopped criticizing him and left Cairo for Alexandria trying to get away from dramatic events in the Egyptian capital. However, Heikal was following the news on Cairo radio, and on hearing that a squadron of Israeli air force jets would meet Sadat's plane in Israel he broke into tears. "I never cried like that since those fearful moments when I stood by Gamal Abdul Nasser's deathbed in 1970," wrote Heikal. "I was following the events like the millions around the world, but a deep sadness engulfed me for many days even after my return to Cairo in the aftermath of that strange show in Jerusalem."[43]

Under pressure from the foreign news media, Heikal could not keep silent any longer. He gave interviews to the French newspaper *Le Monde* and the French magazine *L'Express*. Soon after the publication of these interviews, a Cairo newspaper attacked Heikal in a front-page article under the title "One Man Against Egypt," accusing him of being the only dissident voice in Egypt. Later, Heikal received a personal request from the editor-in-chief of the *Times* of London asking him to make his views on the Sadat initiative known because "the world cannot hear the other view from Egypt." Heikal agreed to talk with the *Times* correspondent Edward Mortimer and the interview appeared on the front page under a 3-column headline: "Mr. Heikal sees trouble in pact without Arab consent; Warning of 'cardboard peace'; Fear of Egyptian isolation." In this interview, Heikal expressed his fears of a deep and lasting rift between Egypt and the Arab world. He said peace reached in these circumstances would be a "cardboard peace." He stressed that he did not necessarily oppose Sadat's initiative as such if it was seen as a "challenge of peace thrown in the Israeli courtyard." But, he said, "this was turned into a state visit, and the state visit got the dynamics of normalization." Heikal believed that a better approach would have been for Sadat to inform other Arab countries of his plans in advance and promise to report back to an Arab summit conference on the results of his visit. Instead, Heikal said, Sadat started to defend his initiative and began attacks on all fronts against the Arabs and the Soviet Union. Heikal thought that Sadat's initiative had been accepted in Egypt for the wrong reasons. By watching the visit on television for 41 hours, he said, war-weary Egyptians had achieved a sense of participation in the event and a belief that peace would lead to a solution of Egypt's economic problems. According to Heikal, this sense of participation in the event by ordinary Egyptians washed away all reservations. But, he said, "peace is not a television spectacular."[44]

After four months of waiting and watching, Heikal decided that he could no longer avoid dealing with the Sadat initiative in his articles. In March 1978 he launched a new series of syndicated articles attacking the initiative. The seventeen articles were printed as a book in Beirut during the summer of 1978.[45] In his introduction to the book, Heikal said the initiative cannot succeed in spite of the intensive mass media campaign surrounding it because "great conflicts of history are too complex to be resolved in front of microphones and television cameras." Heikal believes, however, that Sadat's initiative has produced some "negative benefits" for the Arabs:

1. The initiative has exposed the inconsistency in the thinking of some Arab leaders and their inability to move or act.
2. The initiative has demonstrated the incompetency of Arab leaders to

utilize the extensive resources of the Arab world in facing the Israeli challenge.

3. The initiative has shown that there is no "easy and quick solution" to the Arab-Israeli conflict due to its complex nature.

Heikal argues that the struggle is between two parties over an indivisible land; the Arabs, having the right to the land, may have the power to restore it in the future. The Israelis, having the power to keep the land, will never have the right to keep it. Heikal thinks the Israelis want the Arabs to surrender their rights in Palestine. "Some Arab leaders don't understand this, believing that partial concessions will resolve the conflict," he wrote. "The truth of the matter is that partial concessions are nothing but an Israeli solution because every partial Arab concession would mean a step closer to the complete surrender to Israel." The Arabs, Heikal said, have given concessions "beyond any imagination." The result of this, he believes, is what we see happening in the Middle East today.[46]

Early in 1978 Heikal went on a 10-day tour to some Arab countries to gauge reaction to Sadat's initiative. He purposely chose to visit the Arabian Gulf states, avoiding radical Arab countries such as Iraq, Syria, and Libya. He calculated that the Arabian Gulf area is "politically safer" and that Egyptian authorities might not object to his going there. Nonetheless, as Heikal's statements and interviews received wide publicity in the press and on television, official protests were pouring on Heikal from Egyptian embassies in the Arabian Gulf. "I found this to be ridiculous," wrote Heikal, "at a time when Cairo was receiving tens of Israeli journalists like heroes, and allowing them to express their views in the press and on television."[47]

On returning to Egypt, Heikal stepped up his criticism of Sadat's initiative. He attacked the intensive media campaign to "brainwash" the Egyptian people with regard to the Arab-Israeli conflict. "We made people believe that peace is closer than ever," he wrote. "In our attempt to push people to accept the 'peace initiative' we disarmed Egyptians of their 'right to reject,' thus depriving them of a basic psychological weapon before achieving real peace." Heikal said he could not understand why Sadat launched an intensive media campaign against Egypt's Arab role and her commitment to Arab nationalism. "We believed that by doing so, we show our independent will," said Heikal, "but we are forgetting that we are willingly giving up a strategic weapon that gives our will an effective edge in the Middle East." Heikal believes the Arabs cannot fight Israel without Egypt at their side. He equally believes that Egypt cannot fight without the

Arab nation. A separate peace between Egypt and Israel, he argues, would only reflect the balance of power between them. "I don't believe this is an acceptable situation even from an isolationist, selfish Egyptian view."[48]

According to Heikal, the Arabs are divided because they have different approaches to achieving peace with Israel:

1. One approach to peace does not take into account a peaceful settlement because there could be no middle ground in the struggle between right and wrong.
2. A second approach, championed by the "supporting states" like Saudi Arabia, calls for a peaceful settlement acceptable to the "confrontation states."
3. A third approach, adopted by Syria, understands peace as an end to the state of belligerency with Israel.
4. A fourth approach, adopted by Egypt, requires an end to the state of war, signing of security agreeements, and establishing normal relations with Israel.

Heikal argues that these conflicting approaches to peace will lead to "no peace" because peace is indivisible. He thinks there is no such thing as half peace. To him, a separate peace between Egypt and Israel is no peace at all. He thinks the threat of war on the Eastern front between Israel, Syria, and Jordan may draw Egypt into it. Heikal concludes that Israel will never pay the price of peace unless there is one unified Arab approach to peace.[49]

In another article, Heikal openly questioned Sadat's power and called his peace initiative "a one-man decision." He believed that the Israelis understood this in their dealings with Sadat and tried to exert more pressure on him to get more concessions. He compared leadership power in Egypt, Israel, and the United States to make his point clear. "Our mistake is that we compare the power of our leaders with that of leaders of other countries," he wrote. "We imagine, judging by our own scales, that Nixon, Ford, and Carter possess power equivalent to that of Arab presidents, kings, and sultans. This is a drastic error in judgment because power in most Arab states is still 'tribal power' which allows authority to be concentrated in one person." Heikal believes that most Arab leaders fail to understand that modern states are not "tools of power" but tools for achieving long-range policies based on high-level strategies.[50]

With the growing criticism of his peace initiative, Sadat, in May 1978, began a drive to silence his critics in the press. A public referendum gave him a mandate to curtail political dissent and criticism in the press. His crackdown began when he ordered thirty Egyptian journalists working abroad to return home to face charges of "defaming Egypt." At home, Sadat gave orders that Heikal and four other journalists be barred from leaving Egypt pending investigation of charges of defaming Egypt in the foreign media. Apparently Heikal was included on the list for criticizing Sadat's initiative in the foreign media and for giving two interviews to *Al-Ahaly,* the left-wing Cairo newspaper that was banned on government orders.

In an interview with the *Times* of London, Heikal said he was surprised to see Sadat overreact to criticism and suddenly appear willing to throw away his liberalization policy. "As an Egyptian citizen, I shall continue to express my opinion for as long as I am able," he told the *Times.* He added that internal criticism was inevitable and healthy during a difficult period when Egypt was in transition.[51] Heikal told the *New York Times* a week later that Sadat's plans to purge his leading opposition in the leftist parties were a mistake. "Political parties are an expression of political and social interest," he said. "We are going to push the whole scene underground to explode here and there." Heikal said he was surprised that he would be interrogated for his writing. "It's not done," he said. "It's not harming a man. It's affecting something more."[52]

On June 14, 1978, Heikal was questioned by the socialist prosecutor as part of an investigation to determine whether he had defamed Egypt in the columns he had written abroad. Accompanied by his lawyer, Heikal spent two and one-half hours with the prosecutor in a secret session. When contacted by foreign correspondents after the meeting, Heikal said he was not allowed to comment on the proceedings but said the questioning would continue. In July he told newsmen that he feared the government crackdown could lead to imprisonment of dissidents or sequestration of their property.

Heikal, the Controversial: Pro and Con

THE Arab world has never known a journalist who has drawn so much controversy and admiration as has Mohamed Hassanein Heikal. Throughout his career, which uniquely combined journalistic flair with political influence, he has been the center of continuous controversy. Even after his removal from the editorship of *Al-Ahram* in 1974, Heikal has continued to be a favorite subject for comment by his critics as well as his admirers. It is likely that he will continue to be a controversial figure for some time to come. In recent years the Arab world has witnessed a wave of books and articles either attacking Heikal for his failures or defending him for his achievements. His roles as a journalist and a politician are still analyzed with interest in press circles in Egypt as to their significance and impact on Middle Eastern press and politics. The following is an attempt to survey the pro and con views on Heikal from his critics and defenders in Egypt, the Arab countries, and the West.

As a Journalist

Heikal's superior qualities as a journalist seem to be the only thing that his critics and defenders agree on. The present editor of *Al-Ahram*, Ali Hamdi el-Gammal, believes that history will classify Heikal in the highest ranks of Egyptian journalism. "As a professional," Gammal said, "Heikal is an excellent journalist. But unfortunately, he has mixed his roles as a journalist and a politician, and this involved him in trouble."[1] Another distinguished columnist, Ahmad Baha' el-Din, a former editor of *Al-Ahram*, agrees with Gammal that Heikal mixed up his journalistic and political careers so that it was difficult to distinguish them. "Heikal's journalistic talents should not be attributed to his closeness to Nasser," he said.[2] "Heikal started as a political reporter at his own initiative and later changed to a political writer." According to Baha' el-Din, who is regarded as one of the top political writers in Egypt, *Al-Ahram* gave Heikal a prestigious political position and this started a new phase in his journalistic career. He became a political writer who would take a certain position and defend it in his column. "This created a problem for Heikal's readers," said Baha' el-Din, "because they could not tell Heikal's views from Nasser's views.'' Baha' el-Din believes this also created a complex situation for Heikal himself who wanted to make his readers feel that these were his own views and not Nasser's. He also believes that Heikal's long articles are written in a personal style. ''From a purely technical and professional standard, this is not a good style,'' he said, ''because a writer must be brief, precise, and to the point.''

A strong supporter of Heikal is Dr. Sami Mansour, an *Al-Ahram* columnist who was recruited by Heikal when he took over the editorship in 1958. He worked with Heikal for eighteen years, during which he obtained a doctorate in political science with Heikal's support and encouragement. According to Dr. Mansour, Heikal is the most creative journalist in the Arab world. ''Unfortunately,'' said Mansour, ''no one can reach his journalistic standards when it comes to writing his weekly column.''[3] Mansour thinks Heikal was the first to introduce a style of writing that combined political analysis with reportage and straight news. He believes what distinguished Heikal as a journalist was his alertness, openmindedness, and logical approach to writing. ''Heikal has a beautiful Arabic style through which he creates lucid and clear expression,'' he said. Mansour thinks this comes from Heikal's broad cultural background which is enriched by constant reading and comprehension. ''Heikal is a walking archive,'' he said, ''because he has a phenomenal memory, particularly when it comes to facts, figures, or events that happened a long time ago.''

Dr. Ahmad Hussein Sawi, professor of journalism at the American University in Cairo, believes Heikal is an excellent essay writer who uniquely utilizes information at his disposal. Dr. Sawi credits Heikal with reviving the writing of long columns after they had been on the wane in the Egyptian press. Other writers followed suit and long-column writing became an accepted feature in the Arab press. According to Sawi, Heikal was also a pioneer in news production. Sawi himself had suggested to Heikal that *Al-Ahram* should stop using the old method of writing front-page headlines by a caligrapher. ''The sensational, red-inked streamer on top of the main story was used to inflate news and unnecessarily exaggerate its content,'' he said.[4] Heikal agreed with Sawi and asked him to help *Al-Ahram*'s technicians develop a headline-setting machine to replace the time-consuming job of caligraphy. The idea worked out and other newspapers followed *Al-Ahram* in dropping their full-page red banner.

Former editor of *Al-Gumhouriya,* Mustafa Bahgat Badawi, a poet who works as a writer with *Al-Ahram,* is another admirer of Heikal's journalistic talents. According to him, Heikal coined a new Arabic phrase describing journalism as the ''profession of looking-for-trouble." Badawi says Heikal's contribution to Arab journalism was in his early years as a foreign correspondent. "Heikal built his journalistic glory by following hot news to different parts of the world rather than depending on wire service copy," he said.[5] Badawi says this started a trend in the Egyptian press and many newsmen started to follow Heikal's example of pursuing foreign news.

Heikal and Nasser

According to Ali Hamdi el-Gammal, Heikal under Nasser was a major participant in ruling the country. "He was one of Nasser's pillars," Gammal said, "and this gave him a privileged position through which he monopolized the news."[6] Ahmad Baha' el-Din says though Heikal was influenced by Nasser's thinking, Heikal in turn influenced Nasser's behavior and actions. "In terms of ideology and orientation," he said, "Heikal came under Nasser's influence because Heikal never was an ideologue. He helped Nasser only in application, such as advising him on cabinet formulations and other political decisions."[7] Baha' el-Din believes that Heikal's political stature involved him in the power struggle surrounding Nasser. "Heikal was very loyal to Nasser," he said, "but I don't believe he was after power; Nasser utilized Heikal's talents after discovering his alertness, organized mind, and broad cultural background." Baha' el-Din agrees with Gammal that Heikal monopolized the news in the time of Nasser; however, for this he blames Nasser. He says, "Any newsman in Heikal's shoes would keep his exclusive stories for himself. It was the fault of Nasser who gave the news only to one newsman." According to Baha' el-Din, when he was chairman of the Press Syndicate in 1967, he sent a memorandum to Nasser protesting Al-Ahram's privileged position and its monopoly on national news.[8]

One of the outspoken critics of Heikal is Mustafa Amin, former editor of Akhbar el-Yom. "Heikal built a pyramid and buried the press in it," he said.[9] Amin believes Heikal controlled the press and utilized it for his personal advantage. "Heikal had 'massacred' big-name journalists and kept the 'summit' for himself," said Amin. Amin thinks that he himself could have reached the same privileged position with Nasser as did Heikal, if he had not candidly spoken about Egypt's need for democratic institutions and a free press.

Another staunch supporter of Sadat and critic of Heikal is Mousa Sabri, editor of Al-Akhbar. "Heikal wanted to rule, not to write," he said.[10] "At the time of Nasser, Heikal was an emperor. He defended all of Nasser's dirt. He was a lawyer for all of Nasser's illegal actions.

Everyone was fed up with him but Nasser protected him. When Sadat came to power, he [Heikal] simply couldn't adapt himself to being an editor again."[11]

Ra'id el-Attar is another example of Heikal's vehement critics who airs his anti-Heikal comments openly in *Al-Ahram*'s offices. Attar, a conservative writer with strong religious views worked under Heikal for sixteen years and after Heikal's removal was promoted to deputy editor-in-chief of *Al-Ahram*. "Heikal kept me sitting in *Al-Ahram*'s cafeteria without any job to do for sixteen years," he said. Attar had chosen to stay and fight Heikal from within *Al-Ahram*. "Heikal was not a journalist," said Attar, "but a ruler who used the press to serve the state." According to him, "Heikal was a decision maker who appointed and dismissed cabinet members as he pleased." Heikal's job, said Attar, was to justify Nasser's mistakes. "Heikal was Nasser's Goebbels who brainwashed the public with Nasserite doctrines," he said. Attar believes Heikal knew enough about Nasser's deep secrets to threaten Nasser's power. This explains, according to Attar, why Nasser tried to limit Heikal's power by appointing him minister of information in 1970. Attar thinks Heikal today knows so many secrets that, if revealed, they would harm the memory of the late president. For example, he claims that in September 1970 Nasser gave a "green light" to King Hussein to liquidate the Palestinian resistance movement in Jordan. Attar believes Nasser wanted to crush, or at least control, the Palestinians after they challenged him by blowing up a hijacked jumbo jet in Cairo airport, thus setting an example of defiance to the Egyptian youth.[12]

Dr. Sami Mansour disagrees with Heikal's critics who accused him of monopolizing the news in Nasser's time. "This is a myth that I personally know to be untrue," he said. "Heikal was a participant in the decision-making process, but he never monopolized the news." According to Mansour, Heikal often used to say that he never enjoyed his journalistic scoops because there was no other qualified journalist to compete with him. "Heikal used to know significant news stories," said Mansour, "but on several occasions he decided to keep them to himself to give other newsmen a chance to get the stories from their original sources." Mansour believes no journalist could reach Heikal's standards and talents, and this explains why he stayed at the top for so long. "Ever since Heikal left *Al-Ahram*," said Mansour, "the Egyptian press has been in continuous decline."[13]

One of the leftist writers who owes much to Heikal is Lutfi el-Kholi, editor of *Al-Talia'*. He was jailed seven times as a Communist in Nasser's time, and in all instances Heikal helped him get out. Kholi believes that Heikal never stood in the way of other journalists' efforts to get inside government stories. "Heikal became a distinguished journalist even before he knew Nasser," said Kholi. "He never sought power and preferred to stick to the profession that he loved," he said. According to Kholi, Heikal was a mainstay in Nasser's information system. "Heikal was Nasser's tool by which he waged information battles inside and outside Egypt," he said. "Moreover, Heikal participated with Nasser in policymaking and carried out for him highly sensitive missions abroad."[14]

Mohamed Salmawy, a young university graduate who was recruited by Heikal for the foreign desk at *Al-Ahram*, is a strong believer in Heikal's positive achievements. He believes that Heikal "was definitely a liberalizing force in Nasser's Egypt, not only in the press but in the society at large."[15] According to Salmawy, when Heikal became minister of information in 1970, he lifted censorship on foreign cables going out of Egypt, insisting that the truth was bound to be known.

Heikal and Sadat

Heikal's critics and defenders differ in their interpretation of Heikal's dismissal from *Al-Ahram* by Sadat. Ali Hamdi el-Gammal thinks that Heikal wanted to impose his views on Sadat as he had on Nasser. "When Sadat became president," Gammal said, "he made himself accessible to all journalists, and Heikal lost his privileged position."[16] Gammal believes Heikal could not adjust to the new situation and started to make trouble for Sadat.

Ra'id el-Attar sees Heikal's confrontation with Sadat as a struggle for power. "Heikal was aspiring to become president of Egypt," he said. "After Nasser's death, he thought that Sadat was not capable of carrying on, and Heikal used his influence with the foreign press to circulate a story that he was among the candidates nominated for the presidency." Attar believes that Heikal intelligently concealed his real motives. "Heikal turned *Al-Ahram* into a political party with a newspaper facade," he said. According to Attar, Heikal's political ambitions were aided by Libyan President Qaddafi. "Heikal wanted Qaddafi to fill Nasser's leadership through the suggested union between Libya and Egypt," Attar said. Heikal, Attar believes, was trying to rule Egypt by using Qaddafi who, when he offered to buy *Al-Ahram,* was told by Sadat that Egypt was not for sale."[17]

Mousa Sabri, who launched an anti-Heikal campaign in *Al-Akhbar,* agrees with Attar that Heikal was a power-seeking man. He thinks Heikal was fired from *Al-Ahram* because he was using it for his political purposes. "Heikal wanted to be a key to policymaking," he said. "He wanted to be a statesman."[18]

Ahmad Baha' el-Din thinks *Al-Ahram* was a very strong weapon through which Heikal influenced public opinion. "Heikal utilized *Al-Ahram* for specific purposes such as to undercut someone or expose another," he said. To Baha' el-Din, this made the interrelationship between Heikal's roles as a journalist and a politician unacceptable to Sadat. When Sadat came into power, he asked Heikal to choose between these roles, but Heikal insisted that he was not a policymaker. At a crucial moment, said Baha' el-Din, Sadat removed Heikal from *Al-Ahram* anticipating that he could be forced to accept a government position.[19]

Lutfi el-Kholi does not accept the reason for Heikal's fall as given by his critics. He thinks Sadat and Heikal disagreed on the "style" of dealing with the United States, though both agree on the significance of the American role in Middle Eastern politics. "Heikal expressed his disagreement with Sadat publicly," said Kholi, "and this seemed to embarrass Sadat at a time when he was maneuvering behind the scenes with the Americans."[20] Kholi believes also that anti-Heikal forces from Nasser's time helped worsen the Sadat-Heikal relationship.

Mohamed Salmawy tends to accept what Sadat and Heikal gave as the reason for their differences. He believes Sadat removed Heikal because he was an obstacle to Sadat's intentions. Salmawy thinks, however, that Sadat might have come under pressure from the United States and Saudi Arabia to remove Heikal, because his dissident voice was harming Kissinger's policy. Salmawy does not agree that Heikal grew so powerful as to challenge Sadat for the presidency. "This is untrue," he said, "because after Heikal was deposed, Sadat kept offering him high-level jobs. Until recently Sadat expressed his dissatisfaction with the performance of the press, and at the same time he was trying to woo Heikal." To Salmawy, this is an indication that Sadat would have liked very much to have Heikal's abilities at his disposal.[21]

Dr. Sami Mansour thinks Heikal never sought power for himself. "Heikal and Sadat disagreed after the October War of 1973," said Mansour, "because Heikal disliked the way Sadat ended the war and his exaggerated claims of victory in the battle." Mansour believes the real cause of difference between Sadat and Heikal is not yet known because Heikal is too smart to expose his cards at this stage. "Something happened between them," he said, "and I hope Heikal will reveal it someday."[22]

Heikal himself sees Mansour's interpretation of his difference with Sadat as strange. In commenting on Mansour's statement, Heikal said:

> This is the "conspiratorial outlook to history." People like Mansour and others believe that there must be a secret behind everything in this world. This outlook is prevailing in the Third World today as a substitute to magic. When people can't explain things, they think that there must be something behind them. The fact of the matter is that there is no reason for my difference with President Sadat other than what he has already said and what I have explained in my articles.[23]

Al-Ahram after Heikal

Many members of the editorial staff of *Al-Ahram* believe their newspaper is not the same as it was in Heikal's time. Some feel they are losing the freedom of expression they enjoyed under Heikal. One of these is the leftist writer Mohamed Sayed Ahmad, who spend several years in jail under Nasser on charges of being a Marxist. Sayed Ahmad, who comes from one of the ancient autocratic families in Egypt, has two degrees in engineering and law, two professions he never practiced. In 1964 he was brought to *Al-Ahram* by Heikal and helped Lutfi el-Kholi start the leftist monthly *Al-Talia'*. Since Heikal's departure, Sayed Ahmad feels handicapped because what he writes goes through a filter and he has to twist things around to get his articles through. "I can't write with a logical argument," he said, "because there are certain rules for the game, and as a leftist I find difficulty in accommodating myself to these rules."[24] Under Heikal's editorship, Sayed Ahmad was in charge of the opinion page for eight years.

Mohamed Salmawy believes that *Al-Ahram*'s credibility and prestige has been shattered. "That's not only because Heikal had left it," he said, "but because the instability of its leadership and the constant changes in administration were reflected in its performance and credibility as a source of news quoted all over the world."[25] According to Salmawy, the quick and abrupt changes of six different people, each one trying to leave his stamp on the paper, was definitely detrimental to its performance. "When Ali Amin took over after Heikal, he tried to change *Al-Ahram* from its dignified type into a sensational type similar to that of the *Daily Mirror* of London." Salmawy believes that Ali Amin failed because he was pushed against the wall by his staff and because it was difficult to change the 100-year-old character of *Al-Ahram*.

Dr. Sami Mansour is one of those writers who take a salary, sit behind a desk, and do nothing for *Al-Ahram*. According to him, he was transferred to the center of strategic studies at *Al-Ahram* because the new administration saw no need for the highly qualified editors recruited by Heikal. "When Heikal left us," he said, "we had to fight a battle to save *Al-Ahram* from the new invaders who are completely different from Heikal in their ethical standards."[26] Mansour said *Al-Ahram* had lost Heikal's mentality and brilliant administration, and this is reflected in the lack of institutional spirit and firm organization. "Today there is nobody to care about discipline and cleanliness," said Mansour. "Dirt is all over the building and staff members order hot drinks and refreshments in their offices." In Heikal's time, he said, Heikal himself used to go around and check for cleanliness and gave orders that soft drinks be sent to offices at specific breaks during the day. Mansour believes the loss of Heikal's ethics and talents is also reflected in the decline of *Al-Ahram*'s circulation in recent years. According to him, the daily circulation has dropped 200,000 copies, while the Friday circulation has lost 750,000 copies.

The present editor of *Al-Ahram,* Ali Hamdi el-Gammal, admitted that the circulation declined after Heikal left but says it was restored to a higher level. Gammal thinks *Al-Ahram*'s circulation dropped sharply after Heikal's removal because readers thought the privileged news service had come to an end. "Readers later discovered that we were carrying on with the same standards," he said, "and now we have restored our daily circulation and even passed the level at Heikal's time." Gammal admitted that he was still facing difficulty in raising the Friday circulation. He thinks the Friday edition declined in significance because it lost Heikal's weekly article and because Sadat had stopped the practice of news monopoly by one newspaper and started a new era of press freedom. He believes the significance of Heikal's weekly article came from its inside stories on state policy. Gammal said the circulation of the weekly edition was rising systematically and was expected to reach its previous level during 1977.[27]

Heikal challenged Gammal's statement about the increase in *Al-Ahram* circulation and said the slight increase came as a result of printing "special coupons" to encourage readers to buy *Al-Ahram* and participate in a commercial sweepstake. "I have been told by my friends at *Al-Ahram*," said Heikal, "that this was the only way to increase circulation."[28] According to Heikal, the circulation of *Al-Ahram*'s Friday edition has dropped sixty-five percent. Heikal thinks Gammal's argument about news monopoly is not valid. He said: "The most important fact that Gammal keeps forgetting is that *Al-Ahram* has the best news reporting team in Egypt, but unfortunately he doesn't appreciate what he has at his disposal."

Heikal takes issue with Gammal's claim about press freedom under Sadat. He said journalists are free only to attack Nasser and praise Sadat. "I ask Gammal one question," said Heikal. "Could he discuss vital issues such as Sadat's open economic policy or American policy in the Middle East?" Heikal believes the Middle East conflict has been a stalemate since 1974. He believes Sadat's removal of press censorship is not an indication of press freedom. "Editors still receive a daily list of prohibited topics from the government censor," he said, "and this forces them to impose censorship on their own papers. When an editor censors himself, he is constantly scared to death because at the sign of a slight mistake he is subject to quick dismissal." Heikal gave the example of Ahmad Baha' el-Din, who succeeded Ali Amin in the editorship of *Al-Ahram*. Baha' el-Din wrote one critical article and was immediately dismissed by Sadat. Heikal challenged Gammal and other critics to give an acceptable explanation of the six changes in leadership at *Al-Ahram* Sadat has since made.[29]

The Amin Brothers

When Sadat released Mustafa Amin from jail in 1974, Amin hinted in his newspaper articles that Heikal was behind the charges that lead to his nine-year imprisonment. Amin claimed Heikal wanted to get rid of him as a journalistic competitor and even arranged for his torture in prison by the secret police.[30] In a personal interview with me in Cairo, Amin said he could not accuse Heikal officially without any document to support his claim. "I prefer not to comment on this topic and leave it until proof is produced."[31] Amin said, however, that his release from prison was delayed six months because Heikal told Sadat that Amin was plotting with Ali Sabri inside the prison to write a "black book" against Sadat. "When Sadat learned this from Heikal," Amin said, "he changed his mind about my release." After six months, Amin said, Sadat investigated the matter and found that Ali Sabri and his group were in a different prison sixty miles away from Amin. Amin believes Sadat released him because he was convinced that the charge of being an American agent was untrue. "I know that you are innocent," Sadat hold Amin, "because you had been contacting the Americans with our consent."[32] According to Amin, Heikal monopolized the news and even prevented *Akhbar el-Yom* from publishing its own circulation figures. Amin believes that the circulation of *Akhbar el-Yom* exceeded that of *Al-Ahram* by hundreds of thousands. "While I was in jail," he said, "my staff didn't dare publish this fact because they thought Heikal might retaliate against them."

Heikal denied Amin's claim about circulation and said that *Akhbar el-Yom* stopped publishing its circulation figures because it was lagging behind *Al-Ahram*'s circulation. Heikal also dismissed Amin's allegation about his part in sending him to prison as nonsense. Heikal said he tried to help the Amin brothers because they were his friends. "When I ended my work with them at *Akhbar el-Yom*," he said, "I kept my cordial relations with them in spite of Nasser's warning to me that they were suspected American agents."[33] Heikal said he never believed these allegations against them, and at one time he appointed Ali as a special correspondent for *Al-Ahram* in London. It was not until 1965 that Heikal believed Mustafa Amin was an American agent. On returning to Cairo from a trip to London, Heikal went to see Nasser. "We have arrested Mustafa Amin with all the evidence against him," Nasser told Heikal and showed him the documents, including recorded tapes between Mustafa Amin and a CIA agent in Alexandria. "In one of these tapes," said Heikal, "Mustafa Amin quoted one of my conversations with him, changed its contents and passed it along to the CIA agent as coming from Nasser."[34] From that moment on, Heikal had no doubts about Amin's involvement with the CIA but he thought Amin was entitled to a fair trial.

Following Amin's arrest, Nasser asked Heikal to run *Akhbar el-Yom* temporarily until he found somebody to take over. Heikal found that Amin's salary had been stopped and his family was borrowing money to pay for his lawyers. Heikal said it was unfair to halt Amin's salary while his case was pending in the courts and ordered that his family be paid a certain amount until a court ruling came out. He believed his decision was based on a moral obligation to protect the dignity of the journalistic profession.

According to Heikal, some Arab heads of state intervened with Nasser on behalf of Mustafa Amin. Nasser was not convinced of his innocence and told them he had information that even his brother Ali Amin was working for the British intelligence. In May 1966 Ali Amin wrote Heikal to deny the claim about his connections with the British intelligence and enclosed a letter to Nasser in which he tried to defend himself.[35]

In 1974 Heikal helped Ali Amin return to Cairo after a long period of exile. When he came to visit *Al-Ahram* in its new building, he was greatly impressed and wrote an article about it. Heikal read the article but did not approve its publication in *Al-Ahram*. In the article, Ali Amin praised Heikal for his talents and courage to express his views publicly and said:

I admire Heikal's courage in defending his fellow journalists at a time when other pens had been struck by heart attack. We kept silent when the "ruler" dismissed a reporter, and this gave him the courage to dismiss an editor, and still we kept silent when the "ruler" suspended eight of the top writers and intellectuals from *Al-Ahram*. We are the ones who have turned our "rulers" into tyrants.[36]

Heikal told Ali Amin this was a tough article which challenged Sadat personally, and it was for his own sake that it should not be published.

Heikal said that in all his dealings with the Amin brothers he tried to help them as much as he could, including employing Mustafa Amin's daughter at *Al-Ahram*. He explained the sudden release of Mustafa Amin from jail, however, as part of a deal with the United States. "Sadat released Mustafa Amin in February 1974," said Heikal, "at a time when Egypt was releasing three Israeli spies. Mustafa Amin was released by a special request from the Americans after the first agreement between Sadat and Kissinger."[37]

The American Intelligence

The claim that Heikal was "an American intelligence agent" started as early as 1952. Rumors of his connections with the Americans began in 1969 in a book by Miles Copeland, a former CIA agent in the Middle East.[38] Later Copeland was more explicit in a second book about the CIA and the special relationship the American government has with the world's leading journalists, including some who are cool to the United States, such as Heikal.[39] Copeland said this relationship was based on the understanding that "a journalist can be as harshly critical of American policy as he likes as long as he is generous with his own information and does not misuse the information that the embassy gives him in return."[40]

According to Copeland, "some of Heikal's most bitterly anti-American articles were based on information given him freely by the United States ambassador in Cairo—but on an understanding under which Heikal reciprocated by giving the ambassador details of other relevant information in his possession, complete with explanations as to how he got it." Copeland quoted Ambassador Lucius Battle as saying that Heikal had never played unfairly with him in all their dealings with each other.[41]

Commenting on Copeland's allegations, Heikal said Copeland did not say that he (Heikal) had connections with the CIA. "If he had said that," said Heikal, "I was willing to sue him in the court. All that Copeland said was that I had passed information to the ambassador, who in return passed to me information to use in attacking the United States."[42] According to Heikal, he never had any connections with the CIA, but he had friendly relations with the American ambassador in Cairo. "At any rate," Heikal said, "talking to the ambassador is not the same thing as talking to the CIA agents. Lucius Battle was a very good friend of mine, and we used to see and invite each other quite often." Heikal said the connections with the ambassador resulted from his [Heikal] being an advocate of an American-Egyptian dialogue under "fair rules." Heikal believes that all allegations about his being an American agent or anti-American amount to nothing more than nonsense.

Heikal's alleged connections with the CIA were given wide publicity in the Lebanese press, particularly by the weekly *Al-Hawadeth* and its publisher Salim el-Lozi. In 1973 Lozi conducted an interview with Mohamed Nagib, former Egyptian president who was forced to resign and was put under house arrest by Nasser and his group in 1954. Nagib told Lozi that while he was president, he refused to meet Heikal four times because the Egyptian intelligence service claimed Heikal had connections with the Americans.[43] Heikal threatened to take Nagib to court unless he withdrew his accusations. Nagib later apologized to Heikal and dropped the accusation against him from his memoirs, which he was about to publish.[44]

According to Lozi, Heikal attacked Nagib in *Al-Ahram* and asked President Sadat to stop *Al-Hawadeth* from circulating in Egypt. Lozi answered Heikal in *Al-Hawadeth* and said Heikal had no right to monopolize the writing of the history of the Egyptian revolution. Lozi believed that Heikal considered this a personal attack on him and "instigated an anti-Lozi campaign in Beirut by *Al-Sayyad* periodicals and other Libyan-subsidized newspapers."[45]

At his home in London, Lozi told me that former President Nagib told him personally that Heikal had connections with the CIA in the early years of the Egyptian revolution, and that Heikal had dealt with Kermit Roosevelt, a CIA officer in Cairo, through *Newsweek* correspondent Samir Souqi.[46]

The campaign against Heikal by Lozi was escalated in 1974 when Miles Copeland published his second book in which he referred to Heikal's connections with the Americans. *Al-Hawadeth* quoted Copeland's statements about Heikal and launched a new attack on him. Also mentioned in the article was a story about a meeting between Soviet Premier Khrushchev and Heikal in Moscow in 1957 when Heikal was attacking Soviet policy in the Middle East. According to the story, attributed to Soviet sources, Khrushchev accused Heikal of receiving a handsome amount of money from the CIA during a visit to the United States in the early fifties and told him the exact amount of the check and its serial number. The story said Heikal told Khrushchev the money was a fee from the *New York Times* and the *Washington Post* for articles they had published for him about Korea. Khrushchev, the story continued, was not convinced by Heikal's explanation and thought the fee was too high for newspaper articles.[47]

Heikal believes the story about his conversation with Khrushchev was fabricated by Lozi as part of the campaign against him. "Nobody could believe such a story," said Heikal, "because Khrushchev was trying to woo me as a leading journalist in Egypt." Heikal thinks this was a stupid allegation because "I would not have allowed Khrushchev to talk to me like this."[48]

Heikal explains Lozi's antagonism toward him with the following story. Lozi was receiving subsidies from the Egyptian government to support its policies in his periodicals in Beirut. When Heikal became minister of information in 1970, he discovered a safe in his office that included a "secret fund" to subsidize newspapers in Beirut and specific "information activities" in Egypt. Heikal objected to Nasser and raised the question in the cabinet. "It is utterly unacceptable to my professional ethics," said Heikal, "that the Ministry of Information under my direction be allowed to pay secret subsidies to any newspaper." Heikal then ordered all the "local secret funds" be publicly granted as a bonus to radio and television employees, and the "Beirut secret fund" be taken to the presidency. The next day Salim el-Lozi came to see Heikal and requested $250,000 to help him buy a new printing press. Heikal told him he had stopped the practice of subsidizing newspapers from his ministry and that the "secret fund" had been transferred to the presidency. Lozi thought this was a deliberate move by Heikal against him and Heikal subsequently became one of his targets.[49]

Lozi denied the authenticity of Heikal's story saying Heikal was not a minister when Lozi bought his new printing press in 1969. According to Lozi, he stopped receiving subsidies from Egypt when Nasser was defeated by Israel in 1967. Lozi wrote an article blaming Nasser for the defeat and said the Arab mass media, including Lozi himself, had contributed to the defeat by distorting what they had been telling the Arab masses.[50]

Dr. Mansour thinks that Copeland's allegations against Heikal are part of a broad American campaign to invade Egyptian society. He believes the aim of this campaign is to suppress intellectuals, particularly those in the leftist movement including Heikal who moved closer to the left. "Copeland is still working for the CIA," said Mansour, "and his new role is to work against those national elements who stand up and expose CIA agents."[51]

The United States

Throughout his journalistic career, Heikal was seen by many observers as constantly shifting his position toward the United States. Some of his critics saw inconsistency in his support of United States policy in his early years with Nasser and in attacking the same policy under Sadat.

Lutfi el-Kholi sees no contradiction in Heikal's position because in the early fifties Heikal, like many others, admired the "glittering American model" in the aftermath of World War II. "After the Suez war of 1956," he said, "Heikal and Nasser realized that the United States was an imperialist power that they had to deal with carefully. Since then Heikal started calling for neutralizing America or at least not neglecting her." Kholi thinks Heikal was consistent in his outlook over the years until recently when he disagreed with Sadat on the "style" of dealing with the United States.[52]

Mohamed Sayed Ahmad considers Heikal and Nasser Egyptian nationalists but with no ideological commitments. He thinks that from the outset, Nasser allowed Heikal to contact the Americans and left his options open with them. According to Sayed Ahmad, Heikal carried on the "Nasserite equilibrium theory" which meant striking a balanced relationship between the two superpowers. "When the Egyptian eggs looked to be too much in the Soviet basket, Heikal opposed it," said Sayed Ahmad, "and when the eggs were taken to the American basket, he opposed that too."[53]

Ahmad Baha' el-Din believes Heikal was never anti-American, but attacked American policy in specific situations. "When Sadat decided to deal with Kissinger," said Baha' el-Din, "he tried not to play Nasser's game of double talk." Baha' el-Din also said that Heikal used to attack certain positions with Nasser's consent, at a time when Nasser could deny it and say he had nothing to do with Heikal. Baha' el-Din believes Sadat had no choice but to suppress Heikal's voice because he did not want the Americans to interpret his position as "double talk."[54]

Dr. Mansour believes that Heikal's role as a compromiser has come to an end. He thinks that Heikal's articles in early 1974 brought him closer to the nationalist movement. "In recent years," said Mansour, "the major issues in the region have become either white or black, and Heikal could not stand in the middle anymore." He believes Heikal's sympathetic stand toward the United States changed because the American policy "clashed head on with Arab national aspirations."[55]

Heikal admits that his position toward the United States has changed over the years. He said his articles about the United States in 1951 expressed admiration for American achievements and reservations about certain ills of the American society such as racial discrimination and organized crime. Heikal regarded America as a superpower that Egypt had to deal with according to changing circumstances. "Before 1956," he said, "our main enemy was Great Britain, which became a 'second class' state after its defeat in the Suez crisis. When the United States filled Britain's vacuum, she became the major partner that we have to deal with."[56]

Heikal argues that he still believes there is an American-Egyptian misunderstanding. "Both countries don't see eye to eye," he said. "The Americans have certain objectives in the Middle East, and they are trying to impose a certain pattern on the region's political, economic, and social development, and I see this as harmful to Egypt," he said. Heikal believes that the Americans still do not understand the true national aspirations and the need for development in the Third World, and that they are likely to repeat the same errors as in Asia, Africa, and Latin America. "The Americans usually get irritated at hearing the word *socialism,*" he said. To Heikal, socialism is the only solution to Egypt's problems. He said the Americans and the traditional elements in the Arab world are trying to erase the effects of the revolutionary experiment in Egypt. "Their purpose is to liquidate revolutionary elements in the Arab world, including the new movement toward political, economic, and social independence," he said. He argues that Egypt is exposed today to a deliberate American attempt to corrupt it with what is called "the open economic policy." He thinks that, in the long run, this would be harmful, not only to Egypt, but also to the United States.[57]

Heikal disagreed with Dr. Mansour's argument about "black and white" issues in politics. He believes the options open to him are much broader than this. "My objectives are clear," said Heikal. "I am for three things: (1) secure economic and social development that ensures a certain level of living standard for the population, (2) unity between

Arab countries, and (3) independent Arab security that is related to neither the East nor the West." Heikal disagrees with the leftist argument that the United States represents "a horrible form of imperialism" that should be fought all around the world. "I can't go that far," said Heikal, "because I am not in the crusade against the United States. I am for good relations with the Americans so I can be in a position to make them change the rules of the game in dealing with me."[58]

Personality and Character

Heikal's personality seemed to fascinate many of those who worked with him closely, particularly the young recruits that he trained at *Al-Ahram*. One of those is Husni Guindi, a graduate of the American University in Cairo, who works on the foreign desk. Guindi considers Heikal a sort of "journalistic mutation" which rarely repeats itself in Egypt's cultural history, like the famous lady singer, Om Kulsoum, who enchanted millions of Arabs with her marvelous voice for more than three decades. Guindi believes Heikal has a very charismatic personality. "He is a gentleman in the real sense of the word," he said. "He respected views of others and never changed copy without discussing it first with the writer." Guindi thinks that one of Heikal's distinguishable traits is the high level of his intelligence. "Heikal's intelligence sometimes makes it difficult for others to deal with him," he said, "because they have to keep up to his standards."[59]

Even Ra'id el-Attar, Heikal's outspoken opponent, admired Heikal's charismatic personality. Attar believes, however, that Heikal utilized this charisma to build a "mythical image" for himself. "Heikal is the richest journalist in Egypt's history," he said, "and no wonder he lives like an emperor." According to Attar, Heikal's fortune is estimated by some sources to be between twelve and sixteen million Egyptian pounds ($28–38 million). Most of this money, he believes, came in Nasser's time and from his dealings with Libyan President Qaddafi.[60]

Mohamed Salmawy believes that some people who are put off by Heikal consider him arrogant and self-centered. To Salmawy this tells more about those people than about Heikal.[61] Husni Guindi believes Heikal is a self-conscious man, and this is reflected in his conduct in public places. "Maybe Heikal is a little conceited," he said, "but his conceit is justified within the framework of the high level of his intelligence." To Guindi, Heikal could not forget his outstanding achievements in the press and politics as contrasted with the achievements of others.[62]

Lutfi el-Kholi thinks one of Heikal's negative aspects is his individuality. "Heikal likes to fight his battles by himself," said Kholi, "because he does not like to commit himself to any political organization." Kholi believes Heikal defends himself by being undefensive. "He responds to attacks by discussing public issues and neglecting personal attacks, thus making those attacking him look small," he said. Kholi believes Heikal appreciates the real meaning of friendship, even with those who disagree with his opinion. "Although I am different from Heikal in ideology and orientation," said Kholi, "he stood by me as a colleague and helped me get out of jail seven times."[63]

Mustafa Amin thinks one of Heikal's bad traits is his pretentious personality. "Heikal has an inferiority complex regarding his higher education," said Amin. According to him, Heikal never received a university degree and still claims that he has degrees in politics and economics. "We taught Heikal journalism and English at *Akhbar el-Yom* when he was still young," said Amin.[64]

The Arab World

Like the late President Nasser, Heikal is more popular in other Arab countries than in Egypt. This paradox is explained by the fact that Heikal's critics in Egypt are more numerous than those in other Arab countries. With the exception of Salim el-Lozi and his group in Lebanon, the Arabs in general consider Heikal a great man who is worthy of admiration. Whenever he visits an Arab country, Heikal is treated as a celebrity by the public and local mass media. During Heikal's trip around the Arab world in 1975, the Arab press focused public attention on him, and on one occasion he became the center of controversy in the Lebanese press. The weekly *Al-Hawadeth* criticized Heikal for exploiting the Arab mass media to publicize his forthcoming book about the Arab world, and said:

The Arab capitals have never received a journalist with such a wide campaign of personal publicity as they did with Mohamed Hassanein Heikal. . . . Heikal's purpose of this trip is to convince the *Sunday Times* (which will publish his book) of the profitable deal they will be getting from the book. . . . Heikal has proved himself to be a master of publicity, for himself.[65]

In the same week, an editorial in another Lebanese weekly, *Al-Usbou' el-Arabi,* praised Heikal and said:

This is the week of Mohamed Hassanein Heikal in Lebanon. We in the press see in Heikal more than his political role that he has played over the years. We are proud to see him as a journalist who has kept his original identity as a son of the "fourth estate" and resisted all attempts to draw him into politics. Heikal has not lost his real commitment to words, news, and strong objective views. The real story of Heikal has not been written yet, because in the final analysis, Heikal's story is the story of the Arab press in general.[66]

The leading Beirut daily *Al-Nahar* described Heikal as a "journalist turned historian."

. . . Heikal was a powerful politician, in shade, as well as an influential journalist, in light. From his office at *Al-Ahram,* he used to move, in one way or another, the currents of Arab politics in Egypt's name. . . . He helped Nasser in shaping events during a boiling period of modern Arab history. When you meet Heikal you discover the secret of his success; Heikal's style of dialogue is no less attractive than his style of writing. He never surrenders his desire for accuracy, investigation, and depth. The controversial Heikal is a cool person who never answered any of the campaigns against him during the last decade.[67]

The Foreign Press

Heikal has been a celebrity with the foreign press all through his career. At his office in *Al-Ahram,* he used to meet prominent Western correspondents who sought audience with him and President Nasser. They knew that, without his blessings, Nasser, and later Sadat, would not see them. Even when Heikal traveled abroad, he was received as a chief of state. When he visited London soon after Nasser's death in 1970, Heikal lunched at the Foreign Office, then visited Number 10 Downing Street for a chat with Prime Minister Edward Heath on Middle Eastern problems.[68]

John K. Cooley, foreign correspondent for the *Christian Science Monitor* in the Middle East, has met Heikal several times while on assignment in Cairo. Cooley believes that what made Heikal so powerful was not only his closeness to Nasser and his journalistic talents but also his shrewdness in identifying Nasser as a winner early on.[69] One of the factors contributing to the confrontation between Heikal and Sadat, according to Cooley, was Heikal's pride and Sadat's belief that Heikal was allied with his political foes. Cooley thinks Heikal was consistent in his political analysis of the superpowers' role in the Middle East. "Heikal was consistent in supporting what he felt to be Egypt's best interest at any given time," he said. According to Cooley, the charge about Heikal's "exchange of information" with the Americans was unfair because the same allegation could be made about almost any Egyptian journalist at one time or another. Cooley believes Heikal's final role will depend on future books he writes. "Heikal's *The Road to Ramadan* is the best English-language presentation of the Egyptian side of what led up to the 1973 war," he said. He thinks Heikal has an assured place as Egypt's leading publicist.[70]

A British journalist working for the *Times* of London visited Heikal in 1973 and was struck by the palatial atmosphere of his office at *Al-Ahram,* the size of his cigar, and a casual reference to Roy Thomson. "It seemed to me," the journalist said, "that Heikal wished to project an image of himself as one of an international big league of newspaper publishers."[71] The British journalist, who asked not to be identified, said there was underlying consistency in Heikal's approach to both superpowers. "He never advocated total reliance on either of them," he said, "and always urged that Egypt look for ways to exploit their interests and contradictions to serve the national interest." The *Times* journalist believes Copeland is not a reliable source because "exchanging information" is part of a journalist's job, "but I should be very surprised if Heikal told the Americans anything that could damage Egypt's security." He said Heikal has shown signs of regarding himself as a kind of unofficial leader of the opposition. "I doubt actually if Heikal has the right temperament for a political leader," he said, "nor would he find it easy to play second fiddle now that he has become a major political figure in his own right."[72]

David Hirst of the *Guardian* believes that Heikal was Nasser's most brilliant propagandist. He thinks *Al-Ahram* had become part of Egypt's propaganda machine, at a time when Heikal was insisting on "the need for freedom of speech, the rule of law, more efficiency, less dogma, and a pragmatic foreign policy." "Yet, it is doubtful if he deserves credit," wrote Hirst, "because, enjoying presidential protection in Nasser's time, and immense residual prestige in Sadat's, he could have done far more. In the final analysis he seemed to be doing no more than operate the safety valves of a system of which, basically, he was a pillar." Hirst believes that Heikal may still have a role to play in the future. "It is doubtful whether the experienced and ambitious ex-editor of *Al-Ahram* would take such a defiant position if he did not feel that, proven right, he would eventually earn his due reward," he said.[73]

Edward Mortimer of the *Times* of London believes that Heikal is one of the great journalists of our time. "He is not what is now fashionable to call an 'investigative' journalist," he said, "or at least not primarily that." Mortimer thinks Heikal has made his share of sensational revelations, but what enabled him to do so was his privileged political position. "What makes Heikal a great journalist," he said, "is the combination of a powerful analytical mind, a fluent pen, and a strong sense of the entertainment value of news."[74]

In commenting on Heikal's book *The Road to Ramadan*, J. P. Vatikiotis, professor of Middle Eastern politics at the University of London, said Heikal is at his best as a communicator of an Arab view of Middle East conflict and of world politics. "Contrary to beliefs among some commentators outside the Middle East," wrote Vatikiotis, "what is interesting and important is the fact that Heikal himself subscribes to the mainstream view." Vatikiotis characterizes Heikal as a shrewd, engaging, and witty journalist whose reports are excellent examples of the reporter's eye-witness ("I was there") accounts.[75]

CHAPTER 8

Conclusions and Evaluations

IN removing Heikal from the editorship of *Al-Ahram,* Sadat ended the third phase of a career that uniquely combined journalistic influence and political power. In his meteoric rise to the top, Heikal passed through three distinct stages. During the last three decades, he played a significant role in Farouk's "corrupt" monarchy, Nasser's "socialist revolution," and Sadat's "liberal era." Heikal's amazing talents and shrewdness made him survive the "game of power" over the years by calculating how far he could safely go.

To understand Heikal's role in the power structure of Egypt, it is important to remember that, of about forty million Egyptians, probably more than eighty percent are illiterates. The Egyptian press, therefore, is essentially an elitist institution whose audience is made up of intellectuals and professionals inside Egypt, as well as in other Arab countries. Unlike the press in other authoritarian societies, the Egyptian press has a unique situation in that it is controlled and partly owned by the Arab Socialist Union, Egypt's ruling party, and newspaper editors and staff are, in effect, government functionaries. The press-government relationship in Egypt, however, is much more relaxed than in other authoritarian countries. Although under tight control, the press in the buildup of the Nasserite system was given a privileged status as a "super institution."

The press in Egypt has been given a more important role as an institution than in other societies. The press in Egypt publishes stories that transmit a political line of their own. Quite often, Egyptian political observers can learn a great deal from hints and between-the-line stories that would pass unnoticed by unsophisticated readers. In such a situation, the press becomes more than just a reflective instrument of what is happening; it also becomes an instrument that affects what is happening. Although this has been true in other societies, it has been particularly true in Egypt.

Since assuming power, President Sadat has been calling on the press to become a real "fourth estate," playing a specific role in the nation-building process. This is not far different from the privileged role that Nasser gave to the press, as specifically embodied in *Al-Ahram* as a "super institution." Recently Sadat devised the Supreme Press Council which is, in fact, nothing more than an extra guarantee of keeping things in hand. The government-controlled council can pass journalistic judgments and promote legal procedure against dissenters in the press.

To make the press a state institution, however, requires that it become part of the establishment. This would mean that all people holding the "strings" in the press have to be appointed by the government. Once in charge, they owe their allegiance to the authority that appointed them and cannot criticize without fear of dismissal. In certain key positions of the Egyptian press, however, prominent commentators have been very influential, especially in *Al-Ahram* where writers and columnists are usually more outspoken and expressive of their views, which sometimes challenge government policies.

Mohamed Hassenein Heikal, however, is in a class of his own. Perhaps it is true that Heikal, as some of his defenders say, is a "journalistic mutation" that has rarely repeated itself in Egypt's history. Never in the history of any country has a journalist yielded as much influence and power, for so long, as did Egypt's Heikal. The *New York Times Magazine* has rightly labeled him "the world's most powerful journalist." Heikal's role as Nasser's adviser and participant in the decision-making process far exceeded that of a White House press secretary in the United States. Unlike other editors and columnists in Egypt, Heikal was not "appointed" from above to his post as editor of *Al-Ahram*. Rather, he created his own "world of journalism" and shaped it according to his liking. He owed no allegiance to anybody except to his country and Nasser. Heikal built up his journalistic career and name while covering news abroad without asking for favors from anybody in Egypt. This accorded him a privileged position through which he freely criticized the ills of the Egyptian society.

Heikal could be given full credit for starting a new phase in the Egyptian press. Historically, the press had passed through four distinct phases simultaneous with the political development of Egyptian society:

1. *The translation phase,* during which the press published translated literary works for French writers in the mid-nineteenth century.

2. *The rhetoric phase,* during which the press reflected Egyptian national aspirations in rhetoric as expressed in the Urabi Revolution of 1919.

3. *The gossip phase,* during which the press reflected the Egyptian bourgeoisie and high society gossip with the beginning of the constitutional movement in Egypt.

4. *The modern phase,* which started with the Suez crisis of 1956. Since that date, the press has begun to address itself to the outside world and to reflect the link between revolutionary Egypt and the rest of the world. Heikal was instrumental in this by his emphasis on the news reportage backed with news analysis and interpretation.

Many factors combined to make Heikal a powerful journalist. His eloquent style, fluent pen, and strong sense of news value captivated the imagination of his Arab audiences. This is particularly true in the Arab world where language and words are strong magic, and eloquence is power. That explains partly why Arab poets, novelists, columnists, and eloquent speakers fascinate their audiences and capture their admiration. Heikal was no exception; he developed his own distinctive style and coined new phrases that became accepted "currency" in modern Arab political and journalistic terminology. He introduced a novel and vivacious style in Arab journalism different from the emotionalism and sensationalism of other writers. Just as news columns of *Al-Ahram* were the most informative source about Egypt, his weekly column was read by millions for its reflections of Nasser's thoughts.

Heikal's superior journalistic talents were reflected in *Al-Ahram* which under him became a household word in world journalism. In a few years, Heikal created from a dying newspaper a journalistic empire which is regarded by international standards as one of the half-dozen most advanced newspaper complexes in the world. Under Heikal, *Al-Ahram* became an important source for understanding what was happening in the Middle East. It was quoted daily around the world as an authoritative and dependable source of information about the Arab world. Heikal could elevate *Al-Ahram* to world prominence by emphasizing news as a major selling point and creating a first-class team of news reporters, at a time when other newspapers were stressing sensational news.

It has to be admitted, however, that Heikal's outstanding qualities would probably not have brought him international recognition had he not been close to Nasser. It must also be recognized that it was largely by his journalistic talents that he won that position. Even at the height of his political influence as Nasser's right hand, Heikal did not cease to be a journalist. No doubt, Heikal's closeness to Nasser was a major factor in building *Al-Ahram's* world reputation. This helped him verify the news because he was in a position to see the whole picture. The significance of Egypt as a spokesman for the Arab world and center of events that shaped the history of the entire region also added to the significance of Heikal and *Al-Ahram*. Heikal might not have reached his prominent position if Egypt had not had this influential role in Arab affairs.

Heikal enjoyed immediate access to Nasser and to all secrets of state. Nasser needed somebody at his side on whom to try out his ideas. Heikal always had the nerve to volunteer a response without inhibitions. He insists that in all his dealings with Nasser he kept a dividing line "as sharp as a razor's edge" between his journalistic career and his participation in the decision-making process. This argument, however, does not seem to convince Heikal's critics who believe he mixed his roles as a journalist and a politician. It is hard to believe that Heikal could actually draw a distinctive line between his multirole careers. In his role as a decision maker, it might be humanly impossible for Heikal to isolate himself completely from his role as a newsman. It might be true that he tried to strike a balanced line between the two, but it is probable that this line was not as sharp and straight as Heikal seems to believe. He seemed to have interchanged his roles over the years and wore different hats for different occasions.

Heikal, of course, denies that he was a decision maker like Nasser. He says he only took part in debating the ideas surrounding an issue, and Nasser's thinking might have been shaped by their debates. Heikal could not tell, however, who influenced whom more in these debates, but he denies vehemently that Nasser passed to him ideas and news for his articles. Here, Heikal's argument seems to be more convincing than that of his critics who have accused him of total monopoly of the news. Undoubtedly, Heikal was in the center of events next to Nasser, and this gave him the advantage of knowing highly classified information, but it is doubtful that Nasser deliberately passed to him news for publication in *Al-Ahram*. In fairness it might be said that Heikal sometimes exploited his privileged position to publish news stories of national significance that were not available to other newspapers. But Heikal, as some of his critics have admitted, was not to blame for this, because any other newsman in his position would have done the same. Heikal admits, however, that sometimes Nasser tried to use him as a vehicle to carry his ideas to the public, but Heikal says he tried to keep his independence by seeking only Nasser's news and immunizing himself against his views. It is probably hard to accept Heikal's argument here because it would require a great deal of effort and will on his part to immunize himself against the views of a strong and charismatic leader like Nasser at a time when both subscribed to the mainstream views. Heikal undoubtedly reflected Nasser's thinking because he admired Nasser as a symbol for a cause and national movement. It is more likely that Heikal was influenced more by Nasser's ideological thinking because he himself has never been an ideologue.

As Heikal traveled with Nasser as his companion and adviser, he acquired a broad experience in diplomacy that far exceeded his role as a journalist. Nasser trusted him more and began to depend on him as a diplomatic envoy extraordinary, who carried out highly sensitive missions abroad. Nasser's repeated attempts to draw Heikal into politics failed, however, with the exception of one time when Nasser appointed him minister of information in 1970. It might be true that Heikal was not a power-seeking man, at least in an official capacity. As his critics charge, Heikal might have had more power by staying in Nasser's shadow. The charges leveled at Heikal by his critics, particularly by Mustafa Amin and Ra'id el-Attar, cannot be taken seriously. Most of their charges lack hard evidence to support them. It seems that their personal feud with Heikal made him a target for their allegations.

The confrontation between Heikal and Sadat seems to have more than one explanation. It is hard to believe, however, the charge of Heikal's opponents that he was trying to take the presidency from Sadat or plotting with Qaddafi to help him rule Egypt. In fact, Heikal was instrumental in helping Sadat foil the conspiracy mounted against him in 1971 by Ali Sabri and his group. Sadat did not seem to fear Heikal as a challenger for his power; Sadat was even willing to make Heikal ten times more powerful than he was in Nasser's time. Their differences started to build up gradually after Nasser's death. The following reasons might have had a cumulative effect on Heikal's fall:

1. Sadat challenged Heikal's established role under Nasser and began to interfere in his journalistic autonomy, something that Nasser did not do.

2. Heikal accepted Sadat's challenge and adopted an independent critical line on his policies.

3. Heikal became more outspoken in his criticism of Sadat's policies and began discussing their differences openly in *Al-Ahram*.

4. The gap between the two widened over Qaddafi and how to handle the proposed union with Libya. Heikal has been a strong advocate of a union between Egypt and Libya because he still thinks it might solve a lot of problems for both countries.

5. While Sadat was trying to woo Heikal, he insisted on his committing himself to the state line. Heikal said it was impossible for him to commit himself to a policy he did not believe in.

6. Meanwhile, Nasserism was coming under severe attacks from the conservative camp in Egypt, and Heikal felt that Sadat did nothing to stop the campaign.

7. At a certain point, Heikal felt his fall was imminent, and waited for the right moment to break with Sadat. That moment came during the October War of 1973 when Heikal felt that Sadat mishandled the outcome of the war.

8. Although Heikal moved closer to Sadat during the war, he grew more critical of his excessive dependence on the Americans in seeking a settlement with Israel.

9. Heikal found in Sadat's policy with the Americans a departure from the traditional policy of Nasser and decided to launch a series of critical articles that radically changed his reputation in the Arab world.

10. It is possible that Sadat might have come under pressure from the United States and Saudi Arabia to relieve Heikal who had become a vocal critic of the Kissinger diplomacy in the Middle East.

11. The anti-Heikal forces from Nasser's time might also have played a major part in worsening the Sadat-Heikal relationship.

Many observers in Egypt were perplexed by Sadat's persistence in trying to draw Heikal back to his camp. At the same time they were puzzled by Sadat's failure to control or arrest Heikal. According to Heikal, Sadat believed that Heikal's credibility and high qualifications should be utilized for the good of the country. "President Sadat thinks that I should not be left alone," said Heikal, "because he either tries to draw me to his side or he quarrels with me." Heikal felt that it would be untrue to his profession as a journalist and untrue to himself as a man to accept an official post, because he would have to implement policies he did not believe in. He believed that Sadat could not control him or put him under arrest because he had done nothing against the law to warrant his detention. "If he has to arrest me," said Heikal, "he has to put me on trial for something illegal I have done. I have not plotted against the state nor have I joined any political organization." On the other hand, Heikal thought Sadat would not dare send him to jail without trial "because he would otherwise ruin his allegations about democracy and freedom."

Throughout his journalistic career, Heikal resisted all attempts to draw him into political organizations. When the Nasserites offered Heikal the leadership of their "forum" he refused, telling them that Nasser himself had failed to draw him into politics. "I am interested in politics for journalistic reasons," he said. "There is a difference between my being involved in politics and my being interested in the strategy of my country," he explained. To him, a journalist must be ready at any time to serve his country, particularly at times of national crises. He gave the examples of James Reston and Walter Lippmann who served the United States during wartime. When Sadat offered Heikal a cabinet position before the October War of 1973, Heikal said he would rather serve his country as an ordinary citizen. He recalls that during the Suez crisis of 1956, when Egypt was invaded by troops from Britain, France, and Israel, Nasser and Heikal worked out a plan to go underground if Cairo was to fall to foreign troops. Heikal decided to go underground with Nasser to a small village in the Nile delta to wage guerrilla warfare against invading troops. Nasser ordered that a clandestine radio station and a printing press be transferred to the village and he assigned Heikal to be in charge of them. Heikal bade farewell to his newly wed wife and told her he was going with Nasser if the British entered Cairo. "I had no choice but to make that decision," recalls Heikal, "because I couldn't sit in my editorial chair at *Al-Ahram* and welcome the invasion forces marching through Cairo streets." Later Nasser changed these plans when the invasion forces were stopped at Port Said on the northern entrance to the Suez Canal.

It is regrettable that *Al-Ahram*'s credibility and prestige suffered after Heikal. The changes in its administration that followed Heikal's removal are reflected in its performance and low circulation. Many members of the editorial staff of *Al-Ahram* feel their newspaper needs Heikal's creativity and brilliant journalism. Heikal's team has been handicapped considerably, and many of its most respected writers have been dislodged by the new administration. They pick up their salaries but have put down their pens. The intent seems to be to wipe away all association with Heikal. It is doubtful whether *Al-Ahram* today has the same world reputation and credibility it had under Heikal. It joined other newspapers in praising Sadat and making sure that news coverage and "free comment" did not stray from the official line. The result was a lopsided freedom under which news and especially editorial comment played down, or avoided, important issues. Freedom to criticize or debate became more rigidly controlled and assumed the character of campaigns against the "negative aspects" of Nasserism and corruption in the public sector.

Allegations about Heikal's connections with the CIA have died out for lack of evidence. Miles Copeland has not proved to be a very reliable source, and his two books have been criticized for being full of factual mistakes about the Middle East. It is hard to imagine that Heikal passed to the Americans any information that could harm

Egypt's interests. He was trusted by the all-seeing Nasser for two decades, and it is doubtful that Nasser would not have known he was dealing with an "American agent."

Heikal seems to feel bitter, however, about the lack of American understanding of the true national aspirations of Third World countries. His confrontation with Sadat has brought him closer to the leftist movement in Egypt. Heikal admits he is now in agreement with the left on the goals of the Egyptian society, though he might disagree with them about the methods of achieving those goals.

Heikal is considered by many as a liberalizing force in the Egyptian society. One of the usual charges leveled at him by his critics, however, is that he failed to influence Nasser's thinking with regard to allowing more freedom in politics and the press. This is probably true, because his privileged position with Nasser made it possible for him to speak out far more strongly. Even some of his supporters agree that he could have left *Al-Ahram* in better condition. These maintain that he could have given young reporters the opportunity to "grow up" with him. Some of them feel that he left a wide gap between himself and his staff so that whatever they did he would maintain his position as the only "glittering star" of the Egyptian press. Yet others justify his "limited blows" for freedom on his limited capabilities as a human being. They think he was torn between his loyalty to Nasser and journalism and was unable to devote as much of his time to *Al-Ahram* as he did to politics.

What role might Heikal play in Sadat's Egypt? The answer to this question will depend on which of the two will change his position. Heikal is sure of one thing, however. He will continue writing articles and publishing books outside Egypt. "I am still an active newspaperman," he insists. "I have taken a particular political stand and this had led to differences in opinion with the political leadership in Egypt. I don't believe that in all I have said there is anything that harms Egypt; I might claim that the opposite is true. I am not willing under any circumstances to surrender to pressure or change what I have chosen to believe in." Heikal has calculated that sticking to this position might lead to future risks. "History teaches us that freedom is a choice, each choice is a position, each position is a risk—and the risk alone gives the position, the choice, and freedom their value and honor at all times."

Heikal is still in his mid-fifties, and an active career may be ahead for him. Probably in any future reconciliation with Sadat, Heikal will insist on one provision: that he again become a newspaperman. What Heikal would like to have is a genuinely independent newspaper empire where he could replay his previous role as an influential figure, but without official responsibility.

During the summer of 1978, however, Sadat was cracking down on his critics in the press, and Heikal was facing government pressure to restraih his criticism of Sadat's peace initiative. He was interrogated by the socialist prosecutor on charges that he defamed Egypt in the foreign media. He expressed his fears that this interrogation might lead to his imprisonment. Some of his friends, however, think that Sadat would not risk sending Heikal to jail but they believe he could be expelled from the Egyptian Press Syndicate which would make it illegal for him to publish articles abroad while living in Egypt. At the same time, Heikal was facing an intensive campaign in the Egyptian press accusing him of everything from currency smuggling to being a Russian sympathizer and American agent. In his meetings with foreign newsmen, Heikal was keen to refute accusations of betrayal and to prove that he had no desire to acquire a power base. He argues that, as a professional newspaperman, he does not have a cause but an idea that he feels should be represented to the public. He believes the newspaper business in the Third World is not just reporting but involvement in the whole question of whether "to be or not to be." Heikal says he has nothing but contempt for journalists who are "tame and docile before authority."

As 1978 was coming to an end, the Arab-Israeli conflict was taking new directions. The Camp David Agreements, concluded between Egypt, Israel, and the United States in September 1978, were seen by political observers as a step toward a separate peace between Egypt and Israel. Sadat was reportedly determined to go ahead with his plans to sign a peace treaty with Israel, regardless of protest from other Arab countries. He was keen to silence all dissenting voices inside Egypt, including that of Heikal. It is doubtful, however, that an ambitious and intelligent man like Heikal will fade into obscurity. As a journalist who has made notable contributions to his country's journalism and as a person wielding tremendous influence in the political arena of the Middle East, he has made for himself a sizable niche in the history of this century. And it is doubtful, indeed, that we have heard the last from this astute journalist-diplomat of the Arab world.

APPENDIXES

Dialogue between Mohamed Hassanein Heikal and Henry Kissinger, Cairo, November 13, 1973[1]

KISSINGER: I want to ask you about many things, because I want to know and understand from the Arab point of view more than the mere surface of the practical problems that the crisis forces on our attention. I had not yet opened the file of the Middle East crisis—I thought it would wait its turn. But the crisis has imposed itself on all, including myself, unexpectedly. In this you succeeded, and I am the first to grant you this success.

Heikal suggested that Kissinger's answer to one question was of paramount importance. What role was Kissinger representing in this crisis? In confronting previous problems, such as the Vietnam War or relations with the Soviet Union and China, Kissinger had acted on behalf of a party to the conflict. In the Middle East, however, the United States did not appear to be a direct party or even a negotiator in the conflict.

HEIKAL: You are the first to say that Israel has a will independent of the United States, and although you admit that you have a great deal of influence on her, in the end what you say means that there is a gap between the will of America and the will of Israel. You regard this area between the two wills as being extensive, and it may be that we have disagreed with you and found this area, by virtue of the closeness and the extent of the links, restricted—extremely restricted. But in any case there is an area and this area means that you are not exactly a *party* nor exactly a *negotiator*. If your role is not the role of the "other party," the "role of the negotiator," what exactly is your role? Is it the role of the "mediator"? Again, I do not think so—indeed I am sure not. The role of mediator requires neutrality between the two parties—or at least that the two parties should feel that this neutrality exists or could exist. We do not feel this. Your bias toward Israel needs no proof. The latest indication of it is the air and sea bridge which is bringing arms and ammunition from the United States to Israel. So you are not and cannot be neutral; you cannot be a mediator. Then if you are not a negotiator because you are not a direct party, and if you are not a mediator because you are not neutral—what exactly is your role? I do not ask this question out of mere curiosity but because your answer to it will settle the whole tone of the talk between us.

KISSINGER: I have asked myself this question, and if the question is important to you for setting the tone of the talk between us, it is also important to me for setting the tone of the United States' approach to the crisis. I grant that I do not represent a direct party in the crisis; your conclusion is that I am not playing the role of mediator between the two parties in the crisis. Let us say, and agree to say, that I represent the role of the "concern" of the United States for a grave crisis which is taking place in an area that is sensitive as far as we are concerned, an area in which we have strategic, political, and economic interests—and security interests—and we want to protect these interests. This is in addition, of course, to our concern for world peace and our strong desire for the friendship of the peoples of this area. Let us say the following:

One, we have strategic interests in the area.

Two, the other superpower—the Soviet Union—has interests in this area.

Three, we are trying to establish a new world order based on détente now that the era of cold war is past, but detente will not cause us to leave the area to the influence of the other superpower.

Four, we do not want any crisis to escalate to the extent of affecting detente, because the danger of that would be too grave for humanity to bear.

Five, we have a special relationship with Israel and we are committed to protect her security, and we believe that Israel's security can only be protected by respect for your sovereignty.

Six, if we have a special relationship with Israel, we do not regard it as incompatible with the friendship we want to promote and consolidate with you.

Seven, we do not want to be, either on our own or in partnership with others, guardians of this area. What we want is that the peoples of this area should build their own system of life and security in conformity with what they see fit and in harmony with world facts.

These are the elements of our attitude, as conceived by President Nixon, and as conceived by me, and I agree with you that I am not a "party," nor a mediator. And perhaps you will agree with me that what I represent is American "concern" with the Middle East crisis, a concern that is trying to perform its role to protect its interests without conflicting with the interests of others. I know that I am dealing with a complicated and difficult problem. I find it more difficult than the problem of Vietnam, than opening the doors of China, or than achieving détente with the Soviet Union. The problem here is packed with conflicting and explosive elements—historical, national, and psychological—old and new deposits, and innumerable attitudes inspired by suspicion and fear. I took on the problem knowing what was awaiting me, knowing that I do not constitute a "party" and that I am not a "mediator"; what I do claim is that I am an expression of American concern.

I want to tell you two things about the way I deal with problems. The first thing is that I do not like to approach a problem unless I feel that its basic elements, or at least a large part of its basic elements, are in my hand.

This was the case in the Vietnam War; American public opinion wanted an end to the war. This was also the case in Peking and Moscow, because the facts of the new era were going in the direction I am going. In the Middle East crisis I cannot exactly reckon which of the basic elements of the crisis are in my hand.

The second thing is that I hate failure. I have a credit balance of success and I do not want to throw it away—and I am not talking of the Nobel Peace Prize.

Let me tell you a story. Some of my son's schoolfellows came to him saying: "Do you know that some of our friends are saying that your father doesn't deserve the Nobel Peace Prize, and we were angry with them and told them it wasn't true." But my son said to his friends: "What does it matter? My mother said the same thing."

So my problem in the Middle East crisis is as follows: I do not have enough of the elements of the crisis in my hand, and I hate failure and do not want to fail. The consequence is that I find myself in the midst of the crisis representing American concern for it, but all I have to depend on is my personal reputation, my personal credit balance. It think that in spite of the difficulty of the circumstances there is a chance of success . . . but I want time . . . I want the parties to give me their patience. . . . I admit that I am afraid of Arab romanticism. I fear that the Arabs fancy that the solution is just round the corner. It is my belief that we need a period of between six months and a year to reach the start of something reasonable.

When I met the four Arab foreign ministers during the recent war in the Middle East, one of them said to me: The man who succeeded in solving the problem of the Vietnam War, opening the door with China, and building détente with the Soviet Union can solve the Middle East problem. I said to them: I hope you are not thinking of the last two weeks in Paris, the venue of the Vietnam negotiations, or the last days in Peking or Moscow. Those days were preceded by long years of preparation and work to enable us to reach the decisive weeks and days. I told them that it was not in my power or anyone else's to work miracles, and that international politics is not a series of conjuring tricks.

Some of you in the Arab world misunderstood the proposal put forward on the day after the fighting broke out in the Middle East—my proposal that the conflicting forces should return to the positions they were in before noon on October 6. In making this proposal I was not biased toward Israel, as it seemed to some of you. I had different ideas.

I am going to tell you the whole story. Before October 6 all our information ruled out the possibility of war breaking out, and although there were persistent reports of your mobilization, the appraisal was that the mobilization was for maneuvers, not for war. Then all our experts thought that if you started the war Israeli military force would deal you a decisive blow. When the war did start and it was established that our information was wrong we still believed that our ideas on its outcome were correct. That was when I made my proposal for a cease-fire and for the conflicting forces to return to the lines they held before the fighting started. I thought that it was in your interests rather than in Israel's. Let me put the question to you in another way. If I told you that I was thinking of your interests only, you would think that I was deceiving you, and I do not want to do that, or try to do so, because you can discover the truth. My thinking was on the following lines: The Egyptians had embarked on a dangerous adventure, perhaps driven to it by despair, but Israeli military force would now crush them without mercy. What would happen after that? Egypt would turn to the Soviet Union to rescue her and here were two possibilities: that the Soviet Union would intervene in a way that would oblige us to intervene too, which would confront us with a terrible possibility—us and them together; or the Soviets would not intervene but would enter Egypt in such a way that they would never leave it. This too was a possiblity we did not want.

It was not a question of concern for Egypt alone. First and foremost it was a question of concern for the facts and balance of forces of this era; this is why I made my proposal for an immediate cease-fire and the return of the conflicting forces to their previous positions. Two days later there was still violent fighting in Sinai; our information about your mobilization for war had been wrong, and it is clear that our ideas about your ability for war had also been wrong. I asked for the Pentagon's reports on the progress of the fighting and more than once I asked them: What exactly is going on in the Middle East? Their answer was that the picture looked very different from our previous ideas. I received report after report on your operation of crossing the Suez Canal, and on your soldiers' and officers' will to fight, and on the tank battles in the desert. And the fighting was still going on. I said at the time that circumstances had now become favorable for a cease-fire. The Egyptians had proved their ability to fight; they had changed the situation in the Middle East and there were now new facts which we must take into account. In my view there was no justification for continued fighting after that.

The political goal that the Egyptians had in mind when they accepted the risks of war had become clear. So it was incumbent upon us to strive for a cease-fire and take political action for a fundamental solution of the crisis. I contacted the Soviets; perhaps I have also told you that I sent a message to Cairo. My proposal at that time was for a cease-fire in place; I think that was on October 10.

Here let me remind you of two points: the first is that you may have noticed that we have not given much attention to the question Who fired the first shot? The second is that you may know that it was not easy to offer Israel a proposal for a cease-fire on October 10 or 11. They were furiously angry with us because they estimated that now general mobilization in Israel was complete they were able to change the course of the fighting, but eventually they yielded. As for you, your words reached us through the Soviets— and the British too—to the effect that you were not prepared to accept. In brief, we were unable to achieve a cease-fire in circumstances that I regarded as favorable.

Let me tell you something about my views on the solution of conflicts. If we want to solve a critical conflict, the point we start from must be the point at which each party feels it has obtained something and that to stop there is not a defeat for it. Such a situation was offered us at the end of the first half of October. Egypt had crossed the Suez Canal, penetrated the Bar-Lev line, and advanced some kilometers into Sinai east of the pre-October 6 cease-fire line. Israel had succeeded in checking the Syrian attack—which had been strong and intense—in the Golan and advanced some kilometers northward from the pre-October 6 cease-fire line. Thus each side had obtained some part of what it wanted even if it had not obtained all it wanted. This, then, was the time to stop fighting and seek a solution by political methods.

[Kissinger then stressed the distinction between political emotions and political facts.]

KISSINGER: We are today confronted with a *de facto* situation; whatever its causes, we must start confronting it. . . . It is still a situation favorable to a political solution. Your forces have crossed the canal, and they are in positions east of the Suez Canal. Israel's forces have crossed and they are in positions west of the Suez Canal. We can thus see that the time is still favorable for discussion of a solution—and we cooperated with the Soviet Union, with you, and with other members of the Security Council so that a cease-fire resolution might be adopted.

I want to tell you something else. This time you have behaved differently from 1967. In 1967 you set the world against us—I am talking of what happened then, regardless of whether or not you were right—and the consequence was that a wave of violent hostility for the United States prevailed in the whole area. In this way you destroyed any desire on the part of the United States to perform a role it felt itself capable of performing.

In 1973 President Sadat behaved more quietly and, whether or not we were wrong, you made it possible for us to perform a role we desired to perform and felt ourselves capable of performing. The Soviet Union can give you arms, but the United States can give you a just solution which will give you back your territories, especially as you have been able really to change the situation in the Middle East. Do not imagine that Israel is pleased by what we are doing, but at the same time we do not imagine that you will be pleased by what we are doing. All the same, politics in our age is not a question of emotions; it is the facts of power.

I now want to discuss with you your article on the importance of the American role in the crisis. You believe that, even if he wanted to, the American president would be unable to play any positive role in the Middle East crisis because of the internal pressures on him. Perhaps you will allow me to differ with you. There are problems confronting the White House, but I do not think that Richard Nixon will resign, or that he will be dismissed. The internal pressures on him are strong, but I still believe that the field of movement is open to him, even under these pressures. . . . Since when has Sinai been Egyptian?

HEIKAL: I will send you a number of love letters written on papyrus leaves five thousand years ago. They are from an Egyptian commander in the garrison of El-Arish to his wife, who was a Pharaonic princess, and he says: "I remember you in this distant place where I am waiting to repel the enemy from the frontiers of the sacred homeland." You are at present in the most ancient nation in history. . . .

KSSSINGER: Is King Faisal prepared to go the whole way [in continuing the oil embargo]?

HEIKAL: You are on your way to Riyadh, and you will meet the king. You will find him firmer than many people have imagined—and I admit that I was one of them. He has been wounded by American policy, with which he has been connected for a long time. He is angry at your repeated promises that have not been kept. Also the Arab character of Jerusalem is a subject on which, in his view, there can be no discussion, and on this point the whole of the Arab nation is with him.

KISSINGER: Before leaving Washington I read all his correspondence with three presidents—Kennedy, Johnson, and Nixon—and I feel that Faisal is entitled to feel bitter. I am leaving for Amman and Riyadh tomorrow. I do not expect any problems with King Hussein. I expect all the problems to be with Faisal.

As a consequence of the conversation, Heikal reached the following conclusions:
1. Henry Kissinger is serious in his search for a solution, though I do not believe that he so far has a complete plan that he intends to carry out. What I feel about him is that he is trying to get things moving, and that through the movement he may find a way out.
2. That Henry Kissinger is a Jew will not restrict him; indeed, it may give him immunity against the Jewish pressure groups in American society.
3. Henry Kissinger has a good opinion, so it seems to me, of his ability to move vis-à-vis the present American political situation and in the face of the immense pressures in American society— but for all this I shall be the first to wish him success if he tries and to congratulate him if he succeeds.
4. The Arab future cannot be allowed to depend on the efforts of one man in America, nor are the Arabs entitled to let themselves be dazzled by Henry Kissinger's success in other crises, even if Henry Kissinger is undoubtedly worthy of admiration.
5. There is a problem in his practical view of problems, for he comes from a school which believes that the truth is what we see at this moment, and not what we think or believe as a consequence of what has happened before. This is to underestimate the importance of history in major conflicts.
6. In his estimate, the facts of power take precedence over all other

factors in calculations relative to crises. This point calls for vigilance, because the facts of power do not come to a stop at a precise moment but are a constant debate between events. The practical application of this is that if Israel succeeds in changing the power situation in the field, we may find ourselves called on to accept the new situation as a new basis, and this is exactly the problem that faced us after the Security Council cease-fire resolution of October 22, 1973.

7. The importance of the time factor to us is different from the importance of the time factor to him. This is because we are under pressure from the present military, political, and psychological situation, which pressures cause us anxious days and sleepless nights, whereas for him they are no more than memoranda written on paper, ideas, and possible subjects for discussion at the negotiating table.

8. I am not convinced, in spite of all he said, that the present American president is in a position to exert effective pressure on Israel. I think that if the American president in his present circumstances starts to exert pressure on Israel—supposing that he wants to exert such pressure—the forces of Zionism in the United States will lose no time in defaming him more than he has been defamed already. The American president will need outstanding courage to explain to American public opinion that there are groups in America that do not care if things reach the pitch of a nuclear confrontation which would drown the world in a flood of destruction if this is in Israel's interest. And this in spite of my belief, which has been confirmed by experience and never shaken, in the ability of the United States to exert pressure—indeed compulsion—on Israel to an extent not possible for any other quarter in the world, on condition that the president is leading and not being led.

9. World balances of power are a major factor in Kissinger's estimates; we must therefore recognize without ambiguity the importance of the Soviet role in the crisis. This role must not be an auxiliary or temporary element; it must be continuous and be consolidated in the form of profound Soviet-Arab understanding, and long-term friendship.

10. I do not believe that there is a definite and detailed Soviet-American agreement that we can rely on. Nor do I believe that there is an American guarantee. I do not know what assurance there is for it except comprehensive Arab strength—political, economic, and military.

Editorial of *The Times* (London), February 4, 1974

The Fall of a Great Editor

Short of resigning himself, President Sadat could not have made any change in his team more spectacular than the sudden removal of Mr. Muhammad Hassanein Heykal [*sic*] from the editorship of *Al-Ahram*. Ministers come and go often enough in Egypt, and the appointment of a prime minister has been confidently predicted for weeks without causing any great excitement. But Mr. Heykal is an institution in himself.

In seventeen years under his editorship, *Al-Ahram*'s circulation has risen from 70,000 to 300,000. Its editorials, and particularly Mr. Heykal's own weekly column, "Frankly Speaking," have been quoted and analyzed all over the world, as both an echo and a source of Egyptian official thinking. The newspaper has also made money (reportedly over one million Egyptian pounds a year from advertising). It has moved into lavish new skyscraper headquarters; has sprouted daughter publications and academic institutes; and has become, in law at least, a cooperative company owned by the people who work in it. (Mr. Heykal was particularly proud of this last point, but apparently the "owners" did not have to be consulted about his dismissal.)

All these achievements were the product of Mr. Heykal's undoubted journalistic and business talents but also—and necessarily so—of his close friendship with the late President Nasser, formed when he was a young war correspondent in the Palestine campaign of 1948–49. Nasser made him editor of *Al-Ahram* and frequently used him as a semiofficial mouthpiece; in his last years he appeared also to rely on him increasingly as an adviser, and for the last six months of his life actually brought him into the government as "Minister of National Guidance." At the time of Nasser's death he was thought of as the most pro-Western figure in Egypt's ruling elite, and after the elimination of the pro-Soviet group in May 1971 he seemed assured of an even more dominant position in Sadat's Egypt than in that of his predecessor.

No doubt such predominance carried its own dangers, and sooner or later the new President would in any case have been tempted to get rid of an adviser so brilliant as to arouse jealousy. But there have also been serious political differences. Ironically, the "pro-Western" Mr. Heykal has come to regard himself as the defender of Nasser's radical heritage against creeping *embourgeoisement* and excessive Western influence. Since the October war, especially, he has voiced misgivings about the policy of relying exclusively on Dr. Kissinger's diplomacy to secure Israeli withdrawal.

By moving now to replace Mr. Heykal, President Sadat shows that he is sensitive to these criticisms but unwilling to bow to them. He has in effect staked his whole reputation on the success of the Kissinger policy. That may be right, but dismissing Mr. Heykal is a discouragement for Egypt. *Al-Ahram* under Mr. Heykal has been the nearest thing to an island of free thought and free speech that "revolutionary" Egypt has known. It will be tragic if Dr. Abdel Kader Hatem's brief to take the company in hand in his capacity as information minister means that the official line will now be monolithically imposed on all its activities.

The U.S. Mid-East Role

By Mohamed Hassanein Heikal (From *Al-Ra'i,* Amman, Jordan, May 21, 1976)

In any effort to predict the political atmosphere and the anticipated developments over a period of time, interaction and probabilities can be assessed. The United States now, and for 2 years at least, will remain the international player which will appear most on the stage of the Arab-Israeli conflict. I do not want to discuss here how the United States came to this role or gained its privileged right in view of what we know about its own view of the conflict, or whether this is something right which we helped to achieve or something wrong which we helped to bring about. I do not want to discuss this now since it concerns what has already happened. What preoccupies me now is to discuss what is to be expected and to try to predict it and to draw a picture of its movement within the means available to us.

But the picture will not be in the correct framework unless we specify from the outset a set of controls:

1) If it is true—and it is true—that there is an intense contradiction between the Arab nation and the United States, then the scope of U.S. influence and its means and relationships impose on the Arabs the need to find a special method to deal with their contradiction with the United States.

2) In the conditions of this world and its balances, it is not possible—and no one should imagine that it is possible—to isolate one of the two superpowers—the United States or the Soviet Union—from any world conflict, particularly if the conflict concerns issues of war and peace.

3) Specifically in the Middle East and in its conflicts and crises, the United States and the Soviet Union have immense influence on the course of events due to their strategic interest in the area militarily, economically and politically and in view of the fact that each of them supports one side of the Arab-Israeli conflict.

U.S. Role Exists

I conclude, based on these controls and with extreme objectivity, that the existence of the U.S. role in the Middle East crisis is an actual fact, whether we want it or not. Since this is the case, then we had better want this role and not reject it. The logic in this is that when we "want" it and do not leave it to impose itself on us, we put it to some extent within the framework of "our will" and, consequently, this gives us the relative ability to shape or limit it or at least to check its evils and detrimental effects.

We now move to try to draw the anticipated "picture of the movement" of the U.S. role. We begin with the background to find that it is full of sad shadows, which immediately give an impression which we cannot escape. The impression clearly suggests that we wanted the U.S. role in the crisis at a time when the United States was passing through the worst conditions, which affected its influence, role and even its own spirit and self-confidence. Namely, we wanted a U.S. role in our crisis at a time when this coincided with a time of a U.S. crisis which was perhaps deeper and more intense than our crisis despite its complications and dangers.

We now move to draw the "picture of the movement" of the U.S. role and course in the Middle East crisis. We will go step by step with this role to see how it has moved and how it began its first, second and third steps and where it will go from here.

Nixon's Role

The first step: The U.S. president who made the first step in the U.S. role in the current stage of the Middle East crisis—namely, after October 1973—was President Richard Nixon. We now know who this man is and the circumstances under which he approached the Middle East crisis. The man was the star of the Watergate scandal and his behavior in it fully portrayed his personality. It is enough for us to read four books published recently in the United States about his life in the swamp of the scandal. In these books, the information on which they are based and the documents they contain present horrible pictures and scenes which prompt us to ask: Is this the man whom we confided in and thought would lead the United States to play a balanced role in the Middle East crisis? He was bribed in his office in the White House. He lied after swearing to tell the truth. He forged official papers of the strongest government in the world and in history.

A placard of the election campaign which Kennedy conducted showed a picture of Nixon with this remark underneath: "Could you feel reassured if you bought a used car from this man?" Nixon lost the election and Kennedy won. We should have asked, or rather we must ask now: Should we have left the cause of our struggle and future in the hands of such a man?

Kissinger's Role

The second step: Henry Kissinger was the hero of the second step in the U.S. role in the Middle East crisis.

He saw the weakness of the U.S. president better than anyone else. He wrongly imagined that he could play the role of the U.S. president in U.S. foreign policy. Kissinger did not conceal from his negotiators in any problem or crisis, including the Middle East negotiators, that in the domain of U.S. foreign policy he held the full powers of the president.

I heard it from him personally and no one told me this about him. I heard it from him one night at the Hilton Hotel in Cairo. When he said it, he did so in a tone full of conceit: In anything pertaining to U.S. foreign policy, I am the president and you have to understand that, appreciate it and deal with me on this basis.

I remember that, even with the little I knew about U.S. conditions, I felt concern about what I heard. Some of my concern was for Henry Kissinger personally. I remember I said to him: I beg you to remember that it is dangerous for any person to behave as if he were beyond or above all institutions.

What is important is that Kissinger began acting on this basis. There is no doubt that the man is a genius and knowledgeable, but he simply was not the president of the United States, regardless of his claims. Moreover, due to his previous and subsequent circumstances—about which I do not want to go into detail now—he could not go far with the crisis.

In short, Henry Kissinger, as a human being, could not give up his deep feeling that those in Israel are his people. In short, too, Henry Kissinger, as a professor, could not give up his original specialization, namely, the conflict between the two superpowers.

Again in short, Henry Kissinger, as a mere secretary of state, could not act in the crisis free from the pressures affecting him in view of the circumstances of the U.S. president, the increasing power of Congress and the crisis of self-confidence which swept all of the United States.

Thus, he was not, as I figured, trying to find a means "for solving" the Middle East crisis, but was, I thought, trying to find the means "for calming" and defusing the Middle East crisis.

The third step: President Gerald Ford became president of the United States. Richard Nixon chose him with "his own hand," as the people in rural Egypt say. The U.S. electorate did not choose him first as a vice president. When Richard Nixon was forced to leave the White House after the scandal, Gerald Ford became the U.S. president.

For the first time in history the president was succeeded by an appointed vice president and president, a man who does not possess the legitimate power conferred only by the votes of the electorate.

Ford's Role

What is more important is that Gerald Ford has the ambition—that is his natural right—to become a president in his own right and not on the authority of Richard Nixon, whose situation was known to the entire world including the U.S. people, when he chose Gerald Ford.

In the U.S. presidential campaign, the U.S. president cannot be a source of pressure on the forces which influence U.S. society, but, on the contrary, he becomes the object of pressure from all of them.

Since the votes of the Jews in the United States and the influence of the Zionist pressure groups in U.S. political life is a power to be reckoned with, we thus figure that U.S. actions in the Middle East crisis will be inclined to suit Israel more than the Arabs. The most any U.S. pressure on Israel can reach during this period will be to say to it: You have a chance open to you; do not let it slip by.

This is not the kind of pressure required, particularly by those who possess the legitimate rights—namely, the Arab side—to solve a crisis as serious as the Middle East crisis.

What is to be the course of the subsequent steps from here concerning the U.S. role in the Middle East crisis?

The evidence of any political observations will show us the following:

1) There will be no effective move in the U.S. role in 1976, which is an election year. This is a fact conceded by all, and disputed by no one.

Even if U.S. policy tries to push for another meeting in Geneva to discuss the Middle East crisis, this meeting, by virtue of the current circumstances, will be doomed in advance. Syria will not attend it. The Palestinians are not invited to attend. Most probably, the Soviet Union will be absent. The U.S. role is neutralized by the year of presidential elections.

It will be, therefore, a meeting to fill time or to give the impression of the existence of movement, but without substance because all the forces will either be away or will have been neutralized. Foremost of the neutralized forces will be the U.S. influence by virtue of the U.S. president's preoccupation with his own future rather than the future of the Middle East crisis.

2) Gerald Ford is encountering fierce competition within his Republican party to obtain the party's nomination at its next general convention in August of this year in Kansas City. His present competitor is Ronald Reagan, former California governor and former movie star. Nevertheless, Ford will, more than likely, obtain the party's nomination.

3) The presidential elections will take place on Tuesday, 1 November 1976. There is no firm indication yet who is going to be the Democratic candidate to run against Ford. It might be Hubert Humphrey or Jimmy Carter, former governor of Georgia, or a dark horse might appear in the ranks of the Democratic party at the last moment and obtain the nomination.

Supposing that Gerald Ford succeeds in the presidential elections and becomes a popularly elected president—not a president by nomination after Nixon—he will try in the remaining days of 1976 to build his new independent system and to choose assistants he did not inherit from Richard Nixon.

4) Therefore, the year 1976 will pass without any effective American role in the Middle East crisis. The year 1977 will begin while the new American president, be it Ford or somebody else, is preparing himself to deliver his traditional state of the union address, in the third week of January. The new American president will then begin to choose his new cabinet, to define the relationships of power between him and the Congress and to prepare legislation to leave his imprint on the first hundred days of his rule— and this is an important thing in the United States.

5) Thus in the spring of 1977, the new American president will begin to pay attention to foreign policy affairs. His first priority, of course, is the NATO alliance and its situation, then detente and then the Middle East crisis, which will draw his attention perhaps in the summer of 1977.

6) By the beginning of summer, the new American president will more than likely begin tackling the Middle East crisis and contacting the Arab and Israeli sides.

The Arabs will state their views. Then when it is time for the Israeli side to state its views, the American president will hear somebody from Tel Aviv telling him: Wait, no one here can decide on anything now. We are approaching the Knesset elections, which will take place in October 1977. Before that, we have no one who has the power to say yes or no, or draw a map, or decide on a proposed formula.

The Israeli elections will take place in October 1977, and accordingly the Israeli cabinet will be formed in November or December. Thus the year 1978 will come. And when it comes, we will talk about it.

APPENDIX IV

The Arabs & the World in the Aftermath
of the October War: The New Realities

Address delivered by Mohamed Hassanein Heikal, at the Eighth Annual Convention
of the Association of Arab-American University Graduates,
18 October, 1975 Sheraton—Chicago Hotel, Chicago—Illinois.

The privilege I claim as your guest tonight is to ask one simple question. Do these New Realities in fact have reality? Do they exist?

Tonight, let us stand back and take a wider look at the situation now emerging in the Arab world. Let us look without euphoria and without rhetoric. I suggest that the conclusion we must face is that what we mistake for New Realities are in fact Old Realities. Old Realities present in the Middle East, present in the superpowers' policies, and anticipated by the Arabs, foreseen by them, before the October war. Now these Old Realities are emerging once more, reasserted and confirmed.

Of course, the October war changed things. Nobody would deny that. But let us be careful to identify precisely what changed, and how it changed. Because the other point I want to suggest tonight is that, unless the Arab world is vigilant, unless it pauses very soon to consider what is really happening in the Middle East, these supposed New Realities will operate against, and not for, the supreme interests of the Arab nation.

Take these New Realities. What are they? Three, everyone would agree. The impact of detente on the Middle East. The impact of the oil weapon. And the impact of the new Arab fighting man. Detente—to preserve which, the United States was forced by October to start urgent peace-making efforts. Oil—which seemed to give the Arabs a new global power. And the new Arab—the man who altered the balance of forces in the area by showing that he could fight not just bravely but also effectively.

That is a dangerous list. Dangerous because we distort what happened in October, and we misjudge what is happening now if we think that any of those New Realities is in fact new.

We saw detente. We saw it in action in Europe, even in Vietnam, well before October. I remember discussing the plans for the war with President Sadat. We talked of the importance that detente, and the superpowers' need to preserve detente," had in our calculations. I remember the president saying: "I think we may just catch the tip of the tail of detente." So it was foreseen.

The so-called Oil Weapon is harder to analyze. Harder because two things have been confused, and we must separate them. Before 1973, there were two distinct crises affecting the Middle East. The Arab-Israeli crisis, and the energy crisis.

The Arab-Israeli crisis I do not have to explain, I think, before this particular audience. And this is no time for a full analysis of the energy crisis. Let us only say that the dependence of the West—and especially Europe and Japan—on Arab oil has been apparent, and growing, for more than a generation. The problem became a crisis with the first shortages in the United States in the winter of 1972—a crisis because those shortages revealed that now the United States also was crucially dependent on a free flow of world oil. In the Arab world, the potential that this crisis could forge a weapon in Arab hands had been seen long before. But now Washington woke up. You remember what one State Department expert wrote: "This time the wolf is here."

So the two separate crises of the Middle East were there, waiting. We can say that the Arab-Israeli crisis was looking for a catalyst. And the energy crisis was looking for a detonator. The October war supplied both.

My conclusion is that the impact of detente and of oil are not New Realities. Some people would say: "Does that matter?" They would say: "Surely October changed the way in which those realities were seen." I agree. But I still say it does matter.

In October, and since October, we have seen these realities at work—realities we had foreseen, assessed, taken into our calculations. And we are astonished. We cannot believe that our calculations were right. We have thrown up our hands in amazement. And we are spellbound.

Egypt and Syria are spellbound because they fought creditable campaigns. Most of the rest of the Arab world is spellbound by its new oil wealth.

Now, we can understand this. After a generation of struggle, we can celebrate what October achieved. But euphoria is dangerous. And the danger—I speak frankly—the danger is that while the Arab world stands spellbound, the forces surrounding it are not spellbound at all. They are hard at work. And their object is to limit precisely the freedom of action that the Arabs won in October. But this time the Arabs will be bound in chains of gold.

The chains are the chains of oil. The chains of oil money. The chains of the arms that oil money will buy.

Oil and money and arms. Surely these are symbols of the new Arab power? Weapons, not chains. No. Oil and money and arms can be not only symbols of Arab power but tools of Arab power. But only if they are used to serve an independent Arab will, and a united Arab strategy. So long as the Arab world stands spellbound, so long as it talks of New Realities without looking closely at what is happening in the Middle East, and happening now, then those potential weapons are no more than golden chains.

Let me prove my point. Let us look at the true impact of these New Realities. What has it been? What is our real situation?

Take detente. October showed that detente imposes limits upon the abilities of local powers to take action in local conflicts. That is the necessity of detente, an intrinsic part of it. The limitation applies especially to military action. Local powers can pursue military objectives as far as stalemate. They are not allowed to achieve victory. At that point, a wider balance of forces is affected. And the superpowers step in.

When Dr. Kissinger first came to Egypt after October, he told me: "This is a question which has nothing to do with you, nor with Israel either. This is a question which is directly related to the balance of power between the two superpowers." Dr. Kissinger was talking then of his refusal to let Soviet weapons conquer American weapons. But his comment reveals the whole superpower attitude to the conflict.

So what does detente tell us? It tells us that the Middle East crisis is trapped. Trapped between local powers who cannot seem to solve their problems in peace. And two superpowers who cannot afford to solve their problems by war. The Arabs are caught in the spider's web. That is the New Reality of detente as we see it in action.

Take the oil weapon. I talked of two crises. It is beyond dispute that the energy crisis has used the Arab-Israeli crisis more successfully than that dispute has used the energy crisis. We had a war. Oil prices went up. Then the embargo came down. A few people are getting rich beyond their wildest imaginings. But the West had adjusted to the financial shock, and the Arabs' legitimate demands upon Israel remain quite unfulfilled. And where is this new oil wealth going? Most of it is being handled by three banks. Where? Manhattan.

Do not mistake my purpose. I question the newness of these supposed New Realities. I question their impact. But I do not question what happened in October. Especially, I pay tribute—tonight and always—to the courage and sacrifice of the thousands of Arabs who fought and died in Sinai or on Golan, and to the unsung heroes who dared to act in the occupied lands. We pay tribute to them especially because they were ordinary men. Not politicians. Not journalists. Not oil billionaires. Ordinary men. That is their glory.

But our task, now, is to transform their sacrifice in battle into a New Reality of peace. And I think we betray their efforts if we talk of New Realities as if they somehow fell from the air. Nothing in history happens like that.

The October war accelerated certain forces. It crystallized certain contradictions. But these were already present in the area. And if we look at what is happening in the Middle East now, we will see the truth of this. If we look at how the parties in the conflict have moved since October, what do we see? The Old Realities asserting themselves once more.

At the heart of what is happening is one fundamental objective by the United States. Fundamental, and I think very dangerous. The United States seeks to persuade the Arab world that it alone holds all the cards in the search for a Middle East settlement. Again, let me quote Henry Kissinger. "The Soviet Union can give you weapons," he said. "But the United States can give you a fair and just solution whereby your lands can come back to you."

So what has happened? We have had three disengagement agreements. One advantage—one of the many advantages—claimed for them is that they bring the United States deeply into the search for a solution. This is even claimed as yet another New Reality.

The truth is that the Arabs have always seen the futility of isolating the United States from the Arab world.

The American isolation over the past decade has been largely self-imposed—imposed because the United States refused to accept the forces for change in the area, and refused to accept that the Arabs had a right to economic and social and political independence. So the United States made political gestures. Ambassador Goldberg was deeply involved in the drafting of Resolution 242. Then we had the Rogers' Plan and the Rogers' initiative. Gestures, all of them. Gestures because the truth is that 242 failed when the superpowers chose not to implement it. And Rogers' ideas failed because they revealed no real overall basis for a solution.

But now there is an American commitment to an overall solution. Or so we are told. Very good. But let us ask ourselves some more questions. What price will the Arab world have to pay for this supposed American commitment? What price in terms of what American interests see as a proper solution to the conflict? What borders? What hope for the Palestinians? What price in terms of Arab unity?

You recall Groucho Marx saying that marriage was a marvellous institution, but who wanted to live in an institution. I say we are all in favor of peace, but not if it breaks us in pieces. But that is precisely the objective of present United States policy in the Arab world.

Look at what Dr. Kissinger is doing. We must admit at once that he is the most accomplished player in the game. The objectives of Washington are clear and immediate. Kissinger knows how to manipulate people and events to achieve what he wants. And if we look at the Middle East now, it is clear that he is succeeding.

First, and most important, do not forget the United States entered the crisis with the aim of pacifying it, not of solving it. The American objective, then and now, has been to prevent the crisis from growing into a confrontation of superpowers. The interests of the local parties are purely secondary.

The United States' longer-term objectives are equally clear. It wishes to expel Soviet influence from the Middle East—and again I use Dr. Kissinger's own phrase. We may also suppose that it wishes to consolidate American influence in the area.

But Washington believes that the reason behind the Soviet entry into the Middle East was the Arab-Israeli struggle. So Washington is trying to defuse that struggle. Defuse it, not solve it. How? By trying to revive an old, old idea. The idea that the struggle is a series of separate conflicts. Israel and Egypt alone. Israel and Syria alone. Israel and Jordan alone. Separate conflicts with separate solutions. Washington does not call them that. Washington calls them "partial settlements." The reality is the same.

This policy of separating the Arab parties has two objectives. To hinder Arab unity. And to neutralize the Palestinians. So long as the Arab-Israeli struggle is seen as an all-Arab struggle, then the Palestinians take their rightful place at the heart of the cause. But reduce the struggle to local conflicts between nation states and, by definition, the Palestinians and their rights are removed to the sidelines. More, the Palestinians cease even to be a political issue; they become simply a humanitarian problem.

Why does Washington want that? The answer is clear. Because the United States sees no answer to the Palestinian question within the framework of any so-called solution that Washington will contemplate.

So, under American guidance, the Arab world advances step-by-step. But step-by-step to where?

Meanwhile, the other strand of American policy is to neutralize the one Arab power that Washington does fear, the power of the oil weapon. I have shown my skepticism of the impact of that weapon so far. But for years I have been advocating that, properly mobilized, oil could be a crucial Arab weapon. So the United States is working to neutralize it—working by playing on the fears of some oil producers, by encouraging the prejudices of others. Once again, by working against Arab unity.

Arab oil wealth could be another weapon. So that too is neutralized. Tied up in American banks or on the European money markets. Recycled by the Western governments without reference to the Arabs. Or safely wasted on arms, billions of dollars spent on weapons systems to guard tiny patches of desert. Against what enemy, what threat? Nobody knows.

All this may be a sensible strategy for the United States to follow. Frankly, I doubt if it is. In effect, Washington has invited the Arab world to judge American policy by one criterion—the success of America's search for a just solution to the Arab-Israeli crisis. But that is a solution which Washington shows no signs of even contemplating. So when the search fails— and it will—and when the Arab world sees that it has failed—and it will— what happens to American policy then? I cannot believe that such a fragile strategy is sensible for a superpower. What I am quite sure is that it is not sensible for the Arabs to believe it.

Take the response of the other superpower, the Soviet Union. In the face of the Washington policy, what has Moscow done?

The Arab world finds it hard to look at the Soviet Union coolly. We go to extremes. One extreme would have us base Arab policy on no more than gratitude for the October airlift. The other extreme tries to mount an anti-Communist crusade. I think both extremes are mistaken. Superpowers are not philanthropic institutions. Their aim is to enlarge their sphere of influence. For every gesture of help, they want a price. Our job as Arabs is to weigh the help against the price. On that basis, what is Soviet policy?

During October, Soviet policy was plain. They wanted to regain position after the debacle in Egypt. Hence the airlift. Hence the ultimatum to President Nixon.

When the Arabs responded by opening the door not to them, but to the Americans, the Russians were astounded. The immediate Soviet response was to regain a role. They pushed for Geneva. They continued arms supplies to the area. They cultivated the Arab states still afraid of the American relationship. But the policy gave no results. The Russians had lost the initiative.

So Moscow did a sensible thing—something the Arabs should imitate. The Russians stepped back and reassessed the situation. And I think they reached two main conclusions.

The first was that if the Arabs did not want the Soviet Union to participate in the next phase, the Soviet Union had in practice little choice but to accept that. In public, its attitude became one of more or less benign neglect. In private, of course, the Russians are working as hard as ever.

But—and this is the second conclusion—I think the Russians have also reassessed where to look in the Middle East for friends. I would not be surprised if the Russians were disillusioned with relations simply with governments. I would not be surprised if they turn more toward political allies in whatever country they find them. And American policy presents the Soviet Union with another opportunity too. If Washington does succeed in forcing the Palestinians to the edge of the conflict, then I would expect the Russians to look in that direction as well.

In the meantime, the Soviet Union is concentrating upon the Arab nations at the periphery of the conflict. And its navy prepares to use the Suez Canal once again as the route to the Indian Ocean. So Russian policy too is reasserting Old Realities.

But let us remember one thing. Both strategies, American and Russian, depend upon the United States' ability to persuade the Arab nation that Washington holds all the cards—that a solution can only come from America. But how can this be true? Of course, the United States has taken action. The question to ask is why did it take action?

Kissinger did not suddenly wake up in the Waldorf Towers one morning in October and say to himself: "Today, the Middle East." In fact, we know, he was going to some parties that weekend. No. The answer is clear. Washington stepped in because the Arabs showed that they could now make war. And for no other reason.

But it is equally clear that only the continuing threat of war will persuade Washington to go on taking action. That has been the whole basis of the Arab strategy. The only way in which the Arabs can struggle against detente is to re-fuse to be de-fused. I talked of the Arab world trapped in the spider's web of detente. Yes. Detente prevents us—prevents all local powers—from taking any single decisive step. But there are many options still open to us.

The strategy of October was to threaten detente, to force the superpowers to intervene. October was a demonstration to the world that the old balance of forces in the Middle East was obsolete, and to tell the superpowers: "We know that, in the interests of detente, you will seek to impose a new balance. Very well. Do so. But our price—our price—is a just solution of the Arab-Israeli crisis." That option can still be open to us. The Arabs can refuse once again to accept an imposed balance.

October was never planned as a single act. One war, and finish. The threat of another October if the first did not achieve all we wanted was always part of the strategy. Detente may prevent one single decisive act. But it cannot prevent a series of smaller moves. It cannot prevent the threat of those moves. And the accumulation of those actions will in the end tilt the balance. That is how we must use detente.

But we can only keep that option if we refuse to accept the claim of one superpower that it alone has all the answers. And how can the Arab world, even if it wanted to believe that, how can it believe that any superpower will impose those answers out of goodwill? Superpowers are not like that.

The proof of the fallacy behind American thinking is plain. October itself proves that the United States can never hold all the cards. Was it the Marines who crossed into Sinai? Was it the U.S. Cavalry that stormed the Golan? Of course not.

What did make October possible? To my mind it was coalition of two elements. First was the human element—the new Arab I spoke about earlier. I will return to him in a minute. The second element was an alliance of forces. The force of Arab armed power. The force of Arab oil. The force of public opinion through the Third World, the world to which we belong—opinion which saw the justice of the Arab cause. And those forces were backed by Soviet support and, in the end, by the exercise of a legitimate American interest.

But if I am right, if those are the forces that together made October possible, it is not enough just to identify them. We must preserve the coalition, safeguard the alliance. That is as important in the search for a solution as it was in facing the challenge.

The logic of the American strategy, on the other hand—the objective behind Washington's claim that it holds all the cards—is the breakup of this alliance. And the strategy is succeeding. The coalition of forces is crumbling. The alliance between the Arabs, and between the Arabs and a superpower, is being dismantled. It is the first victim of the false premise that is at the heart of the United States' policy. But without that alliance, the Arabs are left with . . . what? The goodwill of Washington.

Only if you believe that the Arabs gained nothing in October can you view that course as sensible—a course which acknowledges the Arabs' helplessness as a nation. I do not agree. I think the Arabs did win something in October.

It was nothing so immediate as complete military victory. Militarily, no party emerged from the war with what it wanted. The Israelis did not inflict the humiliating defeat to which they were accustomed. The Arabs did not liberate the territory they wanted.

Yet the October war did represent one great Arab achievement. They showed that they are not fossils. They are not doomed to ossify as the modern world passes them by. October showed that the Arabs are a living nation. They can develop. They can acquire the education and culture needed to handle modern technology. They can forge the social coherence, the trust in one another that alone enables men to go to war together and win. October showed that the Arabs can face the challenge of modern times. It showed that, to their quantity, the Arabs have begun to add quality.

Quality is an abstract word. But we are talking of individuals, of men. The Syrians, the Saudis, the Iraqis, the Kuwaitis, the Maghrebis who fought together on Golan. The Egyptian, the Moroccan, the Algerian, the Libyan, the Sudanese, the Palestinian, who fought across Suez. That man is a new

Arab man. He, if you like, is the truly New Reality. But he too has taken a generation of turmoil to evolve. He too we have seen emerging for the past decade. And it is this man, this new Arab, who profoundly alters the prospects in the Middle East.

So I say, October was a message from the Arabs to the future.

Might-have-been is an unprofitable phrase—especially in history. But, against that picture of October, I wonder what might have been if only the parties had moved as forcefully to peace as they had done to war. Appropriately, it was a governor of Illinois, Adlai Stevenson, who had a phrase for what I mean. He said there was a moment when even the most reactionary men became reconciled to change. He said it came just before presidential elections, but I think it comes just after wars. And he called it "the liberal hour."

We had that hour. It lasted a few weeks. After October, with the Arabs still in euphoria, with the Israelis shocked by illusions so painfully shattered, we did—I think—have a fleeting chance to jump several stages in the long process toward peace. We lost that chance.

All the parties thought they needed time. Time to get their breath back. Time to re-equip. Time to assess new political positions. The Arabs, too, needed time to digest the fact that the forces amassed after 20 years of effort were evidently enough to prove a point but not to solve a problem. So no one objected when Kissinger, after the Syrian disengagement said he thought the situation needed time to cool. That may have suited American interests. I doubt that too. But it was a major miscalculation by the Arabs to agree to it. Because as the situation cooled, so the rival positions hardened once more.

That was one miscalculation. The other has been to forget that the heart of Kissinger's concept of diplomacy is the idea that parties negotiate not because they want to but because they have to. The credible threat of force is the foundation of his analysis of international relations. So, we reach the paradox. If the Arabs allow the United States to destroy the alliance that made October possible, the Arabs lose also their capacity to enforce progress toward peace.

The credible threat of force. What does it mean? It means modern armies, sophisticated weapons. And I will say tonight what many experts here know to be true.

To build modern forces you cannot just buy a consignment of planes from here, a few squadrons of tanks from there. Armies, if you will forgive me, are not a Russian salad.

The modern war machine is a system. It has to be acquired as a system, and used as a system. The ancillary parts you can build up from anywhere. But the core of the system, unfortunately, can only come from a superpower. For all practical and political purposes, only one superpower can provide what the Arabs need. I said we must confront the situation without euphoria, without rhetoric. I suggest that is the only possible conclusion we can reach.

So we see that while the other parties in the area are adjusting themselves to the United States' strategy, the Arabs are in danger. For if they accept the logic of the American position, they undermine their ability to make war and their ability to talk peace.

Yet the real battle for the Middle East is only just starting. I believe that. And I think that Israeli policy shows that Israel believes that.

I tell you frankly, I doubt whether Kissinger's efforts will achieve anything meaningful. The reason is simple. After the war of 1948, Israel said it would accept partition—but in return it demanded nonbelligerency. After 1956, Israel again demanded nonbelligerency—threatening this time that it would not budge from Sinai or Gaza without it. But the balance of power at that time, plus the Arabs' own will to fight on, forced Israel to withdraw. After 1967, what happened? Once again, Israel demanded nonbelligerency. What was it offering this time? Most of Sinai. But not the Golan. Not Jerusalem.

Come to the present. After the October war, another plan was floated, suggested in Washington but with Israeli backing. This time, Israel wanted to keep one third of Sinai. Plus Golan. Plus Jerusalem. Plus most of the West Bank. And even for this the Israelis still demanded nonbelligerency.

Now, the Arabs have not even been able to move into the passes in Sinai. For this the Israelis have still demanded effective nonbelligerency.

That is not diplomacy. That is devaluation. How can Israel be serious? Or, if Israel is serious, how can anyone believe the Israelis are also serious about peace?

And look at the price that the United States has been forced to pay, forced by Israel to pay, to buy this last agreement. Because it has been bought. Bought with money and with weapons—hundreds of dollars worth of weapons for every man, woman, and child in Israel. All paid for by the patient American taxpayer. And for what? What is American policy? To build the world's smallest superpower?

And for all this money, all this equipment, what has the United States' push for peace gained? A few kilometers of Sinai, militarily by far the simplest front for withdrawals. If a few kilometers of Sinai cost so much, what will be the price for a meter of Jerusalem?

Washington has not even succeeded in what ought to be its main strategic military objective in its relations with Israel. Washington has failed to prevent Israel from becoming a nuclear power. In this, the United States' failure has been complete and humiliating.

There is no need to waste time on the question if Israel is a nuclear power. Let us acknowledge what every intelligence service interested in the area knows to be true, that Israel has had a nuclear capability for the past five years. If Israel chooses to claim that it does not have such bombs, that means only that some key components are not assembled but are stored separately.

Let us admit some other things which certain people in Washington know to be true. These devices—minus certain components—are almost certainly stored on a particular airbase outside Eilat. There are fewer than ten, but probably more than six. They are heavy and primitive. Their force would be much smaller than most published estimates. That is because of the grade of plutonium that Israel is using. But they would also be dirty bombs. The nuclear poison they would spread through the atmosphere would be terrible. As many people would die of this poison as from the explosion itself.

I said that certain people in Washington know these things to be true. Look at the United States policy record. Washington discovered the Israeli reactor in 1960. There has never been any doubt about its military links. Many of the electronics for it were developed by the Research and Planning branch of the Israeli Ministry of Defense.

By 1961 President Kennedy had settled the policy that Washington has followed ever since—the policy of trying to bribe Israel with such huge amounts of conventional weapons that, in return, Israel will abandon its nuclear research. The first bribe was the Hawk missile in 1962. And the bribes have grown ever since. Because Israel has treated America exactly as it has treated the Arabs over the issue of nonbelligerency—give less, ask for more.

After the Hawk deal, Israel agreed not to build a plutonium separation plant. It did not mean anything. Israel's laboratories were enough for its purpose. And by 1965, President Johnson committed himself to the most massive arms deal so far. For what? In return for a promise from Eshkol to freeze Israeli nuclear development.

Almost at once, Washington knew that this promise was nonsense. The United States was not even allowed to inspect Dimona properly. And in 1968, when the rest of the world at the United Nations was accepting the Nuclear Non-Proliferation Treaty, Isreal did what? Israel asked Washington for special nuclear equipment to be fitted to its first shipment of Phantoms. Not just bomb-racks but special computers too. And by the middle of 1970, the CIA was confirming that by now Israel could well have its own bombs.

Note. I am not talking of the direct help that certain elements in the United States have given to the Israeli scientists. The training it has given them; the laboratory facilities put at their disposal. I am not talking of the report that the CIA gave direct assistance to the Israeli weapons team. But half of Washington is investigating the CIA these days. Why does nobody investigate that report?

I am talking only of the failure of the United States policy. After years of huge bribes to Israel, what has Washington got in return? Israel has still not signed the Non-Proliferation Treaty. And all the evidence suggests that its scientists are working to improve the weapons they have. You remember the proverb about riding the tiger. Perhaps Washington should see what color stripes Israel has these days.

I said that the real battle for the Middle East was just starting. I take Israel's nuclear policy to be a policy of despair, a sign that Israel too sees the changes ahead.

For a generation, the balance of power has been completely to the Arabs' disadvantage. Now, it is shifting. The Arabs themselves—if they follow the correct policies—can shift it further. The slow growth of Arab quality. The potential that oil money—wisely used—brings to the Arab world. The gradual acceptance of the need for unified action, not just military action, but economic, social, and political unity. Above all, the dawning awareness among the Arabs themselves of their potential power and potential importance. All these factors—factors revealed, some fully, some only partially, by October—these factors will in time tilt the balance of forces in the area. And then Israel will face the ultimate strategic realities of its situation. So far, these have been shrouded. The Arabs have talked of "cancelling the effects of aggression." But the real issues go deeper.

The first, to my mind, is that to an Arab nation conscious of its unity, the idea of a land barrier cutting the Arab world clean in half will seem increasingly unacceptable. People do not see that if the Arabs regard Israel as a central problem, that is because Israel is indeed at the center of the Arab world. As the balance of forces in the areas shifts, the Israelis should consider the implications of this.

The second real issue, to my mind, is that the Palestinians are a people. They have proved that they exist. They cannot be washed away, and nor can their recent history. Ancient writings, revered myths and folktales are a necessary part of any people's culture. But you cannot uproot a people in the name of those myths and then pretend that the people will just go away. The Palestinians will not go away. You cannot impose myths upon history.

But this leads me to my third real issue. And that is the nature of Israel itself. It cannot integrate. How many times have its leaders said that Israel will not be "levantinized"—even their word reveals their attitude. If whatever Israel calls "peace" were to come tomorrow, how could Israel tolerate the free intermingling of people and ideas that is the very foundation of the history of that area? To preserve their state, the Israelis must erect permanent barriers—ideological, cultural, educational, even economic barriers—against the Arab sea around it.

How can that be peace? The peace of an armed encampment. An encampment which by its nature has to discriminate.

Perhaps what Berlinguer, the Italian Communist leader, called "the historical compromise" is possible. Perhaps it is not. The burden of seeking it rests, I suggest, even more heavily upon the Israelis than it does upon the Arabs.

I tried to explain why to Kissinger. I pointed out that in all previous conflicts he had tackled, he at least had the same people both sides of the wire. East Germany has Germans. West Germany has Germans. North Vietnam has Vietnamese, and so has the South. But, I said: "In the Arab-Israeli conflict, you are dealing with a phenomenon unique in modern political history. You are dealing with a transplant—a transplant of one people among another people It is a transplant problem that would baffle Dr. Christian Barnard."

I hope I was clear.

In the meantime, we must concentrate. Concentrate our efforts. Concentrate our policies. We must reconstruct the alliance that produced October and still remains our best hope of future progress to peace. We must remember in our social policies, as much as in our military ones, that out of October marched a new Arab man. And he will demand development—

social, economic, and political development—more sweeping and more rapid than anything the Arab world has yet contemplated.

And so at last I come to you, my patient audience. For this is where the problems of the Arab world come to you. No development is possible without ideas and the sifting of ideas. But no sifting is possible without perspective. And you have that perspective.

That too is an Old Reality. In the days of the caliphs, intellectual activity in the Arab world displayed a consistent pattern. Round the caliphs you found the poets. Their function was praise. But in some other city of the empire—a prudent distance from the caliphs—you had the philosophers, the intellectuals. Their function was to pave the way to the future.

Regard yourselves, then, as the lineal descendants of those thinkers. And removed as you are from our modern caliphs, repay your debt to your countries—your debt to the Arab world that is, and will be. Repay it by being a brave, free cell of the Arab mind.

NOTES

CHAPTER 1.

1. Adnan Almaney, "Government Control of the Press in the United Arab Republic, 1952-1970," p. 340.
2. Ibrahim Abdo, *Tatawur el-Sahafa el-Misriya,* pp. 276-78.
3. Almaney, "Government Control of the Press," p. 342.
4. Heikal interview, July 7, 1976.
5. Ibid.
6. Heikal interview, July 6, 1976.
7. Ibid.
8. Ministry of Information, Egypt. *Qawanin el-Matbou'at wal-Sahafa* [Laws of Printed Materials and the Press], (Cairo, no publisher or date given), p. 5.
9. Ibid., p. 8.
10. Heikal interview, July 7, 1976.
11. Almaney, "Government Control of the Press," p. 347.
12. *New York Times,* February 5, 1973, p. 2.
13. Richard M. Smith, "Censorship in the Middle East."
14. *Newsweek,* April 1, 1974, p. 47.
15. Tawfiq el-Hakim, *Awdat el-Wa'i.*
16. *Al-Sayyad,* December 1974.
17. *Newsweek,* April 1, 1974, p. 42.
18. Galal el-Din Hamamsy, *Hiwar Wara' el-Aswar,* pp. 189-90.
19. *Al-Ahram,* March 13, 1976.
20. Mustafa Amin interview.
21. Ali Hamdi el-Gammal interview.
22. *Al-Ahram,* March 12, 1975.
23. Mithaq el-Sharaf el-Sahafi [Journalistic Code of Ethics], Supreme Press Council, Cairo, July 22, 1975.
24. *Al-Ahram,* May 27, 1975.
25. *Akhbar el-Yom,* May 24, 1975.
26. *Al-Ahram,* November 12, 1976.
27. *Akhbar el-Yom,* December 4, 1976.
28. *The Times* (London), June 6, 1978.
29. *The Times* (London), February 2, 1977.
30. *Al-Ahram,* February 4, 1977.
31. *Al-Ahram,* February 11, 1977.
32. *Al-Akhbar,* February 5, 1977.
33. *Al-Ahram,* February 15, 1977.
34. *Al-Ahram,* January 20, 1977.
35. *Al-Ahram,* February 1, 1977.
36. *Al-Ahram,* January 22, 1977.
37. *Keesing's Contemporary Archives,* March 2, 1977.
38. *The Times* (London), December 12, 1977.
39. *New York Times,* May 30, 1978.
40. *New York Times,* May 31, 1978.
41. *The Times* (London), May 31, 1978.
42. *The Times* (London), June 3, 1978.
43. *Christian Science Monitor,* June 30, 1978.

CHAPTER 2.

1. Desmond Stewart, "The Rise and Fall of Mohammad Heikal," p. 89.
2. According to Stewart, "Rise and Fall," p. 88, Heikal was grouching at his salary of 18 Egyptian pounds (high for those days) while working for the *Gazette.*
3. Stewart, "Rise and Fall," p. 89.
4. Fuad Matar, *Bisaraha An Abdul Nasser,* p. 16.
5. Edward R. F. Sheehan, in his introduction to Mohamed Hassanein Heikal, *The Cairo Documents,* p. xviii.
6. Heikal interview, July 6, 1976.
7. Ibid.
8. Heikal interview, July 20, 1976.
9. Heikal interview, July 6, 1976.
10. Matar, *Bisaraha An Abdul Nasser,* p. 18.
11. Ibid.

CHAPTER 3.

1. Ibrahim Abdo, *Al-Ahram: Tarikhon wa Fann,* pp. 621–35.
2. Based on a copy of the original contract between Heikal and *Al-Ahram.* Copy obtained from Heikal in Cairo, July 12, 1976.
3. A Kuttab is an Arabic term meaning an old, informal school system where children met with a religious leader at a mosque or a private home to learn the Quran and other subjects.
4. John C. Merrill, *The Elite Press, Great Newspapers of the World.*
5. Desmond Stewart, "The Rise and Fall of Mohammad Heikal," p. 89.
6. Edward R. F. Sheehan, in his introduction to Mohamed Hassanein Heikal, *The Cairo Documents,* p. xv.
7. Sheehan, in Heikal, *Cairo Documents,* p. xiv.
8. Claud Morris, "The Most Hygienic Newspaper in the World."
9. *New York Times Magazine,* August 22, 1971, p. 12.
10. Sheehan, in Heikal, *Cairo Documents,* p. xxiii.
11. Morris, "Most Hygienic Newspaper."

CHAPTER 4.

1. Desmond Stewart, "The Rise and Fall of Mohammad Heikal," p. 89.
2. Gamal Abdul Nasser, *Egypt's Liberation: The Philosophy of Revolution.*
3. Edward R. F. Sheehan, in his introduction to Mohamed Hassanein Heikal, *The Cairo Documents,* p. xxi.
4. Mohamed Hassanein Heikal, *The Road to Ramadan,* p. 102.
5. Field-Marshal Abdul Hakim Amer, vice-president and commander-in-chief of the Egyptian army until 1967, was said to have misled Nasser and contributed to Egypt's disastrous defeat by Israel in 1967.
6. Anthony Nutting, *Nasser,* p. 305.
7. *Al-Ahram,* June 11, 1962.
8. *Al-Ahram,* May 26, 1967.
9. *Al-Ahram,* December 6, 1968.
10. Nasser's reference to Charles Helu, the former Lebanese president, and Ghassan Tueni, editor of Beirut's leading daily, *Al-Nahar,* seemed to indicate the unfriendly relationship between a cornered president and nonunderstanding journalist.
11. Heikal, *Road to Ramadan,* p. 73.

12. Sheehan, in Heikal, *Cairo Documents,* p. xiv.
13. Ibid., p. xxvii.
14. Nutting, *Nasser,* p. 279.
15. Mohamed Hassanein Heikal, *The Cairo Documents.*
16. Ibid.
17. Ibid.
18. Ibid.
19. Ibid.
20. Heikal, *Road to Ramadan,* p. 58.
21. Ibid., p. 69.
22. Ibid.
23. Ibid.
24. Sheehan, in Heikal, *Cairo Documents,* p. xx.
25. Ibid., p. xxi.
26. Miles Copeland, *The Game of Nations.*
27. Ibid., p. 75.
28. Nutting, *Nasser,* p. 273.
29. Heikal, *Road to Ramadan,* p. 64.
30. Ibid.
31. Ibid., p. 65.
32. Nutting, *Nasser,* p. 457.
33. Robert Stephens, *Nasser: A Political Biography,* p. 537.
34. Heikal, *Road to Ramadan,* p. 93.
35. Ibid.
36. Ibid., p. 102.
37. Ibid., p. 103.

CHAPTER 5.

1. Mohamed Hassanein Heikal, *The Road to Ramadan,* p. 107.
2. Ibid.
3. Ibid.
4. Ibid., p. 112.
5. Ibid.
6. Desmond Stewart, "The Rise and Fall of Mohammad Heikal," p. 90.
7. *Al-Ahram,* February 5, 1971.
8. Edward R. F. Sheehan, in his introduction to Mohamed Hassanein Heikal, *The Cairo Documents,* p. xxvi.
9. Ibid., p. xxvii.
10. Heikal, *Road to Ramadan,* p. 135.
11. Ibid., p. 143.
12. Heikal interview, July 22, 1976.
13. Heikal, *Road to Ramadan,* p. 166.
14. Ibid., p. 177.
15. Ibid., p. 179.
16. Ibid., p. 197.
17. Heikal interview, July 22, 1976.
18. Mohamed Hassanein Heikal, *Ahadeeth fi Asia.*
19. Ibid.
20. Ibid., p. 344.
21. Heikal, *Road to Ramadan,* p. 10.
22. Ibid., p. 24.

23. Ibid., p. 225.
24. Edward R. F. Sheehan, *The Arabs, Israelis, and Kissinger*, p. 51.
25. Ibid. According to Sheehan, Kissinger denied the authenticity of Heikal's story. He told Sheehan that he had talked with Heikal for only ten minutes and that Heikal's interview was largely a fabrication. When Sheehan checked the story with two of Kissinger's aides, they told him that the interview echoed very accurately Kissinger's private statements at that time.
26. *Al-Ahram,* November 14, 1973. The full text of the dialogue between Heikal and Kissinger is in Appendix I in this book.
27. *Al-Ahram,* January 18, 1974.
28. *Al-Ahram,* February 1, 1974.
29. According to Heikal, his prediction missed the actual date of Nixon's resignation by only 17 days.
30. *New York Times,* February 6, 1974.
31. Ibid.
32. Heikal interview, July 22, 1976.

CHAPTER   6.

1. Desmond Stewart, "The Rise and Fall of Mohammad Heikal," p. 89.
2. *The Times* (London), February 11, 1974.
3. Ibid.
4. *The Times* (London) February 4, 1974. For the full text of the editorial, see Appendix II in this book.
5. BBC Files, February 4, 1974.
6. *The Guardian,* February 4, 1974.
7. *Neue Zuercher Zeitung,* February 9, 1974.
8. *L'Orient le Jour* (Beirut), February 9, 1974.
9. *Sunday Times* (London), February 10, 1974.
10. Mohamed Hassanein Heikal, *The Road to Ramadan.*
11. *Al-Anwar* (Beirut), July 12, 1975.
12. Heikal interview, December 9, 1976.
13. Heikal interview, July 20, 1976.
14. *Al-Nahar* (Beirut), November 18, 1974.
15. *Al-Thawra* (Damascus), January 21, 1975.
16. Mohamed Hassanein Heikal, "Pulling Back from Mideast Precipice," p. 41.
17. *Newsweek,* January 20, 1975.
18. *Al-Anwar* (Beirut), July 12, 1975.
19. Ibid.
20. *Al-Anwar* (Beirut), September 4, 1975.
21. *Al-Anwar* (Beirut), July 12, 1975.
22. *Al-Ra'i* (Amman), October 12, 1975.
23. *Al-Ra'i* (Amman), October 17, 1975.
24. *Christian Science Monitor,* October 7, 1976.
25. Special bulletin issued by AAUG, Sheraton-Chicago Hotel, Chicago, Illinois, October 18, 1975. For the full text of Heikal's address, see Appendix III in this book.
26. *New York Times,* October 25, 1975.
27. Ibid.
28. *New York Times,* October 30, 1975.
29. *Al-Watan* (Kuwait), November 10, 1975.
30. Yousef Sabbagh, "Letter from Cairo," *Al-Ra'i* (Amman), March 13, 1976, p. 6.
31. *Al-Siyasah* (Kuwait), October 27, 1975.
32. *Al-Watan* (Kuwait), December 3, 1975.

33. *Christian Science Monitor,* October 7, 1976, p. 35.
34. Talib Abu Abid, "Today's Events" program on Damascus radio, October 16, 1975.
35. Galal el-Din Hamamsy, *Hiwar Wara' el-Aswar,* p. 189.
36. *Al-Anwar* (Beirut), July 16, 1975.
37. *Al-Ra'i* (Amman), March 8, 1976.
38. *Al-Ahram,* June 14, 1976.
39. *Al-Ahram,* April 2, 1977.
40. Ibid.
41. *The Times* (London), October 25, 1977.
42. ABC News, November 17, 1977.
43. Mohamed Hassanein Heikal, *Hadeeth el-Mubadarah,* p. 25.
44. *The Times* (London), December 20, 1977.
45. Heikal, *Hadeeth el-Mubadarah,* p. 25.
46. Ibid., pp. 243–53.
47. Ibid., p. 55.
48. Ibid.
49. Ibid.
50. Ibid.
51. *The Times* (London), May 22, 1978.
52. *New York Times,* May 30, 1978.

CHAPTER 7.

1. Ali Hamdi el-Gammal interview, July 8, 1976.
2. Ahmad Baha' el-Din interview, July 20, 1976.
3. Dr. Sami Mansour interview, July 11, 1976.
4. Dr. Ahmad Hussein Sawi interview, July 15, 1976.
5. Mustafa Bahgat Badawi, *Min Muzakkirat Ra'is Tahrir,* p. 233.
6. Gammal interview, July 8, 1976.
7. Baha' el-Din interview, July 20, 1976.
8. Ibid.
9. Mustafa Amin interview, July 21, 1976.
10. Milton Viorst, "Egypt and Israel: Two Nations and Their Press," p. 33.
11. Ibid.
12. Ra'id el-Attar interview, July 19, 1976.
13. Mansour interview, July 11, 1976.
14. Lufti el-Kholi interview, July 12, 1976.
15. Mohamed el-Salmawy interview, July 21, 1976.
16. Gammal interview, July 8, 1976.
17. Attar interview, July 19, 1976.
18. Viorst, "Egypt and Israel," p. 33.
19. Baha' el-Din interview, July 20, 1976.
20. Kholi interview, July 12, 1976.
21. Salmawy interview, July 21, 1976.
22. Mansour interview, July 11, 1976.
23. Heikal interview, July 22, 1976.
24. Mohamed Sayed Ahmad interview, July 15, 1976.
25. Salmawy interview, July 21, 1976.
26. Mansour interview, July 11, 1976.
27. Gammal interview, July 8, 1976.
28. Heikal interview, July 22, 1976.
29. Ibid.
30. Hassanein Karoum, *Abdul Nasser Bain Heikal wa Mustafa Amin,* p. 6.

31. Amin interview, July 21, 1976.
32. Ibid.
33. Heikal interview, July 22, 1976.
34. Ibid.
35. Ibid.
36. Article by Ali Amin in his own handwriting, shown to me by Heikal in Cairo, July 22, 1976.
37. Heikal interview, July 22, 1976.
38. Miles Copeland, *The Game of Nations.*
39. Miles Copeland, *Without Cloak or Dagger: The Truth about the New Espionage.*
40. Ibid., p. 53.
41. Ibid.
42. Heikal interview, July 22, 1976.
43. *Al-Hawadeth,* August 3, 1976.
44. Heikal interview, July 22, 1976.
45. Salim el-Lozi interview, July 27, 1976.
46. Ibid.
47. Nasha't el-Taghlibi, *Al-Hawadeth,* November 15, 1974.
48. Heikal interview, July 22, 1976.
49. Ibid.
50. Lozi interview, July 27, 1976.
51. Mansour interview, July 11, 1976.
52. Kholi interview, July 12, 1976.
53. Sayed Ahmad interview, July 15, 1976.
54. Baha' el-Din interview, July 20, 1976.
55. Mansour interview, July 11, 1976.
56. Heikal interview, July 22, 1976.
57. Ibid.
58. Ibid.
59. Husni Guindi interview, July 23, 1976.
60. Attar interview, July 19, 1976.
61. Salmawy interview, July 21, 1976.
62. Guindi interview, July 23, 1976.
63. Kholi interview, July 12, 1976.
64. Amin interview, July 21, 1976.
65. As quoted by Badawi, *Min Muzakkirat Ra'is Tahrir,* p. 283.
66. Ibid., p. 284.
67. Samir Atallah, *Al-Nahar,* January 16, 1975, p. 11.
68. Edward R. F. Sheehan, "The Second Most Important Man in Egypt—and Possibly the World's Most Powerful Journalist."
69. John K. Cooley, from a questionnaire sent to him by me in January 1977.
70. Ibid.
71. British journalist (name withheld at his request), from a questionnaire sent to him by me in January 1977.
72. Ibid.
73. David Hirst, "Spiked Editor."
74. Edward Mortimer, "Privileged Journalist."
75. P. J. Vatikiotis, "Lines of Communication: The Road to Ramadan."

APPENDIXES

1. Edward R. F. Sheehan, *The Arabs, Israelis, and Kissinger,* pp. 51–60.

BIBLIOGRAPHY

ARTICLES

Almaney, Adnan. "Government Control of the Press in the United Arab Republic, 1952-1970," *Journalism Quarterly* 49(Summer, 1972):340-48.

Cooley, John. "Nasser's Journalist Aide," *The Christian Science Monitor* (March 19, 1966).

_____. "Cairo's Leading Newspaper—But No Typewriters," *The Christian Science Monitor* (April 15, 1969).

_____. "How Egypt's Top Editor Sees It," *The Christian Science Monitor* (October 7, 1976).

Crabbs, Jack. "Politics, History and Culture in Nasser's Egypt," *International Journal of Middle Eastern Studies* 6(October, 1975):386-420.

Dajani, Nabil, and Donohue, John. "Foreign News in the Arab Press: A Content Analysis of Six Arab Dailies," *Gazette,* 19, No. 3, 1973.

de Borchgrave, Arnaud. "Heikal Breaks Yearlong Silence to Give His Views on the Middle East," *Newsweek* (January 20, 1975).

Entelis, J. P. "Nasser's Egypt: The Failure of Charismatic Leadership," *Orbis,* 18(Summer 1974).

"The Fall of a Great Editor," *The Times* (London), (February 4, 1974).

"Find a Fault in Cairo and You'll Be in Trouble," *The Economist* (February 9, 1974), p. 25.

Godsell, Geoffry. "Nasser's Confidant: The View from the East," *The Christian Science Monitor* (January 31, 1973).

Harik, I. F. "Opinion Leaders and the Mass Media in Rural Egypt: A Reconsideration of the Two-Step Flow Theory of Communication," *American Political Science Review* 65(September, 1971):731-40.

Heikal, Mohamed Hassanein. "Pulling Back from Mideast Precipice," *New York Times* (January 16, 1975).

Hirst, David. "Spiked Editor," *The Guardian* (February 4, 1974).

Kershaw, R. "Egypt after Defeat," *New Statesman* 73(June 23, 1967):864.

Lenczowski, G. "Objects and Methods of Nasserism," *Journal of International Affairs,* 19, No. 1, 1965.

Mansfield, Peter. "Struggle for Power in Egypt," *New Statesman* 74(October 6, 1967):424-25.

Marsot, Afaf L. A. Sayyid. "The Cartoon in Egypt," *Comparative Studies in Society and History* 13(January 1971):2-15.

Moore, C. H. "Authoritarian Politics in Unincorporated Society: The Case of Nasser's Egypt," *Comparative Politics* 6(January, 1974):193-218.

Morgan. J. "Nasserism in Decline? A Report on Egypt after 13 Years of Revolution," *New Statesman* 71(January 7, 1966).

Morris, Claud. "The Most Hygienic Newspaper in the World," *The Times* (London), (May 18, 1972).

Mortimer, Edward. "Privileged Journalist," *The Times* (London), (June 9, 1975).

"No Doubts about Who Is in Charge," *Time* (February 18, 1974).

Peretz, Don. "Democracy and the Revolution in Egypt," *The Middle East Journal* 13(Winter, 1959):37.

Sheehan, Edward R. F. "The Second Most Important Man in Egypt—and Possibly the

World's Most Powerful Journalist," *New York Times Magazine* (August 22, 1971), p. 12.

Smith, Richard M. "Censorship in the Middle East," *Columbia Journalism Review* (January–February 1974), pp. 43–49.

Steward, Desmond. "Nine Years of Nasser," *Spectator* (July 21, 1961).

_____. "Egypt's Embattled Writers," *Encounter* 41(August 1973):85–92.

_____. "The Rise and Fall of Mohammad Heikal," *Encounter* 42(June 1974):87–93.

Vatikiotis, P. J. "Lines of Communicaton: The Road to Ramadan," *Sunday Times* (London), June 8, 1975.

Viorst, Milton. "Egypt and Israel: Two Nations and Their Press," *Columbia Journalism Review* (May–June, 1974), pp. 32–37.

BOOKS IN ENGLISH

Abdel Malik, Anwar. *Egypt: Military Society*. (Translated by Charles L. Markmann.) New York: Random House, 1968.

Berque, Jacques. *Egypt: Imperialism and Revolution*. London: Faber and Faber, 1972.

Copeland, Miles. *The Game of Nations*. New York: Simon and Schuster, 1969.

_____. *Without Cloak or Dagger: The Truth about the New Espionage*. New York: Simon and Schuster, 1974.

Dekmejian, R. Harir. *Egypt under Nasir: A Study in Political Dynamics*. Albany: State University of New York Press, 1971.

Elsheik, Ibrahim. *Mass Media and Ideological Change in Egypt (1950–1973)*. Amsterdam, Holland: University of Amsterdam, 1977.

DuBois, Shirley Graham. *Gamal Abdel Nasser: Son of the Nile, A Biography*. New York: The Third Press, 1972.

Heikal, Mohamed Hassanein. *The Cairo Documents*. New York: Doubleday & Co., 1973.

_____. *The Road to Ramadan*. New York: Ballantine Books, 1976. (London: Collins, 1975.)

Hopkins, Harry. *Egypt, the Crucible: The Unfinished Revolution of the Arab World*. London: Secker and Warburg, 1969.

Joesten, Joachim. *Nasser: The Rise to Power*. London: Odham Press, 1960.

Kerr, Malcolm H. *Egypt under Nasser*. New York: Foreign Policy Association, 1963.

Lacouture, Jean. *Egypt in Transition*. Translated by Francis Scarfe. London: Metheun, 1958.

Merrill, John C. *The Elite Press: Great Newspapers of the World*. New York: Pitman Publishing Co., 1968.

Nasser, Gamal Abdul. *Egypt's Liberation: The Philosophy of Revolution*. Washington, D.C.: Public Affairs Press, 1955.

Nutting, Anthony. *Nasser*. New York: E. P. Dutton & Co., 1972.

Sadat, Anwar. *In Search of Identity: An Autobiography*. New York: Harper & Row, 1977.

Sheehan, Edward R. F. *The Arabs, Israelis, and Kissinger*. New York: Readers' Digest Press, 1976.

Stephens, Robert. *Nasser: A Political Biography*. New York: Simon and Schuster, 1971.

Vatikiotis, P. J. *The Modern History of Egypt*. New York: Frederick Praeger, 1969.

Wheelock, Keith. *Nasser's New Egypt*. New York: Frederick Praeger, 1960.

BOOKS IN ARABIC

Abdo, Ibrahim. *Tatawur el-Sahafa el-Misriya* [Development of the Egyptian Press]. Cairo: no publisher, no date.

_____. *Al-Ahram: Tarikhon wa Fann* [*Al-Ahram:* A History and an Art]. Cairo: Mu'assasat Sijill el-Arab, 1964.

Abu Zeid, Farouk. *Azamat el-Fikr el-Qawmi fi el-Sahafa el-Misriya* [Problem of National Thought in the Egyptian Press]. Cairo: Dar el-Fikr wal-Fann, 1976.

_____. *Azamet el-Dimoqratiya fi el-Sahafa el-Misriya* [Problem of Democracy in the Egyptian Press]. Cairo: Maktabat Madbouli, 1976.

Auda, Mohamed. *Nasseriyoon wa Marxiyoon* [Nasserites and Marxists]. Cairo: Rose el-Yousef, 1976.

Awad, Lewis. *Aqni'at el-Nasseriya el-Sab'a* [The Seven Masks of Nasserism]. Beirut: Dar el-Qadaya, 1976.

Badawi, Mustafa Bahgat. *Min Muzakkirat Ra'is Tahrir* [From the Memoirs of Editor-in-chief]. Cairo: Al-Sha'b Publications, 1976.

Beibars, Dia' el-Din. *Al-Asrar el-Shakhsiya li Gamal Abdul Nasser* [Personal Secrets of Gamal Abdul Nasser]. Cairo: Maktabat Madbouli, 1976.

Hakim, Tawfiq el. *El-Hameer* [The Jack-Asses]. Beirut: Dar el-Shurouq, 1972.

_____. *Awdat el-Wa'i* [The Return of Consciousness]. Beirut: Dar el-Shurouq, 1974.

Hamamsy, Galal el-Din. *Hiwar Wara' el-Aswar* [Dialogue Behind Walls]. Cairo: Al-Maktab el-Masri el-Hadeeth, 1976.

Hamza, Abdel Lateef. *Azamat el-Damir el-Sahafi* [Problem of Journalistic Conscious]. Cairo: no publisher, 1960.

_____. *Qissat el-Sahafa el-Arabiya fi Misr* [The Story of the Arab Press in Egypt]. Baghdad: no publisher, 1967.

Heikal, Mohamed Hassanein. *Ahadeeth fi Asia* [My Talks in Asia]. Beirut: Dar el-Ma'aref, 1973.

_____. *Hadeeth el-Mubadarah* [The Initiative Talk]. Beirut: Matba'at Beirut, 1978.

Karoum, Hassanein. *Abdel Nasser Bain Heikal wa Mustafa Amin* [Nasser between Heikal and Mustafa Amin]. Cairo: Dar Ma'moun lil Tiba'a, 1975.

Malaf Abdel Nasser Baina el-Yassar el-Masri wa Tawfiq el-Hakim [Nassar between the Egyptian Left and Tawfiq el-Hakim]. Beirut: Dar el-Qadaya, 1975.

Matar, Fuad. *Bisaraha An Abdel Nasser* [Frankly Speaking about Nasser]. Beirut: Dar el-Qadaya, 1975.

Mughrabi, Ali el. *Khabaya el-Sahafa* [Secrets of the Press]. Cairo: *Akhbar el-Yom,* 1975.

Murad, Mahmoud. *Man Kana Yahkum Misr?* [Who Ruled Egypt?] Maktabat Madbouli, 1975.

Nagib, Mohamed. *Kalimati lil Tarikh* [My Word for History]. Cairo: Dar el-Kitab el-Namouzagi, 1975.

Sabat, Khalil. *Tarikh el-Tiba'a fil Sharq el-Arabi* [History of Printing in the Arab East]. Cairo: no publisher, 1958.

Shalabi, Karam. *Bisaraha An Heikal* [Frankly Speaking about Heikal]. Cairo: Matba'at Abdeen, 1975.

Tarazi, V. Philip D. *Tarikh el Sahafa el-Arabiya* [History of the Arab Press]. Beirut: no publisher, 1913.

Touni, Mohamed Shawkat el. *Murafa'at An Mustafa Amin fi Qadaya el-Ta'thib el-Kubra* [Defending Mustafa Amin in the Great Torture Cases]. Cairo: Dar el-Sha'b, 1976.

Zakaria, Fuad, et al. *Abdel Nasser wal Yassar el-Masri* [Nasser and the Egyptian Left]. Cairo: Rose el-Yousef, 1976.

UNPUBLISHED MATERIALS

BBC Files, Central Current Affairs Talks, External Broadcasting, London, February 1974.

Heikal, Mohamed Hassanein. "The Arabs and the World in the Aftermath of the October War: The New Realities." Address delivered at the Eighth Annual Convention of the Association of Arab-American University Graduates on October 18, 1975, in Chicago, Illinois, USA.

INTERVIEWS

Ahmad, Mohamed Sayed. Columnist, in his office at *Al-Ahram,* Cairo, July 21, 1976.

Amin, Mustafa. Former Editor of *Akhbar el-Yom,* in his office at *Akhbar el-Yom,* Cairo, July 21, 1976.

Attar, Ra'id el. Deputy Editor of *Al-Ahram,* in his office at *Al-Ahram,* Cairo, July 23, 1976.

Baha' el-Din, Ahmad. Columnist, in his office at *Al-Ahram,* Cairo, July 20, 1976.

Gammal, Ali Hamdi el. Editor-in-Chief of *Al-Ahram,* in his office at *Al-Ahram,* Cairo, July 8, 1976.

Guindi, Husni. Of *Al-Ahram*'s foreign desk, in his office at *Al-Ahram,* July 23, 1976.

Heikal, Mohamed Hassanein. Former Editor-in-Chief of *Al-Ahram,* in the Chicago Sheraton Hotel, Chicago, Illinois, October 18, 1975. Also at his home in Cairo, July 6, 7, 12, 14, 20, 22, 1976 and a taped interview by mail on December 9, 1976.

Kholi, Lutfi el. Editor of *Al-Talia'a,* in his office at *Al-Ahram,* Cairo, July 21, 1976.

Lozi, Salim el. Publisher of the Lebanese weekly *Al-Hawadeth,* in his home in London, July 27, 1976.

Mansour, Sami. Columnist, in his office at *Al-Ahram,* Cairo, July 11, 1976.

Salmawy, Mohamed el. Of *Al-Ahram*'s foreign desk, in his office at *Al-Ahram,* Cairo, July 21, 1976.

Sawi, Ahmad Hussein el, Professor of Journalism, American University in Cairo, in his home, Cairo, July 15, 1976.

INDEX

ABC television, 102
Abdallah, King of Jordan, 30
Abdo, Ibrahim, 15
Abul-Fatah, Mahmoud, 7
Akhbar el-Yom, 30, 38, 41, 115, 116
Akher Sa'a, 30, 38
Al-Ahaly, 22, 25-26, 28, 106
Al-Ahram, 4, 10, 21, 24; centenary, 36,
    101; historical development, 36-37;
    circulation, 37, 41, 43, 114; center
    for strategic studies, 43; world
    reputation, 43, 129; ownership, 47;
    new building, 48-52; evaluated by
    critics, 113-15, 133
Al-Ahram Al-Iqtissadi, 50
Al-Ahrar, 22
Al-Akhbar, 10, 21, 37, 40
Al-Gumhouriya, 10, 15, 37, 38, 40
Al-Hawadeth, 118, 123
Al-Hawadeth el-Yawmiyah, 3
Ali, Mohamed, 3
Al-Masri, 3, 37
Al-Mussawar, 21
Al-Nahar, on Heikal, 124
Al-Nasr Trading Company, 52
Al-Sayyad, 118
Al-Siyasa Al-Dawliya, 50
Al-Talia', 21, 50, 110
Al-Thawra, 44
Al-Usbou' el-Arabi, on Heikal, 124
Al-Waqa'i el-Masriyah, 3
Amer, Abdul Hakim, 33
Amin, Ali and Mustafa: support Nasser,
    7; contributions to press, 11; Ali
    editor of *Al-Ahram,* 11, 14, 91, 92,
    113; Mustafa indicted for spying, 11,
    91, 116; attack Nasser, 15; removed
    from *Al-Akhbar,* 16-17; Mustafa on
    press freedom, 21; Mustafa attacks
    Heikal, 109, 123
Anis, Ahmad, 90
Arab socialism, 62
Arab Socialist Union, 8, 10, 21, 47, 56
Arafat, Yasser, 64, 70
Aref, president of Iraq, 64
Association of Arab-American University
    Graduates, 97
Aswan High Dam, 64

Attar, Ra'id el, on Heikal, 110, 111,
    122, 131
Awad, Lewis, 42, 56, 84
Aziz, Tareq, 44

Ba'ath party, 44, 56
Badawi, Mustafa Bahgat, 108
Baha' el-Din, Ahmad: defends Nasser-
    ism, 16; dismissed from *Al-Ahram,*
    84; on Heikal, 107, 109, 112, 114,
    115, 120
Battle, Lucius, 117
Ben Bella, Ahmad, 64
Bhutto, Ali, 84
Bisaraha (Frankly Speaking), 42, 46, 99
Borba, 44
Brezhnev, 65-66, 79-80
British Broadcasting Corporation: criti-
    cized by Sadat, 27; praises Heikal,
    93; interviews Heikal, 102
British occupation of Egypt, 4, 33, 34

Center platform, 20, 28
Chou En-lai, 83-84
CIA, 101, 116, 120, 133
Communists in Egypt, 5; challenge Sadat,
    20; attacked by Sadat, 23; attacked
    by Nasser, 62, 63
Cooley, John, on Heikal, 124
Copeland, Miles, 66, 117-18, 125, 133
Crowe, Colin, 67

Daily Mirror, 46, 47
Damascus Radio, 99
Dulles, John Foster, 66

Earl, Harold, 30
Egyptian Arab Socialist Organization,
    20-22
Egyptian Gazette, 29
Egypt Petroleum Institute, 52
Eissa, Salah, 26

Fahmi, Ismael, 87
Faik, Mohamed, 68
Farouk, King of Egypt, 5, 6
Fawzi, General Mohamed, 65
Fawzi, Mahmoud, 63, 74, 87, 91